THE ART OF LEAVING

RANDOM HOUSE
NEW YORK

THE
ART OF
LEAVING

A MEMOIR

AYELET
TSABARI

Published in the United States by Random House, an imprint and
division of Penguin Random House LLC, New York.

RANDOM HOUSE and the HOUSE colophon are registered
trademarks of Penguin Random House LLC.

Some of the essays in this work have been previously published
in different form. A publication history is located on page 319.

LIBRARY OF CONGRESS CATALOGING-IN-PUBLICATION DATA
Names: Tsabari, Ayelet, author.
Title: The art of leaving: a memoir / Ayelet Tsabari.
Description: First edition. | New York: Random House, [2019]
Identifiers: LCCN 2018045724 | ISBN 9780812988987 |
ISBN 9780812988994 (ebook)
Subjects: LCSH: Tsabari, Ayelet, | Jewish women authors—
Canada—Biography.
Classification: LCC PR9199.4.T82 Z46 2019 | DDC 813/.6 [B]—dc23
LC record available at https://lccn.loc.gov/2018045724

Printed in the United States of America on acid-free paper

randomhousebooks.com

2 4 6 8 9 7 5 3 1

FIRST EDITION

Book design by Simon M. Sullivan

For my beloved family

Perhaps home is not a place but simply an irrevocable condition.

—JAMES BALDWIN, *Giovanni's Room*

CONTENTS

I. HOME

II. LEAVING

III. **RETURN**

I.
HOME

I sat on the knees of others.
Their stomach was my spine,
their arms—my walls.
I had a home made of people.

—MAYA TEVET DAYAN, "Home"

IN MY DREAMS WE HUG
LIKE GROWN-UPS DO

FOR MY TENTH BIRTHDAY, my father promised he would publish my writing in a book.

"A real book?"

"A *real* book. Put together your best stuff."

I had been writing ever since I learned the alphabet. By the end of first grade, I was crafting books from school notebooks, complete with illustrated cover images and blurbs on the back. I had even started a library of my writings that was frequented by neighbors and cousins. I attached a pocket for a library card to the back of each notebook and fashioned a library stamp by carving letters on an eraser.

My father used to write too; I had seen the scribbling in his bedside drawer—parts of poems, unsent letters, his handwriting artfully drawn and rounded with long strokes, always in black ink. At the bottom of the drawer, I found a yellowing magazine titled *Afikim,* in which one of his poems was featured, his only publication.

That day, after my father made his promise, I locked myself in my room and wrote until dinnertime. After dinner I wrote some more. By the next day, I'd filled a notebook with the tale of a young girl adjusting to a new school. Earlier that year, my family had moved, so I drew the story from my own experience. When I finished, I proudly presented my father with my work. He was resting in bed, leaning against a pile of pillows, recently out of the hospital.

"What's this?" he said.

"A book, like you asked."

He laughed, flipped through the pages. "You wrote all this yesterday?"

"Yes." I puffed out my chest.

He put the notebook aside. "Writing a book should take longer than a day. There's still time before your birthday."

"But you didn't read it!" I protested. "How do you know it's not good?"

He promised he'd read it.

A few days later, as I was walking back from the library, two books clutched to my chest, I saw an ambulance parked on the curb outside our house, its orange flicker lighting up the rosebushes in timed, urgent intervals—a busy signal.

* * *

AFTER SCHOOL, NURIT and I mostly go to her place, because hers is always empty and mine never is. Nurit's house key hangs like a pendant around her neck, and she has pay phone tokens threaded on her shoelaces for emergencies. In my house, unless my mom is visiting my dad at the hospital, she is at home with the baby, and my older sister and three older brothers are in their rooms or in the kitchen or in the living room or downstairs playing Ping-Pong with their friends. Every day my aunts and uncles and cousins come to visit too, for lunch or for an afternoon coffee and cake, or just to chat. "This house is like a train station," my mother often sighs, but she sounds secretly pleased.

On days when Nurit does come over, mostly in the afternoons when my mom is napping, we go up to the roof. From there you can see rain-streaked buildings with protruding balconies, their flat white roofs crowded with crooked antennas, water tanks, and gleaming solar panels. Kids sit on window ledges and dangle legs through metal bars, and strings of colorful laundry smile under windows. Looking east, you can see the end of Petah Tikva, the trees that line the highway leading to the airport, and the hills of Rosh HaAyin in a squiggly line on the horizon. On our west, down the eternally jammed Jabotinsky Road, is Tel Aviv, the big city with its narrow streets and white sand beaches and the promise of the world beyond its shores. Airplanes circle above us like hungry seagulls before landing, and sometimes warplanes zoom by on their way north of the border. The war is far away, but we can see it written on the grown-ups' faces: the tension in their cheeks, the groove between the eyebrows. We can hear it in the music played on the radio, beautiful songs in minor keys about death and the land that fill us with sweet sadness.

Our new house is in Mahane Yehuda, a Petah Tikva neighborhood that was founded by Yemeni immigrants at the beginning of the twentieth century. The main street—a short strip with stumpy buildings propped against each other like a train that has stalled in its tracks—is hidden behind a row of cypress trees, spiky palms with leaves like fountains, and a scary abandoned house with a broken staircase suspended in midair, leading to a nonexistent second floor.

Nurit and I play in my attic, a small triangular alcove under the slanted roof that you have to access through a hole in the wall. Other times, my brother who is three years older than me invites his friends to play music there, which isn't fair because he has his own room and I have to share mine with a baby.

Nurit and I tell each other everything. I'm the only one of her friends who knows her mom had an accident when she was young: her dark, beautiful hair was caught in an industrial fan in the factory where she worked and that is why she now wears a wig. I've never told anyone about that, but every time I walk by a large fan, I imagine my hair being ripped out of my skull. Nurit is also the first person I called after my dad had the heart attack.

Aba's heart attack happened on the first Shabbat of September in 1982, two days after I started fourth grade. I was playing at Keren's, my neighbor who lives a few houses down from us, even though her family isn't Yemeni. There are a few families like hers on our street, lured by the cheap prices and the proximity to downtown. Keren's two brothers are in the air force, so she knows things about the war in Lebanon that started in the summer, when the Israeli troops made it as far as Beirut. In the spring, when we saw Israeli kids kicking and fighting and crying on TV as the army evacuated them from their homes, Keren was the one who explained to me why we were withdrawing from Yamit, which was in the Sinai Peninsula, and how it was a good thing we were returning it to Egypt because now we could finally have peace and go see the pyramids. Once, she lent me a top secret air force book that teaches soldiers how to identify warplanes, and I've studied it carefully in case I see enemy planes in the sky.

We were in Keren's room when my sister came to get me. My sister is sixteen. She wears shapeless embroidered galabiyas she buys from Arab shopkeepers in Jaffa and walks barefoot. She has a poster of Janis Joplin over her bed, screaming into a mic, hair fanning out like an octopus. Her bedroom smells like smoke and incense. In our old apartment, we shared a room, and I would fall asleep to the sound of her turning pages. Now she never lets me into her room. When she's out, I sneak in and search for secret notebooks and letters. I open her wardrobe drawers and try on her makeup and perfume, hoping to rub some of her coolness onto me.

"You have to come home," my sister said.

"Why?"

"Because."

"But why? Ima doesn't mind."

My sister stared at the floor for a bit and finally sat down on Keren's bed. I sat beside her. "Aba had a heart attack while playing soccer," she said. "He's in the hospital."

Keren placed her hand on my arm and told me her father had a heart attack too, a few years ago. He was airlifted by a helicopter to a hospital. "He's fine now," she said. "Yours will be fine too."

Over the next few weeks, as my father goes in and out of the hospital, looking thinner and weaker each time, I keep thinking of Keren's words. I wonder how long it took before her father was fine, but I never ask.

MOST DAYS, NURIT and I talk about boys—boys like Danny, who has hair the color of straw and bluish-gray eyes. Danny isn't popular like my boyfriend, Alon, who is athletic and cool. Danny does not play sports and he's good at math. Nurit thinks he likes me. I wave my hand at that and tell her she's crazy, but inside my chest, my heart does a little dance.

Alon asked me to be his girlfriend last year, in third grade. I had just started in the new school. We were playing hide-and-seek after class under an apartment building on Bialik Street, and when I hid behind a hibiscus bush, Alon knelt beside me. We crouched silently for a while. My palms felt clammy. He glanced at me and said, "Do you want to be my girlfriend?" I blushed and said, "You don't even know me." And he said, "I like what I know." And so I said, "Okay, yes." We stayed for a while and talked, even though the game was over and someone was yelling, "Come out now, everybody." When we joined the rest, my face was flushed and I couldn't stop smiling, and this girl Iris looked at me funny. I didn't know that she liked Alon. I didn't know he used to be her boyfriend in second grade.

A few weeks after that, Iris and some other girls cornered me at recess and told me that I was too bossy and snobby, that I always wanted to make the rules for the games, and that they weren't going to play with me or talk to me anymore. When I came home for lunch, I was crying, and Aba sat on my bed and asked me to tell him everything. Aba always listens to me. He doesn't just nod while folding laundry or washing the dishes, like Ima does. That day after lunch, he took me to his work and bought me a strawberry jam donut, powdered with sugar, from the European deli by his office. On the way back home, sitting in the backseat of his olive-green Ford Cortina, I heard him talking to his brother in English so I wouldn't understand, but I did. He said, "She is sad because the girls say she's acting like a queen."

When I go visit Aba at the hospital, he looks thin and his eyes are tired, but he's still smiling. The nurses beam at him and call him dear, and I can tell they like him. Everyone likes my dad: the people at the deli who give me free donuts; his secretary, who perks up whenever he walks in; the strangers on the street who shake his hand effusively; and his clients, whom I see sometimes when I visit his law office, many of them old people from Sha'ariya, a small Yemeni neighborhood at the edge of Petah Tikva. They thank him repeatedly, overcome with emotion, until he waves his hand, embarrassed, and says, "Don't worry about it. Just pay me when you can," or sometimes, "It's okay. Just pray for me in the synagogue."

Aba asks about my writing and the books I've been reading. Before his heart attack, he wrote the word "masterpieces" on an old shoebox and filled it up with books he thought I might want to read and discuss, like *Around the World in Eighty Days* and *Little Women* and *David Copperfield* and *Oliver Twist*. I want to climb on his bed and cuddle with him but my mom says I can't.

At night, before I go to sleep, I pray to God to make Aba better and hope God listens even though my family isn't really religious and we drive and watch TV and turn on appliances on Shabbat. I hope God remembers that before Aba got sick, he used to go to synagogue every week and helped people for free. When I take off my shoes, if one of the soles faces the ceiling, I fix it right away, because my savta, my mom's mom, who came from Yemen, once told me it is rude to be giving Him the dirty sole of your shoe. Savta peppers her sentences with "God have mercy" and "Insha'Allah," which means "God willing" in Arabic. She looks up at the sky, shaking her head and sighing and slapping her thighs, and I know she is talking to Him, probably listing her misfortunes: her dead husband, her brother who was killed in the war, her mother, who abandoned her when she was only two and no one knows why. I wish I had such a candid, direct relationship with God.

ON YOM KIPPUR, I decide to fast like my mom and my older siblings to make up for stealing my sister's things and for everything else bad I may have done this year and don't remember. I know you don't have to fast before your bat mitzvah, but I want to show God I am serious.

Yom Kippur has always been my favorite holiday, even though it is a day of atonement and you're supposed to be suffering and not having fun. Everything is different on Yom Kippur. For twenty-five hours, nobody drives. No one calls. No television screens flicker blue from open windows. Everyone strolls leisurely along the dark, empty streets, and kids run around and ride bikes, stopping at the traffic lights and pretending they are cars. Ima turns on a few lights before the start of the fast, and we are not allowed to turn them off until it ends. Sometimes, out of habit, I flip the light switch off when I leave the bathroom, and then turn it back on right away so Ima won't notice, which means that I did two forbidden things instead of just one. Maybe three if you count trying to cover it up.

Every Yom Kippur, the kids from our class meet at the park on Rothschild Street. This year, everyone is bringing their bikes, and they're going to ride all the way to the Geha Interchange at the end of the city, on the way to Tel Aviv. Nurit is the only one who knows that I can't ride a bike. Aba bought me a bike after I found the afikomen at the Seder dinner last Passover. The piece of matzo was hidden in the folds of the curtains at Savta's house, and my uncle Aaron, who knew I had never found it before, may have given me an encouraging wink when I started touching the fabric. Aba promised he'd teach me how to ride, but then he got sick and now my bike is collecting dust in the garage and everyone has other things to worry about.

"We can just walk to Geha," Nurit says. "We have all evening."

We start walking after the fast begins. As we crisscross through the city streets, the lights click on, painting the worn pavement a glittering orange. We walk until our legs burn and our feet go numb, and my hunger gnaws at me like little hands pinching my belly from the inside. We walk more than I have ever walked before. I keep moving the spit in my mouth around, hoping it will quench my thirst, but it doesn't. When we get to Geha, the overpass looms above us, larger than it appears through a car window, a gray, silent monster, the exits on both sides like curved arms. The traffic lights continue to change in timed intervals, illuminating the asphalt a different color every time, like party lights. The atmosphere is festive: kids circle on their bikes and form groups on the curbs and sit in the middle of the highway, just because they can. We are all giddy to have taken over this adult territory, and nobody thinks about remorse or forgiveness. Then someone yells, "Ambulance!" and we all shuffle to the side and watch the ambulance barreling past. It could be a new mother being rushed to the delivery room, but the sound of the siren quickens my heartbeat, and for the rest of the evening, I am solemnly atoning.

The next morning, I wake up and accidentally let some water slip into my mouth while I brush my teeth. It's not even enough to quench my thirst but I already feel like I cheated. Later, numbed by hunger, I eat unwashed grapes while standing in front of the open fridge, lit by its cold fluorescent light.

THE FOLLOWING WEEK, it's Sukkot and we're having a holiday dinner at Savta's house. Savta lives in Sha'ariya, only five minutes' drive from our house. For some reason—maybe because it's on the margins of our city or because it was populated by newer immigrants—Sha'ariya feels like a different country, what Yemen must be like, rustic and old and perpetually infused with the aroma of Yemeni soup—turmeric and fenugreek and cilantro and ginger. Savta's house has no toys or candy, no books or movies. She wears large dresses that hang, a headscarf over her graying hair, and thick-lensed glasses that magnify her cynical glare and permanent grimace.

There is a yellowing, black-and-white family portrait hanging in Savta's living room that I love looking at. My grandmother, my grandfather, who died when I was little, and their six children, all clad in their best garments, everyone smiling charmingly except for my mother, the petulant child in the corner, black curls held by a pin, one shoulder raised, lips down-turned, forehead scrunched. My aunts all laugh and say that this is where I got my sulk from. I know my mother inherited that expression from her own mother, but in the picture, Savta is smiling wider than I had ever seen her do in real life, face open and unwrinkled, eyes warm. She looks young, beautiful, and happy. I wish I had known that woman.

My uncles carry the dining table and set it inside the sukkah they've erected in the front yard, with white sheets slung between poles for walls and dried palm leaves for a roof. Holiday drawings my cousins and I made are pinned on the sheets, and colorful paper garlands are strung across the ceiling. Everything else is the same: one of my uncles does the kiddush in an undulating, singsong Yemeni accent, and we all chant "Amen" in unison. We pass along the wineglass and sip a little bit of the dark red sweetness, which stings our throats and warms our bellies. One of my cousins throws the lahoh—the sticky Yemeni pita that is dappled with holes—on her face so it looks like a silly mask, and the rest of us giggle into our bowls of yellow soup.

After dinner, my mom, aunts, and female cousins pile up the dirty dishes and carry them inside while the men stretch their legs and argue about things like politics and the war in Lebanon and the huge protest that happened the week before in Tel Aviv and whether Ariel Sharon should resign as minister of defense. They crack sunflower seeds and spit the shells into little mounds by their coffee mugs. I watch my cousins climb into their fathers' laps, cozying tiredly into their wide chests, and I feel like there's a bone stuck in my throat that won't go down. When no one is looking, I crawl under the table and sit there hugging my knees and watching their feet, biting my nails until it hurts. I make myself small, invisible. I'm good at that. I'm flexible and agile and can squeeze myself into the smallest spaces, like in the niche at the top of the stairs leading to the roof, or inside the laundry chute, or in the back, between the olive trees, in a small path I cleared under a bush. Once I fell asleep in the gap between the couch and the wall, and everyone went crazy looking for me.

Savta pulls up the tablecloth and nudges me, nodding toward the kitchen. I crawl out, drag my feet, back hunched, but instead of going in, I watch the women through the window: they are loud and curvy and strong-minded and effortlessly charming, their curls bouncy or blow-dried or hennaed, their throaty "het" and "ayin" melodic—syllables I swallow, flatten, learned in school to pronounce incorrectly, like an Ashkenazi. They fill that tiny room with motion and perfume and chatter and bursts of laughter. Water is running and food is placed in bowls and stacked in the fridge. It is a secret sorority to which I've been granted entrance, invited to bask in their womanly prowess thanks to my DNA and gender. They seem happy, content to be doing what they're doing, to share in one another's company, but I hate washing dishes and I don't like the smell in Savta's kitchen, years of spices that have ripened and soured. My aunts tell my mom that it is her fault I am so lazy, that she spoiled me because I was her baby for seven years before my brother was born.

I look back at the dirt road. The darkness teems with nocturnal wildlife: crickets chirp deafeningly in the background and things rustle in the trees and in the shadows. The other sukkahs on the street glow brightly, floating squares of light in the night, and the people inside them are silhouettes, like in a shadow-puppet show we saw in school. They raise their glasses, their plates and forks clink. They sing holiday songs, voices booming through the crisp air. I'm standing in the dark, watching their lives.

. . .

IN OCTOBER, WHEN it starts to get cool in the evenings, Ima pulls down the gas heater and bags of warm clothes smelling of mildew and winter from the top of the closet, and I find the sweater she knitted me last year, when she had time to knit, with blue and pink stripes. Inhaling its scent, I remember the times I wore it, back when Aba was well, when Ima was happy. Every single item of clothing is now a souvenir from better days.

At a class party on Friday, Alon and I slow dance among the other couples and the space between us feels solid, like there's an extra body in there. We can't seem to move in sync: one of us is always a little too slow to catch up. Last week after school, I ran fast and scaled a fence, and Alon said, "Why do you have to act so tough all the time? Like you're a boy?" I close my eyes and for a moment imagine dancing with Danny instead.

At recess, I sit on the stone bleachers and watch the boys play soccer. Alon scores and then circles the field, grinning. His arm extends up like he is Oded Machnes on TV, the best soccer player in the whole country. Alon is such a show-off. He used to wave at me and I sat taller, proud that he was my boyfriend. He never does that anymore. My gaze wanders, scans the crowds for Danny. He and Yoel invited Nurit and me to work on a group project after school. I spot him hanging out with the geeky kids on the barricades. He is the complete opposite of Alon: he is humble and soft-spoken, and he is the first of many boys and men I will fall for because they seem to possess my father's sensibilities. He looks up and smiles and I stare at my feet, cheeks burning.

Danny lives in a new high-rise opposite school. The stucco walls outside are still white, yet to be blackened by years of smog and rain. From his room, you can see the orange groves that border our city. He has a blue wall-to-wall carpet instead of tile floors, and its touch is ticklish under my feet. I curl my toes to grasp at the strands. Danny's mom serves us chocolate wafers and raspberry syrup with water. We study and then play Monopoly for a while, and Danny steals glances at me when he thinks I'm not looking. Nurit says he's too shy. He hardly ever speaks in class, even though he's really smart and knows the answers to almost everything. He's funny too. We get each other's sense of humor, which is a lot more than I can say about Alon, who doesn't really have a sense of humor at all.

Sometimes, in my dreams, we hug like grown-ups do.

WHEN ABA RETURNS from the hospital after a few weeks, my brother and I are so excited that we bounce on his bed until Ima yells at us to stop. I snuggle up to Aba and read him my new poems. His body feels brittle and bony. We take short walks and sometimes we run into people, and Aba stops and talks to them at length and I try to be patient and not fuss. Everyone knows my father in the neighborhood. They hold his hand in both their palms and then pinch my cheeks and pat my head.

One night I wake up to urgent voices from the living room, heavy feet climbing up the stairs. I tiptoe out of my room and watch from the landing. There are paramedics in the living room and Aba is lying on a stretcher. Ima holds his hand and nods at the paramedic with a furrowed brow. Aba has been home only a week.

The nights after Aba returns to the hospital, I hear stifled sobs creeping through the walls.

MY AUNTS TELL Ima that she should go see a special rabbi, a mekubal, who can help lift the curse. "Someone put the evil eye on you," the younger sister says, smoking out the open window, her kinky curls tied in a messy bun.

"Nonsense." Ima waves her hand.

My aunts' faces are a variation of my mother's, like artwork that was reproduced with slight modifications. They are all beautiful and weary, their skin marked with years of raising many children, of cooking and cleaning and shopping and breastfeeding and not sleeping. Despite their hardships, their beauty only seems to deepen with the years. I wish I had inherited the good looks from my maternal family instead of their sulk and bad temper.

They sit around the kitchen table, drinking Turkish coffee with milk in glass mugs—the grinds heaping thickly on the bottom—and eating my mom's ka'adid cookies, crumbly and freckled with nigella seeds. My oldest aunt, Rivka, bounces my baby brother on her knees and he squeals and giggles. Ima frowns at her coffee. Her cheeks are sunken now and her skin is sallow.

Eventually, my aunts go to the rabbi without her. When they come back, they say the rabbi knew that the incident had happened in water. "But it didn't," Ima says. "He was playing soccer."

"By the swimming pool!" my aunt says.

The rabbi also said we must check the mezuzahs on all the doorframes. I can hear the resolve in Ima's voice weakening. Later that week, unsmiling men in beards and kippahs unscrew the mezuzahs affixed on our doorposts and pry out the scrolls that are rolled inside like tiny SOS notes. They unfold the parchment papers and inspect the neatly scribed Torah verses through a magnifying glass.

They tell us the scrolls were faulty—they found typos in them—and must be replaced immediately. I'm relieved that the source of our troubles has been identified, and awed by the power of the written word.

. . .

WHEN WEEKS PASS and Aba doesn't get better, my aunts go back to the rabbi and return with another remedy. The rabbi concluded, based on numerological calculations, that we must legally change my baby brother's name. Many years ago, my aunt had changed her own name following a rabbi's advice and her luck turned, though her sisters never stopped calling her by her birth name. My mother gives in more quickly this time. At night I stand over my brother's crib and watch him sleep and I am flooded with sorrow. He is only one year old and he's perfect, with his tiny button nose and round face, his skin dark like my dad's. I like his old name. I don't want things to change.

ALON SLIPS ME a note in class. "I want to ask you to stop wearing jeans with holes. I don't want people thinking my girlfriend is poor."

I write back without thinking. "I'll wear whatever I want. I am not your girlfriend anymore, so there."

When I get home, the front door is locked. I walk to the back to see if the car is there, and I find Ima sitting in the driver's seat, head over the wheel, shoulders quivering. I steal away without her noticing me and go to Nurit's.

ON A SCHOOL trip to the Galilee, while everyone is frolicking in the aisle of the bus, singing and laughing, I watch the road winding up and down lush hills and remember the trips we used to take up north as a family before my baby brother was born, all seven of us cramped into my dad's Cortina, and me always stuck in the middle because I was the littlest. Back when we lived in our old place, Aba used to take me out of school sometimes and bring me to work with him. We'd drive to the court in Haifa or Jerusalem or Netanya, and I'd get to sit in the passenger seat like a grown-up. On the way there, we'd stop at a bookstore so I could pick a book to read while he worked. Once, we parked on the side of the highway and watched migrating birds and Aba told me about their journey. Another time, we walked along the seawall in Netanya and the breeze made my hair crazy, and even though I was already too big for it, he carried me for a bit, and it was nice to feel small because Ima was already pregnant and soon I wasn't going to be his baby anymore.

The tears come all at once. I press my face against the cool window so no one will see me and wipe my tears as soon as they leap out. From the gap between the window and the armrest, I suddenly see Danny watching me from a few seats down. I quickly move away from the window. When we get off the bus, we don't speak but his eyes search mine and stay on me a moment longer.

MY COUSIN MALKA, who is old enough to be my mom and teaches at my school, suggests to my mother that I see the school counselor. At the counselor's office, Malka sits behind me, by the door. The counselor's name is Rachel and she has a sympathetic smile plastered on her darkly painted lips. It looks fake, like a joker's mask. "I know this is a difficult time for you," she says softly. "I know you are very close with your father. Would you like to talk about it?"

I turn to look at Malka. She gives me an encouraging nod. The distant echo of a teacher's voice travels in through the open window. I don't want to talk about my father, because talking would make this real. Because then I would cry and I don't want to cry. I don't talk about it with anyone. Not my siblings. Not my mom. Not even Nurit. I don't even write about it in my diary.

I know about death. Savta Sarah, my father's mother, died two years ago, and my father didn't shave for thirty days afterward. He was sad and strange-looking, and I was sad too, but mostly for him, because I didn't really know her. I was one of many grandchildren that filled her tiny house in Sha'ariya every second Friday. She didn't speak Hebrew well and I didn't speak her dialect of Yemeni Judeo-Arabic. Their home was dark and cramped and smelled of cooking and of basil, which grew wild in their yard among the weeds and broken things that lay there in disarray.

I know about death because in the news they keep reading names of soldiers who die in Lebanon, and every Remembrance Day we grieve the heroes who gave their lives for our country, and every Holocaust Day we mourn the six million Jews who perished in the camps. Our country is haunted by its dead, weighed down by loss and remembrance.

When I was younger, I'd wake up some nights breathless from dreams so vivid I would later confuse them for memories, dreams in which I fell off the balcony or was run over by a car. I would race over to my parents' room, sobbing, "I don't want to die." My parents hugged and soothed me; they said everything was okay, I wasn't going to die for a very, very long time.

The counselor is waiting for me to say something. Finally, I say, "I'm worried."

Rachel leans forward, her smile now softer, sincere. "What are you worried about?"

I look at my lap and bite my nails; they taste like pencils and dust. "I worry he'll die," I say. It just slips out. I feel like I broke some spell by uttering those words, and now my throat is full of tears and I don't want them to burst out in front of this woman I don't know, in front of my cousin, who is probably going to tell my mother, but the tears stream out anyway now, silently, so many of them that they are dripping from my chin and my nose into my lap.

The counselor says some empty, sympathetic things. She urges me to go on, but I can't. I can't tell her of the awful thoughts I've had since I allowed myself to imagine. Like how the girls in class might be nicer to me if he died, how they might treat me more kindly, feel bad for what they did to me last year. I don't tell her how, for a brief moment—not even a second, really—I almost thought it wouldn't be so bad. And how hard I tried to take that thought back, erase it from my mind, but like trying to undo my turning on the light on Yom Kippur, I couldn't. The past could not be changed. My sins could not be rewritten.

DANNY AND I are alone in his room one afternoon when he says, voice shaky, "I have to tell you something." My heart races. But then Yoel walks in with a glass of water.

"Did you tell her?" he asks. Nurit walks in too.

Danny quickly says, "No."

"Tell me what?"

Danny fiddles with a thread of carpet. "My father got a job in America," he says, the way he says everything, softly, with a little smile. "We're moving there." He looks everywhere but at me.

I swallow. In my head, I try that sentence on. *My father got a job in America.*

Nurit glances at me. "When?"

"Next month." For the first time, his gaze lands on me, but I stare hard at the carpet, afraid that if I look up, my face will tell him everything.

"It's just for a year or two," he hastens to add. "We're coming back."

A lifetime.

. . .

DANNY WILL COME back for a visit the following year. By then, everything will be different. My father will die in his hospital bed on an ordinary Friday in the spring. He will die in the same hospital I was born in almost ten years before. I will sleep an entire night ignorant of that loss, and the next morning, I will wake up still unknowing, un-orphaned (and for the first few weeks after his death, every morning will begin with the same blissful amnesia before I am hijacked by remembering).

That morning, Shabbat morning, my mom will call me from her bed and I will be happy to snuggle up to her, to soak up the comforting softness of her body. But the room will be dark and airless, and the figure on the bed that is my mother will look like a broken, withered version of herself, and she will have terrible news.

That moment, crystallized in my memory through the fog of grief, will be the fork in the road where my future splits in two: what could have happened had he lived and what happened because he didn't. And as I grow up, I will try to live as wildly and loudly as I can to outdo the enormity of this moment, to diminish it.

Later that day, my childhood idol, Ofra Haza, will win second place at the Eurovision Song Contest, dressed in a glittery outfit and singing "Israel is alive" in Munich, of all places. The war in Lebanon will continue. Soldiers will die. It will rain, obviously, because what else could the sky do?

Later still, summer will come, bully its way in as it does in our country, with its cruel heat and glaring sun. My mother will pine away until she becomes a shadow, a faded replica of her younger self, and I will miss her all the time, even while she's around. And every time the doorbell rings, my baby brother's eyes will light up and then dim right down when someone who isn't our father walks in.

I will spend those months making deals with God, promise to forgo writing on Shabbat, to stop stealing from my sister, to wait the appropriate length of time between meat and dairy, until the futility of my prayers will dawn on me and I will feel stupid and hollow—like a cavity inside of me once filled with God has split open and the emptiness is gnawing at me like my hunger on Yom Kippur.

I will have a new boyfriend, Yariv, an only child to older Holocaust survivors whose house is even ghostlier than mine has become, and he will be sweet and effeminate and gay—I will somehow know that already then—and I will not love him the way I loved Danny.

By the time Danny comes, I will have discovered how easy it is to skip school, and I will hang out in parks to kill time, sit on benches and write poems about Aba, about wanting to die because then I could be with him. I will write because writing will be the only thing that makes any sense at all.

Danny will show up at recess, just for a short visit. Like many people who come back from a prolonged stay in the land of plenty, he's gained weight. Excited to see him, and flustered, I will blurt out to a group of kids, "Danny is back. He got fat," and then turn to see him standing behind me—perhaps coming to speak to me—and he'll be smiling that default smile of his but his face will be frozen in a wounded expression. And there will be nothing in the world I can do to fix this either.

I will watch Danny walk away, disappear into his parents' car and back to his new life in America, watch him with heart crumbling, but also with envy, a new yearning to be in his place. I will wish I was the one leaving, because that would be better than being left behind.

A SIMPLE GIRL

I N THE MID-EIGHTIES, after an impassioned campaign led by my
brother and me, my mother had pirated cable installed in our
house. One day, two burly men, unshaven and smelling of cigarettes, climbed on our roof and tinkered with the antenna. We
weren't the only delinquents; everyone on the street did it. Israeli
television operated only one state-owned channel, which had just
begun broadcasting in color and offered limited programming for
about ten hours a day, most of it dreary. The only show we
watched religiously was Friday night's Arabic movie: tear-jerking
Egyptian melodramas featuring voluptuous, smoky-eyed, big-
haired starlets my mother often scolded for their bad choices.
More often than not, I preferred reading books to watching television. The arrival of illegal cable changed everything; it broadcast
twenty-four hours a day, screening movies and miniseries rented
from the local video store, and some late-night erotica I snuck
downstairs to watch after everyone fell asleep.

One afternoon, during my mother's daily nap, I turned on the
TV and was delighted to happen upon the 1979 Israeli flick *Shlager*
(*The Hit*), showcasing Ofra Haza and the song that launched her
career, "Shir HaFreha" ("The Freha Song"). I sat cross-legged in
front of the screen, mesmerized by Ofra's younger incarnation.

Fresh-faced and still unknown, she looked a little bit like family, like one of my more beautiful cousins.

In the years since the movie was released, Ofra had gone on to become wildly famous, winning second place in the 1983 Eurovision Song Contest (another television event we watched dutifully). Later, she would become Israel's biggest musical export, even to this date, selling millions of records around the globe and earning a Grammy nomination. Later still, a tragic figure whose story would haunt fans long after her death.

Even without a developed Yemeni identity, I knew enough to be proud of Ofra Haza. The young singer from HaTikva Quarter—the impoverished neighborhood in south Tel Aviv—youngest of nine children born to Yemeni immigrants, was my community's Cinderella and one of few Mizrahi artists who made it into the heart of the Israeli canon. Ofra's humble beginnings gave me hope, for I wanted to be a singer and an actress when I grew up, just like her. I was already in the school's choir and had taken several drama classes, and I had the right genes. I may have never heard of a Yemeni author (which made my other dream, that of becoming a writer, seem a bit far-fetched), but everyone knew that Yemenis were great entertainers. The three times that Israel won the Eurovision contest, it was represented by Yemeni singers. Despite the glaring recording-industry bias against artists of Mizrahi descent and the radio's systematic exclusion of Mizrahi music—a genre inspired by Middle Eastern and North African musical traditions and rhythms—those Yemeni singers were seen as great ambassadors for Israel's image. European viewers went crazy for their "exotic" looks, their dance moves, and their kinky Yemeni curls. Our singing voices and our cuisine—spicy, doughy, often yellow with turmeric and fragrant with fenugreek and cilantro—were our greatest contributions to Israeli culture.

THE ART OF LEAVING · 25

In the movie, just before Ofra breaks into "The Freha Song," she asks her date, a boring-looking, suit-wearing Ashkenazi man, to dance with her, and he replies with contempt, "Are you some kind of a freha whose head is between her legs?" Even at eleven, I knew what frehas were—knew I didn't want to become one. The freha looked a lot like the starlets in the Egyptian movies we watched every Friday. She wore dramatic makeup and elaborate accessories ("Wherever the lights are, that's where I'll go, with the nail polish, the lipstick, and other show-offs"). She wasn't very smart ("I don't have a head for long words"), liked to party ("I want to dance, I want to laugh"), was promiscuous ("I want during the days, I want during the nights"), and knew, deep inside, that she would never escape the poor neighborhood she came from ("At the end of every freha hides a small housing project, a husband, and air pollution from a thousand directions").

I also knew that the freha was Mizrahi—not just because in the movie she was portrayed by a Yemeni actress, or because the term originated from a name common among women of North African descent (derived from the Arabic word for "happiness") but also because I had seen frehas in my neighborhood, older girls from the technical high school down the street who sat on the barricades holding cigarettes with thin manicured fingers, laughing loudly, their bodies bursting from their tight, revealing outfits and their gaits assured and all-sex. I had seen them on the outskirts of Sha'ariya, in the newer additions to the traditional Yemeni neighborhood where both of my parents grew up and my grandparents still lived. Sha'ariya made me uneasy, alive with aspects of my identity I wished to distance myself from: the loud Mizrahi music blaring from car windows, the elderly women in their headscarves who squinted at me when I walked by with my cousins, asking in their peculiar syntax and thick accents, "Bat mi at?" *Whose daughter are you?* Similarly, the teenage frehas I had seen there, loitering by the falafel stand or at the park, always surrounded by lusting boys, brought to light a part of me that I was conditioned to reject. Though I thought myself better than them, smarter, more versed in the ways of the world, I secretly admired the confidence with which they carried themselves, as though they knew something I didn't, something about boys, or their bodies, or sex, or about how to be happy. They were only a couple of years older than me, but they appeared to be women already, while I was still a girl.

"The Freha Song" had swept through Israel in a frenzy, remaining at the top of the charts for five weeks. Even after this big break, and despite singing mainstream pop that did not fall under the Mizrahi label, Ofra struggled to find lyricists and composers willing to write for her. Eventually, her manager, Bezalel Aloni, began writing her music, and later in her career, Ofra composed her own songs. Her fans voted to award her Israel's Singer of the Year for five consecutive years, and her albums broke sales records, but the radio rarely played her music. "I don't know why they don't give me a chance," she said in an interview. Bezalel Aloni, less diplomatic, simply said, "The radio is for Ashkenazi singers."

*　　♪　　♪　　♪*

"I CAN'T WEAR that," I told my high school friend Yael. She was offering to lend me one of her short, tight skirts for the night. We were going dancing at the Liquid Club in south Tel Aviv, a large, smoky hangar that played new wave, pop, and punk. The evening had just begun and I was already far outside my comfort zone: I was wearing Yael's stylish button-up blouse, and my curly hair was huge after I allowed Yael to blow-dry it upside down while I was bent over the sink. I didn't know what one did in clubs. I didn't know how to talk to boys. I didn't own the right clothes and I couldn't dance—unless, of course, I was at a wedding with my family and traditional Yemeni music started playing. Despite my aversion to popular Mizrahi music with its undulating voices and corny lyrics, my body had a visceral reaction to Yemeni beats, to the sound of tin drums, like a buzz coursed through it, compelling me to rise to my feet.

At that point, my obsession with Ofra had simmered down to a mature admiration. In junior high I had removed Ofra's wholesome posters from my walls and replaced them with Madonna's. Hypersexual and provocative, Madonna was the mother of all frehas, and as a newly proclaimed feminist, I found her empowering. My horrified mother sighed wearily whenever I left for school dressed in lace and ripped stockings, neck laden with chains, arms dangling with silver bangles that tinkled loudly every time I flipped a page in my textbook, irritating my teachers. Thankfully, that phase was over.

Ofra, too, had matured and turned in a new musical direction. In 1984, she recorded *Yemenite Songs*, an album of remixed traditional Yemeni tunes, devotional and secular, in Hebrew and in Arabic—songs her mother, who used to perform at henna ceremonies back in Yemen, had sung to her growing up. Ofra appeared on the cover in a traditional Yemeni wedding gown, an ornate golden hood over her head. The record was met with bewilderment. Not until the album was released in England to great acclaim, and European clubgoers began hopping to the same Yemeni beats I had danced to at family weddings, did Israeli media take notice. Her subsequent Yemeni album, *Shaday*, sold more than a million copies worldwide and won her the New Music Award for Best International Album of the Year in New York in 1989.

My friend Yael held the skirt in front of me. "Why not?"

"Because I'd look like a freha," I said. Animal prints were also out. Certain shades of lipstick, such as blood red and neon pink. Dangly, large earrings. Anything gold. Anything with rhinestones. Bleached hair, a popular trend among my fair-skinned friends, was an absolute no-no. A Mizrahi girl with blond streaks was as freha as one could get.

"That's crazy. You're not a freha," Yael said with conviction. "So nothing you'll ever wear will make you look like one." Yael's parents had come from Poland. She could wear anything.

For a moment, I reconsidered. Then I remembered how wearing the wrong things in junior high during the ill-fated Madonna phase got me attention from the wrong men—older Mizrahi men who wore thick golden necklaces and tight T-shirts and too much gel in their hair. In other words, arsim, the male counterparts of frehas and plural for *ars*, the colloquial Arabic word for "pimp." They would inch by me in their cars, lean out the window, and say uninspired things like, "You're a flower that needs a constant gardener," and "Did it hurt when you fell from heaven?"

At fifteen, I had just developed a set of hips and an ass that drew more attention than I cared for, especially in contrast to the rest of my scrawny body. Those hips, if I wasn't paying attention, swung from side to side when I walked, in a manner I soon discovered could be read as "asking for it." I didn't even know they did that until a boy at school pointed it out, laughing and bellowing, "Look at her meantezet!" using an Arabic slang word to describe my hip-swaying walk. I had a vague notion that the use of an Ara-

At first, my hippie-ness was mostly expressed through my fashion choices: long flowery skirts and dresses, trench coats, and vests. I perused the flea market in Jaffa for silver earrings, chiffon scarves, and harem pants. I stopped brushing my hair and came to school dressed in conversation pieces. If I wasn't going to be popular, at least I would be memorable. Then I began catching up on music I figured I should listen to in order to grant my image more cred, music far more sophisticated than Madonna or Ofra Haza, like Janis Joplin, Carole King, Led Zeppelin, and Pink Floyd.

When strangers asked—judging by my newly cultivated look—if I was from a kibbutz or a moshav, Ashkenazi strongholds in Israel (in the same way that developing, impoverished towns were predominantly Mizrahi), I took it as a compliment. When meeting new people, I casually mentioned my disdain for Mizrahi music, made references to Chekhov or Lorca, worked my writing career and love of theater into conversation, and flaunted my impressive vocabulary so they would know I had "a head for long words." I shared progressive political views that were not necessarily in line with what you'd expect a Mizrahi girl to have, as Mizrahi traditionally vote for right-wing parties. At one demonstration I attended, a couple of men gaped at me: a Mizrahi hippie girl carrying a peace sign. "Look at this little sh'hora." They spat their words with derision. "Who do you think you are?" I'd been called black before—once, by a disappointed boy Yael had set me up with, to whom she'd neglected to mention my Yemeni background. In a society that idealized a Western beauty standard rarely found within its vicinity—blond, light-skinned, blue-eyed—I looked all wrong. And yet, I had always been fair for a Yemeni. Fairer than many of my female cousins who had been taught by their mothers to fear the sun. Fair like my grandmother who, raised in a culture imbued by shadism, was admired for her

light skin while her twin sister, Saida, was nicknamed "Aswada"—
"black" in Arabic.

Bored and restless in school, I started doing freha impressions
during class, to my teachers' displeasure and to the delight of the
back row. Making fun of frehas ensured, so I thought, that no one
would ever mistake me for one. Lacking the confidence to sing
onstage, I had long given up on my musical aspirations, but playing a role granted me a welcome hiatus from my unhappy, awkward teenage self. And the freha was an easy act: I combed my
hair with my fingers to give it volume, chewed gum with an open
mouth, blew bubbles, and dumbed down my language. My classmates were entertained.

Then I wrote an entire freha monologue and acted it out in a
couple of auditions for commercials and movies. The freha monologue got me the small part of a vulgar, angry wife for a Turkish
coffee commercial. It made the judges for the coveted army entertainment group, which performed at remote bases to raise soldiers' morale, laugh out loud. It got me past the first cut and into
the second selection process, even after my nervous, stilted singing performance. This was no easy feat. Inconceivably, Ofra herself had never made it into the army group. "I guess she didn't fit
the *style*," her manager said dryly.

Later, I performed the monologue on demand at parties. "Do
the freha," my friends would implore, and I would, enjoying the
laughter, high on the attention—not once stopping to think
about the girl I was mocking. My own inner freha began escorting
me everywhere, my sidekick, always ready to make an entrance.
While I was often insecure around new people, she was chatty
and too stupid to care what people thought of her. Sometimes, in
social situations, I'd slip into her momentarily for laughs, making
a comment or an inarticulate observation accompanied by a hair

toss. People who didn't know me sometimes confused her for me, exchanging glances with their friends and rolling their eyes. And though I should have regarded it as the best compliment to my acting skills, I was mortified, and quickly made sure they knew I was kidding. That wasn't me. I wasn't her.

* * *

PEOPLE IN ISRAEL like to say that the compulsory army service is the country's biggest melting pot. Young men and women from different backgrounds and social and economic status are brought together, mixed, and blended at high speed. In reality, there is also a great measure of segregation, reminiscent of, and likely originating from, a tracking system that directs Mizrahi youth toward technical schools, gearing them for trade and service jobs as mechanics, cooks, and secretarial staff.

At the end of basic training, the army decided the best way to use my skills was to station me as a secretary in an administrative base. I knew I'd scored high in the army classification tests in twelfth grade. I had peeked at my printout sheet during one of the appointments in basic training, noticing, also, that it said "Yemen" under family origin even though I was born in Israel and so were my parents. For weeks, I cried over my assignment. I had been working as a prolific journalist from the age of fifteen, and my test results were high enough for me to have become a pilot had I been a man. Surely there was a better way the army could have used me; I could have been a writer for the army magazine or a reporter for the army radio station, two sought-after positions I was a natural candidate for, yet I was unable to apply, eliminated in an initial selection process rumored to be impelled by nepotism. Not to mention I couldn't type properly, file, or make coffee. I wasn't even a high-ranking officer's secretary, but everyone knew that to be in those offices, you had to be thin, pretty, and preferably blond, because you were the face of the Israel Defense Forces.

Since its creation in 1948, Israel has never had a Mizrahi prime minister and only three Mizrahi chiefs of general staff, with the first one coming into the position thirty-six years after the founding of the country. And while you'd be hard pressed to find a Mizrahi pilot (considered the most elite position one can attain in the IDF, as the air force's slogan claims "The Best for Pilotage!"), it was apparent that most drivers, janitors, quartermaster clerks, and sentries in the army were of Mizrahi background.

After a year as the army's worst secretary and after giving up on the army entirely (arguably, it gave up on me first), I found myself in one of these lowermost positions, pressing buttons that opened and closed the gate to the base.

A friend from school came to visit one day. Ilanit was an officer now: it was evident in her step, her newly acquired poise—her confidence boosted by those rectangular pieces of metal sewn on her shoulder straps that indicated her rank. The pity in her eyes was palpable. While she was there, I got into an unnecessary argument with one of the janitors and he yelled, "Shut up, you dumb freha."

Ilanit's cheeks reddened. "How dare you?" She fumbled for words. "Do you know who she is?"

"Yeah," the guy said. "She presses buttons at the gate."

"She's a writer!" Ilanit said, but the guy snorted and walked away, waving in dismissal.

"It's fine." I pulled her away. "I don't care."

I was in khaki like everyone else. But I was on the bottom rung of the army ladder, and I was Mizrahi, and a girl, and it was the only slur that fit.

* * *

"YOU'RE A SIMPLE girl," a guy I met on a beach in Sinai once said to me, with a paternal smile. My (Ashkenazi, kibbutznik) boyfriend, Gilad, and I had come to Sinai for a vacation after completing our army service. We slept in a straw hut by the sea, struck up conversations with strangers, made friends with other backpackers in the huts next door. This man—educated, well-off, Ashkenazi, and slightly older—was one of them.

"I am not simple," I snapped. "You don't know me."

"I didn't say it was a bad thing," he said.

I glared and said nothing.

"I just don't get it. Why would he think of me as simple?" I asked Gilad later.

He flipped a page in his book. "Who cares about this guy?"

The World Dictionary of Hebrew Slang by Dan Ben-Amotz and Netiva Ben-Yehuda describes the freha as "a simple girl, vulgar, uneducated and lacking in class, who dresses according to the latest fashion." All that effort and still, to this man, I couldn't be anything else. With or without the hippie clothing, with or without the kibbutznik boyfriend.

"I AM A simple girl from HaTikva neighborhood," Ofra had said in an interview once, unchanged by her fame or fortune. "A Yemeni girl with legs on the ground who enjoys life, loves her parents, and thanks God."

Ofra was known for her gentle manners and great constraint. She didn't party, she didn't date. Her makeup was subtle and her attire conservative. If anything, Ofra Haza was the anti-freha.

There was something almost unreasonably pure and innocent about her. She found joy and purpose in simplicity, in being grounded, in being connected to one's roots—qualities I had failed to appreciate or possess. I had spent a lifetime proving to unimportant people that I was complex, slipping into yet another patronizing label, that of a mishtaknezet—a Mizrahi who's trying to "pass" as Ashkenazi, as if being cultured, educated, and articulate were qualities reserved for Europeans. It had been so much work to keep apologizing when I hadn't fully understood the accusation. I couldn't see that by striving to prove myself different, I was estranging myself from my heritage, my history, myself.

*   *   *

IN MY EARLY thirties, I started working at a Lebanese restaurant in Vancouver. Mona's was a hub around which the Middle Eastern community in the city assembled, a new Middle East to which I—the Israeli, the Jew—was graciously permitted entrance. At Mona's I looked like everyone else. "You look more Arabic than I do!" Mona often said with a chuckle. The music they played, the food they served, the language they spoke were familiar and comforting. The family quickly adopted me, and I celebrated holidays and birthdays with them. I was half a world away from my country, and for the first time since I'd moved to Canada, I felt at home.

The groups of young women who came to Mona's to dine and dance and smoke water pipes often looked like what I imagined the actresses from the old Arabic movies would have looked like today. They reminded me of the teenage girls from Sha'ariya, exhibiting that overstated expression of womanhood that made me—the late bloomer who couldn't walk in heels, who found skills such as applying eye shadow or blow-drying one's hair inscrutable and foreign—feel like an impostor.

During my six-year stint at Mona's, their magic started rubbing off on me. It was around that time that I also began discovering my own Arabness, my way back to the Yemeni identity I had rejected as a teen, as though my body retuned itself, gave up the fight. Perhaps feeling at home in my own skin had made me more at ease with my femininity too, made me care less about what people might think or what they might call me. Or perhaps it was the acceptance of oneself that comes with age. Some days, I wore miniskirts to work, revealing blouses over push-up bras, long dangly earrings or large hoops, dramatic, ornate jewelry, sometimes even gold. I learned to apply makeup, had my eyebrows threaded at the Iranian aesthetician they recommended, cut my hair at the Lebanese hairdresser who specialized in curly Middle Eastern manes. I strutted with my trays across the floor, hips swaying, and belly danced to Arabic pop much like the Mizrahi music I had once snubbed, embracing the sensuality of the dance, allowing the natural movement of my body to take place, for my body to take up space. Never had I spent as much time on my appearance as I did while working at Mona's. And though I did not pull it off as well as my young tutors did, never with the same effortlessness, during those years at Mona's, I felt more beautiful and womanly than ever before.

* * *

THE LATE DR. Vicki Shiran, a Mizrahi scholar, activist, and poet, wrote once about the twinge she feels when she hears the word *freha*. "I see you," she wrote, "a Moroccan woman standing embarrassed, and behind your back the shimmering ugly face of the Israeli mob who took your beautiful name and made it synonymous with a vulgar woman whose heart is rough . . . Took your name and used it to mock my daughters and your granddaughters."

It's been forty years since "The Freha Song" took over Israel, and probably twenty years since anyone has called me by that slur. Things have changed in Israel: the disparities between Ashkenazi and Mizrahi have narrowed, partly because of intermarriages; popular Mizrahi music has found its way into the heart of mainstream radio; and activists have begun calling the media out on their under-representation of Mizrahi characters, demanding to see more brown-skinned people in advertising and entertainment, and not just in the role of frehas, arsim, criminals, and workingmen. Young Mizrahi poets have sidestepped the gatekeepers by crowdfunding their own books and launching their own poetry readings, and in 2015, Erez Biton became the first Mizrahi poet to win the Israel Prize for Literature. Subsequently, the Israeli government asked Biton to head a new committee that recommended adding Mizrahi content to the school curriculum. Still, only 9 percent of the academic staff in Israel are Mizrahi, and most key positions in places like the Supreme Court and the media are held by Ashkenazi. And while Israeli slang has evolved and changed, *freha* shows no signs of waning.

In recent years, some young professional Mizrahi women in Israel have decided to reclaim the term. They created a Facebook page defiantly named "Who Are You Calling a Freha?," its cover photo asserting, "This is not Europe." Their About section reads, "Do you love wearing animal prints but they twist their face at you in university? Do you enjoy rhinestones but people call you freha?" and their photos showcase women with long manicured nails dressed in bold fashion statements.

When I watch Ofra singing "The Freha Song" now, I see there

is something unconvincing about her delivery that I couldn't see then, a little flinch in her eyes whenever she utters the words "Ani freha." For a while, I wanted to believe it was subversive and brave of her to be singing those lyrics, an act of reclaiming the demeaning label as these young women in the Facebook group try to do today. But the song was never truly hers: "The Freha Song" was written by Assi Dayan, son of the legendary Israeli defense minister Moshe Dayan and a tortured artist with a penchant for drugs and women—a privileged Ashkenazi man who knew nothing about the freha experience.

Despite Ofra's wholesome image, "The Freha Song" is one of the tracks most associated with her. But the song, and the controversy it spurred, was also a roadblock in her career. Officials at Galei Tzahal, the popular army radio station, considered banning it, concerned with its inappropriate content. Some Israelis found it racist and offensive. Toward the end of her days, Ofra refused to sing the song, distancing herself from it and from what it represented.

OFRA'S DEATH IN 2000 from a disease later revealed to be a complication of AIDS shocked everyone. She was young, recently married, and at the height of her career. By then, I was living in Vancouver, working part-time as a barista, mostly stoned, and achingly lonely. It was in the days before social media, and I was becoming disengaged from my country, its pop culture, its gossip and news.

Listening to Ofra's CDs in my West End apartment in the days following her death—the West Coast granite skies migrating in through my sixth-floor windows—I found that I still knew all the words. Her voice stirred forgotten childhood memories, an old nagging ache. I had always held an irrational conviction that one day I'd meet her in person. Even after she sang for DreamWorks' *The Prince of Egypt* and sat on Johnny Carson's couch, she felt so close, so human and real, as though I could run into her at any minute on the streets of Sha'ariya.

Now, I thought, I would never get to tell her what she had meant to me growing up, how much she had inspired me, given me hope, empowered me—because in a world where the actors on TV were Ashkenazi and the singers on the radio were Ashkenazi and the models in magazines were Ashkenazi, there was Ofra, the simple Yemeni girl from HaTikva neighborhood whose star shone brighter than anyone's, who made it against all odds, and who looked like me, or like one of my more beautiful cousins. Like family.

YOU AND WHAT ARMY

ON MY NINETEENTH BIRTHDAY, I was lying on a yellowing patch of lawn in front of an army dormitory, waiting to be questioned by the military police. I was dressed in a khaki uniform that was a tad too tight, the button of my pants pressing against the folds of my belly. Around me, other girls in uniform were chatting and waving away flies. Others had fallen asleep.

We'd been here since before dawn, when we'd rolled out of our beds for our 4:00 A.M. patrol to discover that two guns had gone missing. Soon after that, military police officers showed up at our dorm with grave faces, stretched bright orange tape at the entrance to our room, and declared it a crime scene.

Now, a few hours later, it was a typical Israeli spring day, intensely bright and overexposed. The sky was a faded pair of acid-washed jeans. I leaned my head back on the grass, closed my eyes, and gave in to the warmth of sun on my eyelids, willing myself to fall asleep. The inside of my eyelids was orange and paper-thin.

Slipping into a drowsy daze, I drifted back to my eighteenth birthday. On this day last year, my friends and I went to a beach party outside Tel Aviv. The day was warm and breezy, smelling of fish, salt, and teen spirit. I danced barefoot in the sand in a flowing red dress and drank beer I had purchased without having to lie about my age. I had just graduated from high school a few days earlier, after three turbulent years. I was nearly expelled twice, and had earned an unprecedented E in behavior and a reputation of being a teacher's worst nightmare. With high school behind me, the air was sweeter, the beer colder, the boys better-looking.

Back on the lawn, I opened my eyes, depressed by the stark contrast. I was nineteen and a soldier, trapped in a hideous outfit on a dreary army base. It had been seven miserable months since I joined the army, and I had seventeen more to go. This was the second-worst birthday I'd ever had. The worst one, my tenth, was a month after my father's death.

A dark shadow eclipsed my sun. I squinted and made out a military police officer towering above me. He spat a list of seven digits, like shots fired from an automatic weapon. It was a mysterious jumble, a couple of sevens here and a couple of threes there, mixed with an eight, a nine, and a six. This thoughtless arrangement, which was impossible to memorize, was my number. My official army ID. My new name. Huddled closely against one another and uttered with a dash of disdain, the numbers sounded like an accusation. In a daze, I replied, "Yes?" and then quickly stood up, cleared my throat, and saluted. "I mean . . . Officer. Sir."

"Come with me." He turned on his heel.

I followed him to a dark dormitory room, temporarily converted into a police office. Inside, high-ranking officers in neatly ironed uniforms stared at me grimly. One of them spoke, demanding to know if I'd heard something—anything at all— during the night, if I had any idea who might have stolen the guns, if I'd noticed something suspicious over the past couple of days. "Anything, anything at all," he said, almost pleading. I said no, again and again. They stared at me a little longer.

The next day, a military police officer summoned me to an investigation. I was now a suspect.

I JOINED THE Israel Defense Forces at eighteen, a few months after my high school graduation and the end of the first Gulf War. Saying I "joined" the IDF makes it sound as if I did it on a whim, like taking tap-dance lessons or signing up for a book club. Really, I had no choice. In Israel, the army service is mandatory, and I lacked the foresight to claim pacifism or lunacy and get myself discharged. Somehow, I romanticized the army service. When you grow up in a place that has never known peace, where the army is what you do—what everyone does—after high school, you can develop strange ideas about what the military is. You might tell yourself that it's just like college days for Americans, or that it's a great way to meet boys and get out of your parents' house. You might push aside thoughts of war and occupation, forget that throughout history, millions of young soldiers have died in combat and innocent civilians have been killed by their bullets. You have to, because this is your life. This is your home.

And so I pictured myself stationed in a secluded base in the south, where I'd meet a cute boy who'd sneak into my tent at night. I dreamed of becoming an instructor in an all-male fighters' unit, like Kelly McGillis in *Top Gun,* terrorizing a group of hot men while watching their perfectly toned bodies gather sweat under my command.

Instead, our basic training camp was in a female-only base in the desert, where the only thing to sneak into my tent was sand, coating my hair and skin and creeping into my orifices. We were assigned to tents and beds with sheets and scratchy blankets neatly tucked into them, the smell of desert dust and gunpowder sweetened by girls' moisturizers and lotions. We were each handed an Uzi: we had to take it everywhere, sleep with it, wake with it. "Treat it like your boyfriend," the sergeant, deceivingly diminutive and strikingly beautiful, said. That night, lying with the cold metal poking under my lumpy pillow, I cried myself to sleep. Outside the tent, the wilderness swarmed with unfamiliar sounds and wandering beams of light.

We tumbled out of our beds at four o'clock every morning to days filled with repetitive drills and grueling duties: we scrubbed bathrooms, scoured the base's grounds, washed mountains of dishes, and guarded the base at night. During the day, we ran. We sat in class. We did jumping jacks. In the evenings, we stuffed ourselves with chocolate and candy in the canteen and talked about sex and boys and our mothers' cooking. Some nights, we were woken up from sleep for more drills, ordered to get dressed, clean our rooms, disassemble and reassemble our guns. Groggy and stunned, we scrambled to follow the sergeant's orders while she timed our performance, which was almost always inadequate.

By the end of the first week, it felt as though I had known the other girls in my tent forever, especially Shelly, a tough girl from the south with tragic eyes and fiery curls who slept in the bed beside mine. I had learned to fire an Uzi, surprised by the painful impact as it dug into my shoulder with each shot, leaving a purple bruise. I could take my Uzi apart and reassemble it within seconds, cleaning it until the barrel was smooth and gleaming when the sergeant inspected it, tilted up toward the light. I learned self-defense and first aid, and discovered that despite consistently skipping physical education classes, I could, when put on the spot, erect a tent in minutes and run for kilometers with a stretcher on my shoulder. I also learned that I couldn't charm an officer, that I couldn't get away with anything, and that I had to do what I was told. The army and I were all wrong for each other.

My post after basic training was in the army ombudsman's office in a large administrative base in Tel Aviv. A colorless cluster of concrete buildings with trees and bushes placed in an orderly fashion, it was a world of serial numbers, strict regulations, and abbreviated lingo. For the first few months, I came home every day, locked myself in my room, and cried into my pillow. I walked through the base in awe that other soldiers could laugh or enjoy small talk with each other. My only saving grace was Shelly, who had been stationed in the same base, in an office not far from mine, but she seemed as shell-shocked and depressed as I was. Sometimes I took off my glasses and wandered blind, hiding in the blur, like a child who puts her hands to her eyes and believes no one can see her. Without my glasses, the base appeared softer, an abstract watercolor painting in cool shades of pale gray and khaki green.

Over the next few months, things got progressively worse. I developed a minor eating disorder, and a juvenile crush on Amos, an aging married officer who showed a fatherly interest in me. I collected a record number of court appearances for breaching army regulations: I neglected to tie my hair in a proper ponytail, untucked my shirt, lost my ID, and misplaced my cap. On my long daily commute to my mother's house in Petah Tikva, I wrote short stories about miserable female soldiers whose lives were falling apart.

My nineteenth birthday fell on my weekend watch duties, a monthly task I dreaded. I had to spend the entire weekend at the base, patrolling the fences with an Uzi, making sure no one tried to break in to, say, steal guns. Unlike in civilian workplaces, I couldn't ask to switch shifts, and nobody cared that it was my birthday.

I arrived in the girls' dorm on a Friday and settled into the bare narrow room, which was framed with rows of metal bunk beds. The girls occupying the other beds unzipped backpacks and pulled out lotions and hairsprays, sweets and snacks, Walkmans and fashion magazines. Some changed into lounging clothes, revealing lacy bras and G-strings underneath the khaki.

Netta was the last to arrive. When we saw each other, we gasped and fell into each other's arms. Many years earlier, Netta and I had been best friends. I had lost my father in fourth grade and she lost hers in fifth grade. She had four miniature pinscher dogs that munched on my feet when I slept over. Her mom used to make figurines out of avocado pits. Netta had that hot soldier look going for her, a look I never mastered. Her cotton uniform was worn-out, fitting her bum snugly, as if it were a perfect pair of jeans, and her button-up shirt offered a glimpse of cleavage that just barely met with army regulations.

I got the top bunk, by a smeared window overlooking Tel Aviv streets. That night, as my birthday officially began, I lay awake and watched cars filled with young partyers on their way to the clubs, arms leaning on window ledges, fingers flicking out cigarette butts, long hair blowing in the wind. Music blared as they stopped at the light, and then faded away as they sped off. The traffic lights from the nearest intersection cast a tricolor slideshow on our white walls, and the whining of sirens sawed through the starless night, sneaking into our dreams.

It was still dark out when the officers' hollers woke us up for our two-hour watch. I put on my uniform, then grabbed my Uzi from under my bunk and flung it over my shoulder. Netta reached under the bed for her Uzi. "Hey, girls," she said slowly. "Where is my gun?"

"Oh my God." Another girl patted the space under her bunk with increasing panic. "Mine's gone too."

. . .

ON SUNDAY MORNING, the first day of the week in Israel, I was back at the office. After the phone call from the military police, I packed my bag and cheerfully informed my boss that I was a suspect in a gun theft investigation and I must leave everything and go. Of course, the army police had already informed him. "I probably won't be back today," I said with a large grin. My boss was a lieutenant colonel with a protruding belly and freckled face whose rank was all he had going for him. I was the worst secretary he'd ever had. My coffee was barely drinkable, my phone manners were a disgrace, and I typed with one finger and refused to get better at it. He waved me out of his office with a dismissive sigh.

An hour and a half later, I arrived at the military police headquarters. Away from the city, the sky was bigger and bluer, and the breeze sifted through the row of cypress trees that lined the barbed wire fence.

Waiting on the wooden bench outside the investigation room, I tried to make out the muffled conversations. When the door finally opened, a cute, skinny soldier with spiky hair and thick-framed glasses—just my type—gestured me in. The room was small and windowless and smelled of a typical canteen lunch: cheesy and fried. The soldier—a detective, I soon determined—joined a female detective, who raised her head briefly from behind the large desk and then continued to jot notes on a scratch pad. They were both about my age. Finally, the girl looked up, intertwined her hands on the desk, and studied me. I smirked.

They started with questions similar to the ones I had answered at the scene, then repeated them, differently phrased. They seemed to have borrowed their investigating techniques from a *Starsky & Hutch* episode: they paced around the room, shooting questions at me with narrowed eyes. The girl—who had dirty-blond hair and beady eyes—was playing Bad Cop, and the guy was Good Cop. Every now and then, they exchanged meaningful glances or scribbled quick notes in my file. I sprawled in the chair in front of them with my legs stretched out and my arms crossed, smiling with my mouth closed, as though I found the entire thing highly entertaining.

"How long have you had an overdraft?" Bad Cop bent over the desk with both hands firmly planted in front of her. I bristled, suddenly less amused. How did they know that? What else did they know? It was clear, even to me, that I had a solid motive. Selling guns would certainly fill the bottomless pit that was my bank account.

"When was your credit card revoked?" Good Cop leaned against the front of the desk with his hands in his pockets, facing me. His voice was soft and his eyes kind. I gave him a generous smile with my answer, and checked him out as he turned around. An image flashed in my head and I indulged it for a moment: Good Cop clears the desk with one swift motion, clouding the room with flapping paper. He flings me on the desk, rips my khaki shirt open to reveal a bra much sexier than the one I am actually wearing. My buttons fall to the floor in quick succession, like the shells of an Uzi.

"How exactly are you planning to cover your debts?" Bad Cop snarled, killing the moment. I suspected her family was well-off. I was willing to bet that her daddy took care of her debts.

I told them that due to financial hardship, I was granted a special permit to work outside the army, and that I had an evening job in a little movie theater that screened foreign films. I watched every single movie, ate heaps of free buttery popcorn, and cried at all the appropriate parts and sometimes at other parts as well. Since I worked for minimum wage, my paychecks were a few drops of rain to a desert soil. Still, instead of eating free lunch at the base's dining room, I'd take myself out to a café in town, order pasta in cream sauce and a chocolate cake for dessert. Outside the base, on a sunny patio surrounded by civilians on their business lunches, I let my hair down, unbuttoned my shirt, and pretended I was free.

Over the next few weeks, I returned to the military police headquarters several times. I'd go about my day at the office until they called—cold official voices ordering me to appear for an interrogation immediately. The sessions all seemed to blend into one. They repeated the same questions, exchanged the same glances, wrote notes in my ever-growing file. Sometimes we sat in different rooms. Sometimes new officers came to question me. I was bored and let it show, yawning liberally, staring at an imaginary speck of dust on my pants, weaving hormone-saturated fantasies in my head.

One day, I ran into Netta in the waiting room. She gave me a quick guilty look, and I could tell that she was frightened. We didn't talk about it, but we both knew that we would never tell them how we had teamed up to commit our very first crime. We were eleven; it was a couple of months after Netta's father died. We stole a chocolate bar from the supermarket by our school, then ran to the park and ate it greedily, our hearts racing and our cheeks flushed. We were astonished by how easy it had been to fool a store full of adults. We went back a few more times after that, becoming more daring, pushing the boundaries further. We were never caught.

A COUPLE OF months into my investigation, I sat at a police station in front of an officer with a bushy mustache. It was a gray morning in Tel Aviv. Fall had just arrived, heralded by the first rain, a heavy downpour that washed away the summer dust and turned the roads into slippery mirrors. I was wired up to a lie detector, strapped in with two rubber belts over my breasts, a few wires attached to my fingers, and a big cuff wrapped tightly around my arm. I couldn't help but find it kinky.

This was a civilian police station: a maze of long corridors with closed doors, filled with the echoes of dragging feet, clanking handcuffs, and persistent phone rings. This officer was a real cop, much older than those young army detectives, and not the least impressed by my attitude. As far as he was concerned, I could be a gun thief. Why not me, who had barely finished high school? Whose behavior sheet was littered with regulation breaches? Who had nine disciplinary trials in the past year? Who clearly lacked money management skills?

"Sit straight," he barked.

I reluctantly sat up.

"I'm going to ask you a few questions before we begin," he said as he browsed through my file. His voice was tired and monotonous. "I need to know if you ever stole anything."

My eyes widened. "Like, ever?"

"Yes."

I'd been a small-time thief as a kid. Sometimes I stole things I desired but couldn't afford, like books and magazines. Other times I stole for the thrill of it: candies and pop, the occasional scarf or sunglasses from a large department store. I was good at it too. Never got caught. "Yes, I have stolen things before."

"Have you ever stolen anything from the army?"

I hated the army, and I was broke. There were the pens and paper, the occasional binder, and maybe a couple of stamps. I told him that. He glared at me. "Are you so strapped for money that you have to steal from the army?"

I looked at him blankly, the way people do when they have nothing to lose. "Are you here to perform a test or are you here to question my morals?"

And so we proceeded.

He asked a set of questions to establish my reactions when answering truthfully: my name, my rank, my age. I watched the needle move erratically as I answered, wishing I was one of those people who could manipulate lie detectors, who had control over their anxiety and perspiration. Then he asked, "Did you ever steal anything from the army except for what you already told me?"

I shifted in my chair. What if I'd forgotten something? "I don't know. I'm not sure."

"This is a yes-or-no question."

Hesitation. Could I possibly fail the lie detector test? Could I really be charged with gun theft? Until now, it was all a joke, an entertaining anecdote, a way for me to get out of the office. Now I was thinking of Kafka, remembering *The Trial,* which I had watched earlier that year at Habima, Israel's national theater in Tel Aviv. It was around that time that I began throwing the word *Kafkaesque* into conversations and was pleased by the intellectual air it bestowed upon me.

Finally, I said, "No."

This would be my last interrogation, but I didn't know that. They would never tell me I was off the hook, but after the polygraph, the phone calls stopped. I stepped outside the station to a city renewed by the first rain, smelling as fresh as clothes off the laundry lines. I ran into Good Cop in the parking lot—he must have been there to collect my test results. It was the first time I'd seen him outside the investigation room. He smiled at me. We chatted. I blushed. Still, I didn't see it as a good sign. I didn't feel relieved.

Instead, I gave up trying to pretend that I gave a shit. If this was happening, if I was truly a suspect in a gun theft and accused of treason, I figured I could get away with pretty much anything. I concentrated on being rude, talking back, and lying. I was often late and always grumpy. After I neglected to complete an archiving job my boss had requested and lied about the reasons for it, he finally decided he had suffered through enough of my bitter coffee and bad attitude and threw me out of the unit. When I said goodbye to Amos, the aging officer I fancied, he shook his head at me with disappointment. I had grown inured to these kinds of reactions from people foolish enough to have faith in me. I was relocated to another unit in the same base, where the office was duller, the men older. Within a month, I managed to get myself kicked out of that unit as well.

I had now paved my way to the base's recycling bin, a transit unit consisting of misfits and rejects, troubled and authority-challenged soldiers. Soldiers who ended up there were assigned to the dirtiest and most mindless jobs, mostly cleaning and standing at the base's gates. I noticed most of us were Mizrahi.

My new job required no training and no skills. A seven-year-old could have done it just as well, or in my case, maybe better. It involved standing by the gate and following an armed military policeman's hand signals. When a car approached, the policeman authorized it and waved at me to open the gate by pressing a button. Once the car passed, it was up to me to push another button to shut the gate. Long hours of standing in the heat made me daydream of traveling to tropical islands with names that rolled in my mouth like candy. Mozambique, Martinique, Mauritius. I dreamed of making love to exotic men who fed me pineapple and coconut on sandy beaches.

I damaged two cars in a two-week period. The first one was a little Fiat. The gate was the kind that dropped like a drawbridge onto the ground for the car to drive over. Once the Fiat had passed, I pressed a button to lift the gate back up. Except the car was still passing. I heard the metallic clatter of the gate lifting and a loud thump as it met with the bottom of the car. The little Fiat bounced several times, bumping the angry driver's head against the roof.

A week later, I was standing at another gate, which closed like elevator doors. Distracted by an imaginary world filled with romance and sweets, I shut it while a brand-new Volvo belonging to a high-ranking officer was still driving through. The heavy metal gate closed on it three times, denting the car's back doors repeatedly. I heard somebody calling my name like in a dream and turned to see my finger on the wrong button.

It became clear I wasn't good at pressing buttons. Following another round of investigations, this time with the road safety department, they—the faceless voices on the phone, the scribbled signatures on official documents—recommended that I be transferred to another unit, where I wouldn't have access to button-operated machinery. But before they had a chance to do so, I managed to get myself into more trouble.

That day, the meanest officer in the base, notorious for his bad temper and ruthless punishments, came by the gate for a routine check. Soldiers avoided eye contact when he walked by, urgently tidying up their uniforms in an attempt to look inconspicuous. Something about my attitude ticked him off. He wasn't impressed by my sloppy salute and my unkempt appearance. He yelled at me to stand straight, to fix my shirt, to retie my ponytail. And why was I sitting at the gate? Shouldn't I be standing? His face was so close to mine that I could smell digested falafel on his breath. My body grew tingly, my anger simmering. Other soldiers congregated at a safe distance to watch the show.

The blood rushed into my brain like a burning fuse, and then my rage erupted—a white-hot, blinding flood of it. "You can't talk to me like that!" I shouted. "This is not about officers and soldiers; it's a basic human interaction! Maybe you should take a human relations course that will teach you how to treat people!"

The crowd emitted a collective gasp. For a moment, nobody spoke. I heard an impatient car horn, the clamor of a gate opening, my own shallow breathing. Then the officer exploded. His face turned from red to purple. I took a small step back and cowered as he roared, "Get out of my face! To the major's office! NOW!"

Waiting at the office of the female major I'd visited many times over the past year, my trembles began to subside, my heartbeat slowed, and my body resumed a normal temperature. I hesitantly approached her secretary. She was browsing through a fashion magazine with a bored expression, twirling a curl around her finger.

"What do you think is going to happen to me?" I asked.

"Don't worry," she said without looking at me. "They'll probably just demote you. They won't put you in jail."

"Demote me?" I snorted. "I press buttons at the gate."

"Oh." She raised her gaze to examine me in the light of this new information. "Then I really don't know."

They didn't put me in jail, but I was now on probation. I'd been grounded, fined, and given warnings before. But this was the first time I'd been put on probation. I almost felt proud. I almost wanted to go to jail.

Once again, I was transferred. This time I had outdone myself: I got myself thrown out of a unit they usually threw people into. I was in limbo, floating between temporary units. In the mean-

time, the army decided to conduct a full security check on me.
My friends were summoned for an interview. I was strangely flattered.

My best friend, Shira, who was an officer now, looking sharp
with her ranks and an M16 casually slung over her shoulder, was
losing her patience. "Why can't you just make the best of it, like
the rest of us?" she asked. In the interview, she told the intelli-
gence officer, "Her biggest problem is that she *will* drive you crazy.
I don't see that being a major security threat."

One Friday afternoon my mother and I sat at the kitchen table.
Chicken stew steamed on the stove and the sun painted the cabinets gold. I was reading the weekend papers and didn't look up
when she asked, "Why are you doing this to yourself? Why are
you fighting so hard?"

I blurted without thinking, "Because I'm smarter than them."

"Oh, honey." My mother looked at me wearily. "But they are
the ones calling the shots. You can't fight a whole army."

NEAR THE END of my service, I was assigned to a new unit, working under a colonel who was willing to take a chance on me and
whom I didn't hate so much. I made a friend in the new unit,
Elsin, a punk rock kid from south Tel Aviv who hated the army
as much as I did. Going to work was not so dreadful when she was
around. Sometimes we even had fun. One day, while our boss was
out, we invented a game called "put things back in their place." It
involved stretching the phone receiver cord to the other side of
the room and hurling it back, trying to place it in its cradle. On
hot days, we took extended lunch breaks and went to the beach,
folded our pants, removed our army shoes, and dipped our feet in
the water.

I was also in love, which seemed to have mitigated my rage. My first real boyfriend, a soft-spoken, blue-eyed kibbutznik named Gilad, served with Shira in the north of Israel, and I lived for the weekends, when he was on leave and we could be reunited. Once I finished the army, we were going to move in together, live in his studio apartment in the kibbutz, and work to save money for the customary after-the-army trip. I just had to keep my head low for a few more weeks.

By then, I was the most senior soldier in my unit, with a new rank—a sergeant, granted solely for my length of service—sewn onto my sleeves. My new position afforded me a level of respect among newer soldiers and an unspoken license to slack on my duties. But I was still outranked by officers, no matter how young and inexperienced they might be. Resentful of the arbitrariness of military hierarchy, I made no effort to conceal my disregard for these young officers' command, but never went as far as to risk disciplinary action.

A few weeks before the end of my service, a young, cocky officer from our unit marched into the office and told me to go clean the grounds with the rest of the staff. Tomer was handsome, Ashkenazi, and entitled, and he suffered from a classic case of sagemet. Derived from *sagam*, for "second lieutenant"—the rank awarded right after officers' course—sagemet was a common malady among young officers, who, buoyed by their new rank, began conducting themselves with an inflated air of importance.

Tomer wasn't my direct superior, so he rarely had reason to boss me around, but when he did, it drove me crazy. Perhaps it was the affected tone of authority, the forced deepening of his voice, the smug smirk on his face. He just seemed to enjoy it way too much. That day I looked up at him and flatly said, "No."

"Why not?"

"I'm busy. I'm eating a carrot," I said, taking a bite and staring at the computer screen. Elsin, standing behind him, stifled a giggle.

Tomer glared at her, then crossed his arms and cleared his throat. "Get up now."

"I have to stay at the office," I said, and as I spoke it aloud, my rationale began to make sense. "The colonel is out."

"You can lock the office for a few minutes."

"I don't think so."

"It's an order."

I snorted. "Um, no."

He stormed out of the room fuming and came back waving the written complaint for disobeying his order. My tenth trial.

Gilad exhaled loudly over the phone. "You promised to stay out of trouble! You're on probation! Do you want to go to jail? What were you thinking?"

But I wasn't thinking. As with my screaming at the high-ranking officer—the incident that had gotten me on probation in the first place—defying Tomer wasn't rational. I was so desperate to maintain a semblance of autonomy and dignity in a system designed to repress that it got the better of me.

A few days later, I appeared in front of the female major who had grown to despise me over the last two years. When I walked in, she sighed deeply, eyebrows raised in a "now what?" expression. She went through the routine protocol and then asked, "Do you agree to be judged by me?" I looked straight ahead, voice steady, and said, "No."

The noncommissioned officer who accompanied me elbowed me in the ribs.

The major looked up. "Excuse me?"

"I'd rather not," I said.

The major scoffed. She scrawled something on paper and said

that my case would be passed on to her superior, the highest-ranking female officer in the whole district. "Do you understand that her decision will be final?" I did.

Asking to transfer the trial was a right available to all soldiers, but very few took advantage of it. I had nothing to lose. I knew the major would have likely sent my sorry ass to jail. With a new judge, one who wasn't biased against me, I still had a chance.

The trial was scheduled three weeks before the end of my service. I forwent my contact lenses that day in favor of black-rimmed glasses, braided my hair neatly. It was the same "good girl" look I had donned for my interview with the colonel, in the hope that it would offset the impression my behavior sheet made.

The lieutenant colonel eyed me and then read the complaint aloud. "How do you plead?"

"Not guilty," I said.

She leaned back in her leather chair while I gave her my rehearsed defense. I explained that I was the only secretary left at the office, and that the one time I had left it unattended, I had been charged with abandoning a post.

The officer perused the complaint again, then gazed up and studied me. I stood as straight as I could, chin up. Then she told me to step outside while she called the unit to verify my story.

It was the only time in my military history that I was acquitted. I never went to jail.

WE HAD A cold parting, the army and I, a limp handshake with no eye contact. I didn't have a goodbye party as many soldiers did. There was no cake made, no cards exchanged, and no tears shed. I packed my things in a hurry and left, worried that if I stayed another minute, I would somehow find a way to fuck everything up again and end up in jail. As I walked out into the sunny afternoon, I waved at the new girl who pressed buttons at the gate, and then stood for a moment on the busy Tel Aviv street with my eyes closed against the warm sunshine. Buses and cars zoomed by, music pouring out from their open windows. From a nearby patio, I heard the clatter of dishes, the tinkling of cutlery, the soft hum of conversation. A woman walked by, her heels tapping purposefully on the tattered pavement. I inhaled the city air—car exhaust, cigarette smoke, perfume, swirled with a touch of salty breeze—and felt lighter, younger, and freer than I had known possible. This, I thought, is what the rest of your life could be like.

A SLEEPLESS BEAST

I AM SITTING IN THE PASSENGER SEAT of a dusty pickup truck next to my friend Shelly's father. I'm eighteen and a few months into my mandatory army service. Shelly is asleep in the backseat, long freckled limbs, auburn ringlets hiding her eyes. Leonard Cohen is playing on the tape deck. Outside, the luscious greens of Tel Aviv give way to smeared yellows. Water bottles roll at my feet, crinkling empty bags of chips and Bamba. An open can of Coke and a Styrofoam cup with fragrant coffee are lodged in the cup holders between us. I sit back, stretch out my legs. My lungs expand and my muscles soften; my body unwinds, changing gears into desert mode.

Shelly's father had picked me up from the army base first. Shelly's unit had the day off and her place was closer to the highway, en route to Eilat. When I walked out of the gate, he rolled down his window, smiling widely at me as if we knew each other already, and then got out of the car to throw my backpack in the trunk. He was in his mid-forties, fit and spry, with dark, ropy legs in white shorts, a thick salt-and-pepper beard, and Shelly's intense eyes under thin-framed glasses. He seemed cool enough, for an old guy. When we started chatting, traversing Tel Aviv's mad traffic on our way to pick Shelly up from her rented apartment, I found him laid-back and friendly, a lot like Shelly.

"I need to change from my uniform," I said, eager to transition from soldier to civilian on vacation. "Can we stop somewhere with a bathroom?"

He glanced at his watch, and then at the jammed traffic. "Why don't you just change here?" he said casually. "I won't look."

So I did. Unbuttoning khaki and slipping on a T-shirt, wriggling out of my pants in favor of a cotton skirt, letting my hair down. As he promised, he didn't look.

WHEN SHELLY HAD called to ask if it was okay if her father joined us on our weekend trip to Eilat, I was not thrilled. We had planned to hitchhike—the uniform was good for catching rides—and sleep at the youth hostel downtown. We planned to swim, drink, and meet cute boys.

"He's really cool," Shelly said. "He's not like a regular dad. And it means we won't have to hitchhike or pay for a hostel: we can just camp somewhere. He's going to bring food and a pot for coffee. He can make fire. We can still do the same things. He promised not to be in the way if we got with some boys."

Really? I had no personal frame of reference—my father died before I was ten—but I suspected he would not have been that cool. Sometimes, I tried to imagine what our relationship would have looked like, how our closeness would have survived my rebellious teenage years, the emergence of my sexuality. I marveled at fathers, curiously observing my friends' dynamics with their dads, envying their intimacy, their disagreements, even their fights.

"It would just be easier," Shelly said. "But whatever."

The idea of not having to hitchhike or pay for accommodation was appealing. Halfheartedly, I agreed.

Now, after we stopped for gas and some food, Shelly has fallen asleep. Her father and I talk about music and travel. He loves Eilat, and he loves the desert, as do I. I'd been going to the southern desert town regularly since I was sixteen, when *Maariv LaNoar*, the magazine I had worked for, sent me to write a piece about a scuba diving course. As an angst-ridden teenager, my work at the magazine had been my salvation. It offered a sense of accomplishment I had not found in my studies and provided me with the pocket money my mother couldn't afford. Once the editors recognized my dedication and dependability, they began rewarding me with assignments such as that one, introducing me to the luxuries most of my friends took for granted. I returned from Eilat changed, in love with the desert, with the Red Sea—so unlike my former love, the murkier, shallower Mediterranean—and with scuba diving. Diving, for me, was the ultimate escape, a world so unlike anything we know, where nothing works the way we expect it to, where even our most basic needs are altered: the way we move, communicate, breathe. On land, I talk too much. I don't know what else to do with myself around people. Underwater, I relish the silence, the buoyancy, find the rhythmic sound of my measured breathing comforting, meditative. Diving is the closest to feeling at peace as I may ever get.

For the last two years of high school, I had gone to Eilat almost every holiday, sometimes with my friend Shira and sometimes alone, always staying at the windswept, musty youth hostel at the diving club. In Eilat, I was free to be anybody, blend in with the tourists, the backpackers, and the adventure divers. In Eilat, I bravely kissed boys I'd just met and flirted with handsome instructors in their twenties. In Eilat, sandy-haired tourists from Nordic countries, to whom the ordinariness of my olive skin and black curls was a novelty, told me I was beautiful. And I was: my hair smoothed by the dry desert air, my skin tanned and showing in the dead of winter, because in Eilat, it was warm year-round. I was a better version of myself in the desert.

When I was a child, the arid landscape had inspired different emotions in me. Every time my family drove south, my stomach tightened as soon we left the city and the desert unfurled in front of us like an unrolling rug. The vastness had seemed menacing, the heat and silence as absolute as death, the desolation a mirror of my own loneliness. Now, my chest is filled with exhilaration. The desert feels extreme, but in a good way, and loving it is radical, a thrill. I love how simple it is, clean-lined, raw, and—similar to the depth of the sea—uncomplicated by human interventions. I love the hint of threat and mystery, the risk inherent in it.

To love the desert is to love a beast.

The road winds around hills and drops into canyons and craters. Then a long, faded asphalt narrows down into a haze—an arrow pointing south, surrounded by an expanse of nothing and the largest, bluest sky. The mountains of Jordan loom in the far distance, unattainable. The towns and kibbutzim we cross are dusty mirages; even their trees appear un-green, coated with wandering sand.

Growing up, I watched Hollywood movies and envied the magnitude of America, coveted its open roads, wished I could just drive off whenever I needed to get away. In a country so small that you could travel north to south in less than seven hours and east to west in two, hemmed in from all directions by inhospitable neighbors and shifting, elusive boundaries, where the only firm border, ironically, was the sea, a four-and-a-half-hour drive to Eilat was the closest one could get to feeling "on the road."

Deep into the Arava plains, Israel's small stretch of middle-of-nowhere, the desert is already embedded into my skin. Wild aca-

cia trees pepper the dusty savanna, and tumbleweeds roll across
the wavering asphalt. I am feeling free and relaxed, optimistic
about this weekend, enjoying the soft music, the wind in my hair,
and the calmness of the desert on my eyelids.

Then Shelly's father reaches over as if to grab the coffee between us, but instead, he takes my hand and begins stroking it.

I freeze in my seat.

SHELLY AND I first met in basic training. We slept on neighboring
beds in the same tent, sharing the same air, and by the end of
basic training were as intimately close as two girls who had spent
a month in extreme conditions could be. We had other things in
common: anger issues, a history of loss, a cynical outlook. There
was a hint of mystery about Shelly that both intimidated and intrigued me. She didn't talk about her life much, but I knew she
didn't have it easy. Her mother had died when she was little, and
she grew up with relatives. She didn't mention why she hadn't
stayed with her father and I never asked. I wondered if it was her
rough upbringing that made her so fierce, someone you didn't
want to mess with, someone you wanted on your side. I wished I
were that resilient, that cool, and was pleased she chose me as a
friend.

When we found out we were both stationed at the same large
base in Tel Aviv—I at the army ombudsman's office and she at
human resources, a short walk from my office—we were overjoyed. At first, our relationship was limited to office hours. We
chatted on the army phones and took coffee breaks and lunches
together, bitched about our officers and our jobs. Sometimes, she
was sent to fetch files from our archives and we'd sneak a shared-
moment break while she smoked on the front steps. As time
passed, our friendship deepened. The civilian life I'd once had,

my writing career, my high school friendships, seemed to be halted. Most of my friends were posted away from home and returned only on weekends. This base—this uniform, these people I saw daily—had become my world.

I was assigned to a senior adjudicating officer whose job was to arbitrate complaints soldiers made about rights they were denied or unjust punishments they were given. As his secretary, I filed complaints, set up meetings, and made calls to pre-interview plaintiffs and defendants, most of them young men. Too insecure about my looks and inexperience, I found the anonymity of the phone to be a safe space to experiment with flirting. Soon, I was carrying on elaborate phone affairs, usually with the defendants— young officers whose confidence, arrogance, and dark side I found alluring. They were not accused of legal infractions, mind you; no real crimes, only moments of poor judgment and abuse of power. And though I was sympathetic to the plaintiffs who were treated unfairly—always cheering for the underdog—I was fascinated by the defendants' questionable morals, enthralled by their hunger for power, their failure to be good officers, their failure to be good. In that way, they were like me. Flawed. Human.

Most of the affairs ended in disappointment and heartache once we met, and I became awkward and shy face-to-face, unable to maintain my on-the-phone confidence. There was a marine officer who drove all the way from Haifa to my mother's house in Petah Tikva. "I'm coming right now," he said. I said no. He said yes. And then he was there, climbing up the stairs to my room while I preened in front of the mirror, tossing my hair one way, then another. Once he was there, in my room, impossibly handsome, I couldn't look him in the eye, didn't know what to do with my hands.

There was that artillery sergeant who was witty and charming over the phone, and appeared sweet and unassuming in person when he came to pick me up for a party in his kibbutz. We drank and danced in a large, smoky barn that had been converted into a bar, and then teetered outside. The trails were wet and the air tasted like it does after rain, fresh and cool and full of promise. We ran into a girl he knew, and he said, "Hey! This is . . ." and then paused and stared at me, unblinking. I waited for a minute, because I thought, No way. This is not happening. The girl smiled at me with pity. I punched his arm, which seemed to jolt his memory, because he laughed and said, "Ayelet! I'm sorry, I'm drunk."

And then I made out with him anyway.

Then there was Amos from my unit, on whom I had developed a ridiculous crush. A married officer with a potbelly, Amos was smart, kind, and old enough to be my father. It was the one time in my life when my desire for a father figure had manifested in such an overt way. One day, I found an excuse to stay in the office while he was working late. It was dark out by the time we finished, and he offered me a ride to the bus stop. Before I got out, we sat for a while, chatting, and the longer we stayed, the two of us side by side in that dark, warm, enclosed space, the tenser and weirder things got between us. Then I reached over and kissed him goodbye on his cheek, and he kissed me back on mine, and gently caressed my arm, and suddenly it was real, a moment of no return. This was a good, decent man. What was I doing? I quickly opened the door and left.

At eighteen, these non-affairs and the boys I kissed on Eilat's beaches summed up my experience with men.

BEFORE SUNSET, THE yellows blushing into deep reds, Shelly's dad stops the car by the side of the road for a coffee break. He steps out, stretches his arms over his head. Shelly wakes up, rubbing her eyes. She looks out the window. "Where are we?"

"Close," I say. I glance at her dad, now crouched by the side of the road, heating water in a small pot over a portable gas stove, then back at Shelly.

She yawns and sees me looking, breaks into a smile. "What?"

I shrug and give her a half-smile. This is the first of many chances I will have to speak up. I choose to say nothing.

IT'S AFTER SUNSET by the time we roll into Eilat, and the red mountains bleed onto the sea, their reflections rippled in the waters of the bay. Lights stud the large hotels along the shore, monsters of concrete that are the stepchildren of the desert. The night smells of sunscreen and fish and beer. Red-faced tourists throng the bars on the seawall, stagger along the strip. I inhale the dry desert air with relief.

We pitch our tent on a deserted rocky beach near the border with Egypt, outside of the city. Sitting around the fire, we look across the gulf at the glimmering lights of Aqaba, Jordan's Eilat. It's 1991, three years before Israel and Jordan would sign a peace agreement, before Israelis could visit Aqaba and watch the lit shore of Eilat from the other side. Shelly's father cooks pasta in tomato sauce and then brews dark Turkish coffee sweetened with heaps of sugar. Leonard Cohen's "I'm Your Man" is emanating from the truck's tape deck, and Shelly's father sings along, his face glowing orange from the fire. He glances at me and I stare into the flames.

When the night grows deeper and stiller, we head into the tent. Inside, it seems smaller than I expected and Shelly's father insists on sleeping in the middle, "to keep us warm," he says, half-joking but then not. We lie there for a while chatting, giggling to cover up for the uneasiness. Shelly turns a couple of times, agitated, until finally she flings her blanket off. "I can't sleep," she says, crawling outside. "I'm going for a walk."

WHEN I COME back from Eilat, I don't talk about it. I don't tell anyone, not even Shira, to whom I tell everything, what happened in the tent that night. Even though it's nothing. Nothing at all. But still, I would rather not speak of it; do my best to forget it. My plan works. The less I talk, the less real it becomes. The silence covers the memory with a blurry screen, a rain-washed windshield in a moving car, so you can't make out the details, so you can only see the broad strokes. Much later I realize this was how Shelly would have seen us if she happened to look through the fabric of the tent, the silhouettes of two people lying closely together, the undecipherable whispers, an impression of intimacy.

When I finally tell Shira an abridged version of the story months later, I make it sound as if it was something that had just happened, a careless, casual fling, something I must have wanted too. Because that is a story I can live with. She can't understand why I would hide it from her for so long, can't place the source of my shame. Is it because he was older? A friend's dad? "Do you think I'd love you any less?" she asks, confused.

My plan worked, because two decades later, my memory—usually exceptionally sharp—fails me, details elude me. When I read my diaries from that time for more clarity, it's my guilt that strikes me. "I really didn't want to," I wrote. "I don't understand how I let it happen. I feel terrible." I kept lamenting over it for pages: Why didn't I leave? Why didn't I stop it sooner?

This is what I piece together eventually, from my diary entries and my adult recollections. After Shelly leaves, I turn my back to

him, ready to sleep, though the coffee surges through my blood-
stream, though I already get the sense that I'm trapped, already
wish I had left with Shelly. He starts touching me, stroking my
legs. I freeze. "Shocked, frightened" are the words I use in my
diary. When he persists, becoming bolder, I ask him to stop.
"Why?" he asks, and I consider my response, actually concerned
with his feelings. "Because you're Shelly's dad," I say finally.

He laughs. "Do you think she doesn't know? Why do you think
she left?"

My heart chills before it breaks. I have known Shelly for only a
few months. What if I didn't know her at all? I always sensed a
shadow in her, some cloudiness in her eyes, something wild and
unpredictable in her face. It was partly what drew me to her; I
thought it made her a deep, tortured soul. But could she be that
perverse? Setting me up with her father? Leaving me alone with
him when she knew what he was capable of? Was that some
twisted agreement they had? He agreed to leave if she got with
boys; she agreed to leave if he got with me?

"Did you mind when I caressed your hand in the car?" he asks.
"It's the same thing. Doesn't it feel good?"

Is it? Does it?

Somehow, I stay there. Where would I go? He keeps touching,
cajoling. Maybe I don't say no loudly enough, clearly enough,
often enough. His beard is scratchy, sandy, and reeks of tobacco. A
line from "I'm Your Man" keeps playing in my head, something
about the moon, a chain, a sleepless beast.

Things like this happen. They happened to me. There was that
time when I walked home in a skirt, feeling pretty. I was just a
kid—twelve? thirteen?—and two boys around my age walked by,
and in a quick millisecond, no longer than a pulse, one of them
lifted my skirt, moved my underwear, and slipped the tip of his

finger right in there, so swiftly that neither he nor I could believe it had happened, without seeing, without even stopping. He hollered to his friend, laughing wildly at his brazen violation of my body, while I kept walking, shaking with rage and shame and tears, swearing I'd never wear a skirt again. For a while, I didn't.

And there was that guy in the dorm in Eilat, a nice guy, handsome, Ashkenazi, who climbed into my top bunk one night while I was sleeping and patted my legs and my bum, despite me telling him, nicely, that I wasn't interested, until I had to literally kick him off me, off the bed. The next morning, when I told his friend, a beautiful, blond hippie girl who slept on the bunk beneath me, she hardened and told me that it couldn't have happened, that I must have imagined it. And what I heard was, Who are you kidding? He would never go for you.

Or the forty-something photographer from the teen magazine who I thought was my friend, until we went to cover an out-of-town music festival—one of those festivals I wouldn't have been able to afford if it weren't for my job—and he drank too much and pinned me against the wall, panting in my ear, hand snaking under my shirt. When I tried to get away, he grabbed me again. Harder. "Come on," he said. "Won't you give the photographer a kiss?"

These things happen. Not just to fatherless girls, although it may have felt that way at times, as though the lack of a protective male figure in my life made me more susceptible to predators. Other women I knew had it worse. Compared to them, what happened with Shelly's dad was nothing at all. Nothing but poor judgment. Abuse of power. Maybe I was remembering it wrong. Because when did I ever let people push me around? Why else would I have let it go on? Maybe I was still seeking a father figure. Maybe I begrudged Shelly that relationship, the closeness she shared with her father, the same way I envied little girls on their fathers' shoulders on the street. Maybe a part of me was drawn to the beast. I had tried to impress him on the drive there, tried to appear mature, sophisticated. I must have sent the wrong signals.

In the end, tears in my eyes, I say no loudly and firmly enough. In the end, he stops. I fall into a broken, watchful sleep. When I wake up, my mouth tastes foul. My skin feels slimy and foreign. I crawl out of the tent and shuffle along the abandoned beach. The day is hazy as if sand has infiltrated the air. Holding up my dress in a tight fist, I plod into the water. The sea is cold and unwelcoming but I keep treading anyway, staring down at my body underwater, morphed and misshapen. I throw water on my face, salt tingling in my pores.

I find Shelly sleeping in the truck, curled on the backseat, a frown wedged in her forehead.

Somehow, we manage to drink coffee together, the three of us quiet. Somehow, we go on with our day, eat, read books, swim, drive to town to promenade along the seawall. It is agony. I want nothing more than to be home, for this to be over. Shelly is grumpy and distant all day. Not like I could have confided in her, anyway. If I learned anything from that girl in the dorm room, it's that women don't want to hear these things about the men they love. Throughout the day, whenever Shelly is out of sight, her father grabs me, gropes me. I keep pushing him off. In the tape deck, the Leonard Cohen cassette is on repeat. Whenever "I'm Your Man" plays, he sings it to me, feigning a heartfelt delivery, ruining this beautiful song for me forever.

We drive back to Tel Aviv that evening. We are back at the base the following day. Shelly doesn't look at me and I can't bear to look at her. Something between us has been broken beyond repair.

. . .

MORE THAN A decade later, while living in Vancouver, I get a message from Shelly on an Israeli social media site: "I'm sorry about the fight. I realized you were right and I was wrong."

I write back. I say I don't even remember what we fought about, though I vividly recall choppy images from it, the sick, helpless feeling in my gut. It was a few weeks after our trip to Eilat. Things between us had been strained, the unsaid so loud it left no space for other words. Shelly started avoiding me, coming by less often. Sometimes days would pass without us seeing each other. That day, she came by for a file and we went to the archive to search for it. I remember her yelling at me, arms flailing. I remember being surprised at her anger. I remember trying to calm her down with simple words, but it only seemed to fuel her fury.

A few weeks later she left the base for an officers' course, after which she was stationed up north. I did not see her again for years.

MONTHS AFTER OUR correspondence, while I'm in Israel for a friend's wedding, Shelly catches me on Messenger and suggests dinner. I agree.

When she spots me from across the restaurant and waves, I almost don't recognize her. It has been more than a decade, so change is to be expected. The first thing I notice is the hair: her spectacular auburn ringlets are gone, cut short. "It's easier with the kids," she says, rubbing her head when I comment on it. When we used to know each other, she was willowy and athletic, something I envied while struggling with the extra kilos I had gained during my service. Now, after three pregnancies, the added weight has softened her features, brought a warm glow to her cheeks. Meanwhile, I am the thinnest I've been in years, a virtue I attribute to a steady diet of alcohol and cigarettes and long shifts as a waitress at a high-volume restaurant. She used to chain-smoke then; her energy was always nervous, fidgety. Now I am the one asking the waiter for an ashtray and digging for smokes in my purse, fiddling with my lighter, avoiding her eyes.

It is a nice restaurant on the outskirts of my hometown, Petah Tikva. The tables are illuminated with tea candles, and behind the bar, the liquor bottles are backlit with red and purple. When I grew up, you used to have to drive out to Tel Aviv for this kind of dining experience.

Shelly leans on the table and gazes warmly into my eyes. She's still beautiful. Her face seems more open now, without the dramatic framing of her locks, and the hardness in her eyes is gone, mellowed by age and motherhood. Meanwhile I feel stronger than ever. Stronger, partially because of what happened that night. After the shame and self-blame subsided, I vowed to toughen up, harden, become the kind of girl you don't want to mess with. A rock. My father was gone; my mother was occupied with surviving. No one was watching over me. "We are essentially alone in this world," I used to tell people dramatically. "Once you accept it, it becomes easier to face life." And as the years passed, and I left home and began traveling alone, I became fiercer, more resilient. A tough chick. Or so I wanted to believe. Last year, while I was walking on Commercial Drive in Vancouver in midday, an inebriated man grabbed at my breasts, and I swung at him and screamed, "What are you doing?" By a stroke of luck, two policemen were not far from the scene and I reported him immediately. The man spent the night in jail for assault. It has been one of my favorite stories ever since.

The power balance between Shelly and me has shifted now. I am no longer the insecure girl who admired her. It should offer me some comfort. It doesn't. For some reason, I find her transformation unnerving. She looks calmer, at peace, like she's got it together. Next to her, I feel like a child still, stuck in my twenties, with my waitressing job and my refusal to procreate. I flick my lighter on repeatedly, tap my pack of cigarettes, already wanting another.

Over drinks we reminisce about people we knew from basic training and from the base. "Remember that time we were on patrol duty together?" she says. "And you had the key to your office?"

I lean back and laugh. "Oh my God, yes! It was freezing that night!"

"We sat by the heater inside your office for like half the patrol."

The waiter places salad bowls in front of us, but now we are so excited that we can hardly eat.

When Shelly mentions her mom in conversation, I pause. "Your mother? You mean stepmother?"

She cocks her head, puzzled. "No, my mother."

"You told me your mother had died when you were a kid."

"I did?" Shelly puts down her fork. "Wow. I'm sorry."

I stir the lettuce, stung. I always thought we were both members of the dead parents' club. I thought it made us honorary sisters.

"Well, I guess I could see why I said that." Shelly leans back in her seat, frowning. "My mother and I are estranged. I was raised by my grandmother. When she died, it felt like my mother died."

I confess the crush I had on Amos.

"Amos?" She stops chewing. "Seriously?"

I bury my face in my palm. "I know." All these years and I'm still blushing.

I'm drinking more wine, then coffee. Shelly is ordering tea.

Our candle has burnt off. We decide to order dessert, for old times' sake. We reminisce of the lunches we used to take outside the base, at Tel Aviv cafés, the extravagant chocolate cakes with whipped cream we often ordered for dessert, drowning our sorrows in sugar.

"I am so sorry about that fight," she says.

"Why did we fight anyway?" I ask lightly. The wine has loosened my tongue, let my guard down.

She looks up, eyebrows raised. "Because of my father," she says, and my heart stops.

For a minute, I stare hard into my cup. At once, my façade is collapsing. I realize I still carry the shame with me. I rarely speak about that night. Most of my friends don't know about it.

"But you never told me that," I say finally, my voice catching in my throat. "We never talked about him."

"I didn't?"

"No," I say. "We were looking for a file in the archive, and you freaked out at me for something trivial. I don't remember what." I don't tell her that she shoved me with both hands, that I staggered backward and landed against the metal shelves. I don't tell her that I was scared of her.

"Ha. I always thought we spoke about it," she says. "I guess I didn't have the guts to confront you. You know, I should have known he was lying. I should have known it wasn't your fault."

"My fault?" I swallow. "How could it have been my fault?"

"I'm sorry. That's what he told me." She lowers her chin, swirling her tea. "We both know what he's capable of. Already on the way there, he started saying stuff to me. When you were in the bathroom, he said, 'Your friend is hitting on me. She changed right in front of me. Your friend is all over me. She couldn't keep her hands off me while you were sleeping in the backseat.'"

This was planned, I realize. This was the work of a careful pred-ator. He manipulated us, turned us against each other, ruined our friendship. And for what? I light a cigarette instead of talking, grateful for the diversion. I am not angry at her for believing him, for thinking that I could do something like that. After all, at one point, I thought the worst of her too. I choose not to tell her that. I choose, once again, to keep silent.

Until now.

ON THE WAY home, I'm listening to Galei Tzahal, the army radio station, playing its melancholy late-night music. As a soldier, I used to borrow my mother's car some nights and just drive. As long as they had good songs on the radio, I kept going, savoring the solitude and being on the move, watching the world reveal itself from the windshield in all its heartbreaking beauty and feel-ing morose and alive.

Outside my window, the city is painted a wet, diffused street-light orange, and the music washes over me, elicits a sadness that feels old, misplaced. I miss the exit to my mother's house and keep driving south on the Number 40, the highway leading to Ben Gurion Airport. I keep driving until the good songs end.

II.
LEAVING

You're walking on the edge of a very narrow road over a boiling crevice and you might fall in; and, in fact, you will fall in.

—Cynthia Ozick, from an interview in *Writers & Company*

MY AMERICAN DREAM

An air-conditioned bus takes me and my beat-up backpack from JFK Airport to downtown Manhattan. I am twenty-two and flat broke—in the airport I had no change for a cart or to call my friend and had to use my overdrawn Visa to purchase a ticket for the shuttle bus. I'm also in love with two men, neither of whom is here with me now.

It is a sweltering July day, so hot that the view outside my window seems to shimmer. These oppressive Tel Aviv–like temperatures are a surprise; having never been to the U.S., I had expected a cool, polite North American summer. That heat, paired with jet lag, culture shock, and travel-induced exhaustion (a seventeen-hour flight from New Delhi via London), makes everything appear a bit surreal, as through a film of fog.

The American highways are sleek, fast, and so new, unlike back home, where history is everywhere, written on buildings and soaked into the earth; unlike India, where the roads are narrow and potholed and jumbled with vehicles. When the Manhattan skyline appears in the distance, a row of solemn gray buildings like soldiers snapped to attention, I straighten in my seat and search my heart hard for emotion. This is it, I tell myself. Don't miss it. Hurry. Feel something. But the bus rumbles on through underpasses and over bridges, and the skyline grows and diffuses into individual buildings and streets and traffic. The moment is gone. The only thing I feel is heartache, and it's been with me for months now, like an exotic, undetected bug, a stowaway riding along with me from Israel, through India, and all the way here.

At fifteen, I drew the Manhattan skyline across my bedroom wall with teenage fervor and hopefulness. I painted the buildings white and the sky in swirling grays and blacks. I used a dinner plate to shape a milky full moon. On the top right corner of my mural, a small window opened to a square of Israeli skies, sultry and thick, misplaced. At night, I would fall asleep gazing at the stars on my wall and imagine that I lived there. New York. Because of Madonna and Paul Auster and *Catcher in the Rye*. Because if I'd learned anything from the subtitled Hollywood movies I had watched at Shalom Cinema on Herzl Street, with its ever-creaking wooden seats, its floor littered with peanut skins and sunflower seed shells, it was that New York was where people went to start over, reinvent themselves, and that the American Dream was for everyone, even for a little girl from a Yemeni neighborhood in a tiny, messed-up Middle Eastern country. It was a dream I could adapt, steal, make my own.

OUTSIDE GRAND CENTRAL Station, I sit on my backpack and wait for Shira. I haven't seen her since the last time she came to visit me at the northern kibbutz where I lived with Gilad, my first love. Shira was the one who inadvertently introduced me to him. I had called the army base where she served, on a sparse hilltop by the border with Lebanon, and he answered: the new guy, fresh out of the officers' course. He was smart and funny and flirty on the phone, and after a few days, I was no longer asking for Shira.

Gilad and I lived in a tiny studio apartment crammed with

books, a short bike ride from the beach and steps to cornfields and swarming fishponds. In the winter, a pecan tree bloomed outside our window, and every morning, I collected the nuts into a blue bucket and we cracked the soft shells with our teeth. We rode bikes through the fields with our fluffy-eared dog galloping behind us. We woke up in the middle of the night from the sound of rain and made love. We were so in love that some days we felt sick with it, drained by the intensity of emotion, anguished and tormented when we were apart. Did everyone feel this way? They couldn't possibly. Surely our love was unique and remarkable and beyond any love anyone else had ever experienced.

Other days I was plagued by anxiety. It had to end somehow, I knew. He was probably going to die. That's what happened to soldiers and men in this country—men like my father, and my sister's boyfriend. Men we love. I was twelve when my sister's boyfriend died in the army: a gentle boy with a shy smile and long bangs that nearly covered his eyes. An early morning phone call. My mother and I both answered the phones by our beds; my sister was bawling on the other end of the line. I went to school that day and silently wept through everything. I sat in the back of the classroom hearing the teacher speak, but I couldn't make out the words.

Whenever Gilad was late for his weekend leave from the army, he'd find me sobbing in bed; I had already visualized the headlines, his picture, black-framed in the paper, the announcement on the radio, his funeral service. At night, I'd dream of his death, and the loss was so real, so devastating, that I would wake up inconsolable. At times I picked fights for no reason, accused him of not really loving me. Anything to make this unbearable happiness a little less consuming, a little more manageable, so that once it ended, which it must, it wouldn't destroy me.

By the time Shira visited, our pecan tree—a biennial—was not blooming, and I was flirting with Avishay, this guy I had met at my job writing for a business magazine in Haifa. I told Shira about Avishay in a lighthearted tone, like it was no big deal. Gilad knew about him; he was fine with it. It was harmless flirting, after all.

At twenty-two, Avishay wore suit jackets, carried a briefcase, and owned a car. He had longish, wispy blond hair, broad shoulders fetchingly slouched in an apology, and wire-framed glasses. His lips were thin and colorless, and he smelled faintly of milk. He had never dated a Mizrahi girl, he'd said to me with surprise in his voice, as though his attraction to me—my brown skin, my Yemeni heritage—was some kind of fetish. He hadn't met any Mizrahi girls in his white, affluent neighborhood on top of Mount Carmel, or in the elite, prestigious high school he attended. He was the kind of guy—charming, rich, blond—who never would have given me the time of day in high school, and I was intoxicated by his attention. He wrote me poetry, played me Tori Amos and Joni Mitchell over the phone. "Why aren't you mine?" he said, sad, wanting, adorable, like a puppy. "Life isn't fair."

On a bench outside the kibbutz, waiting for the bus to take her back to Tel Aviv, Shira searched my eyes. "Gilad loves you so much," she said. "You know that, right?" Then her bus rolled into the stop and I didn't have to say anything in response.

That was only a few months ago.

Now, Shira's shadow falls on me, and I stand up, collapse into her arms in a sweaty embrace. She takes a moment to look me over and hugs me again. "Welcome to New York," she says.

My home for the next few months (longer, if I choose) is a studio apartment tucked in the back of a four-story redbrick building on Thirty-seventh Street, between Third and Lexington. The rent is miraculously cheap. The air conditioner just broke and the air inside is still and damp like an unstirred cup of tea. The apartment is tiny, one room that slants into a galley kitchen, a single window facing a narrow courtyard. No TV. It will do. Shira and I have shared small spaces before: we slept cuddled on a ferry deck to Greece, in windswept rooms on Mykonos and Ios, in a sinking walk-up overlooking a canal in Amsterdam, on flea-infested mattresses in Sinai.

We stay in all day, talking. Outside, it is bright and noisy and humming. She has a new boyfriend. She spends a lot of time in his apartment, so I will have the place to myself often. She doesn't ask about Gilad or Avishay, and I'm sick of talking about them anyway. In India, stoned, I told everyone who'd listen the convoluted story of my affair with Avishay and its aftermath, entertaining strangers on restaurant rooftops and riverside cafés with overly intimate details, thinking that by turning it into a story, I could gain distance somehow, make it hurt less, free myself from the guilt, stop thinking about Gilad. Then Avishay. Then Gilad again. It didn't work.

An image is seared on the insides of my eyelids: the look in Gilad's eyes—so blue, so disappointed—on the evening it ended. After we took a break, during which I stayed at a friend's studio apartment in Tel Aviv. After I met Avishay for a drink in the city, let him hold my hand as he walked me back to my friend's place, and then invited him upstairs for the night. After Gilad took me back despite everything, and I kept answering Avishay's desperate calls even though I promised Gilad I wouldn't. That evening, I walked into the room after yet another phone call, and Gilad turned on his swiveling chair, his face wounded and resolute, and said, "Why did you hang up? Might as well call Avishay back and tell him to come get you and your stuff." That scene has been playing on repeat, just one of many in this unforgiving movie projector in my head.

Like that one from the morning I left. Gilad lying in bed, tears streaming, while I packed my things, moving through our apartment in slow motion, as though searching for something I'd forgotten. And then Gilad at the window, wrapped in our checkered duvet like some ancient Hebrew king, our dog clawing at the glass beside him, whining, as I pedaled away on my rickety blue bike for the last time, the same bike on which Gilad had taught me to ride.

The day I called Avishay to tell him I'd broken up with Gilad, he was silent for a moment too long, his panic transmitting like static through the phone line. "I didn't break up with him because of you," I said, defensive, trying to reassure him and maintain a semblance of dignity at the same time. Was it true? Later, as the two of us strolled along a pale, wintry beach in Haifa, hugging against a bitter wind that threatened to blow us over, an old man with a dog stopped by and said, oddly, "You take care of her, will you?" and Avishay laughed, eyes shifting. Something stabbed in my chest. How could I have been so stupid? The signs had been there all along. Avishay had told me early on that he was addicted to the ache of unrequited love, that he sometimes wished it were possible to die of a broken heart. I thought he was being a romantic, a poet. I looked at him on that beach in Haifa and knew it was already over—that now that he had me, he was going to leave, which he did, a few miserable weeks later, in the most cowardly way. One day he stopped calling, didn't answer his phone, vanished from my life as though he was never there.

And then I left too. Because staying was unthinkable. Because suddenly, through the murkiness of grief and heartache, the choice to leave presented itself in brilliant clarity as the answer to everything. I withdrew my meager savings and flew to India, my heart cracked in two places.

SHIRA AND I sleep together in her queen-size bed, swathed in yolky yellow sheets. When I wake up, she's gone.

I open the window, make coffee. It's Friday morning, Friday night back home; my siblings are gathered at my mother's for our weekly Shabbat dinner, arguing and laughing and tossing dish towels at each other from across the table. It's strange how much I miss them and how badly I need to be away from them right now. Maybe it's because around my family, I can only be who I've always been: the angry, tantrum-prone, oversensitive child who fought her way through adolescence. Maybe I need to do my growing up away from them. Or maybe I love them so much, it feels safer to walk away. Because you never know what might happen to the people you love.

Then I remember. Our dinners are different now. I can no longer rely on my memory to conjure the correct image. On my last week in India, I called home from Ladakh, a moonscape province near the border with Tibet, where Buddhist monasteries cling to the side of tooth-colored cliffs. When my little brother told me that my mom wasn't there, on a Friday night, my heart began pounding. "Why not?"

"She has a boyfriend," he said. "They're gone for the weekend."

The red numbers on the meter were adding up. It was costing me a fortune just to think, to be speechless. My mother had been a widow for twelve years. She had never—not once—dated.

I called again from New Delhi. Since I'd left, phone conversations with my mother, sporadic and brief, had grown more intimate. There was no time to argue or talk in circles; the urgency made us more honest, more open. Now she sounded younger, buoyant; she giggled. I had missed the sound of her laughter. "My life has changed," she said, "a hundred and eighty degrees."

I had been gone only three months. My mother was back, and I wasn't there to see it.

AFTER DAYS OF traversing the city, traipsing up and down steep subway stairs, my feet begin to ache. It is a peculiar pain, as though the earth is kicking my sole with every step. My feet throb, pulsate, forcing me to pause, out of step with the whirlwind that is New York. While I rest on park benches, the city assaults my senses in all its glamour and grit: giant signs blind me with neon, large screens flicker, department stores glimmer and rattle with escalators, taxis and cars and buses whiz through broad avenues, and subway trains rumble and clang under my sore feet. The city is electric with agency, as though hooked up to an amplifier in the sky. And the people, steady streams of them, slicing through intersections on their rollerblades with purposeful, graceful swipes, dashing by with their shopping bags, flagging taxis with urgent hand gestures. Everyone seems to have a place to go. Everyone belongs here more than I do.

I have never been to a place where everybody speaks English, and I feel like I am living inside a TV show. I imagine drama in people's tone, because they couldn't possibly be chatting about the weather in their television English, with that drawling accent. Communication, one of my strongest suits, has become a handicap. I hate being misunderstood, am frustrated at not being able to tell stories, to string words together in an elegant way. In New York, I am not witty or funny or articulate or a writer. I am that person who struggles to order food at the bagel shop. What on earth are scallions?

Then other days I feel lifted by the lack of vocabulary, find freedom in the constraint, the same way I sometimes relish being broke. I have said enough, I think, resigning myself to my compulsory silence, enamored with the stoic new me who emerges.

I check the mailbox every day, empty it of flyers, take-out menus, and bills. I haven't heard from Gilad since I found a dispassionate letter from him in New Delhi's poste restante. He was talking about heading to the States with Nadav, his best friend from the kibbutz, buying a cheap car, and traveling from coast to coast before heading south. It is the trip we had planned together.

Before I left Israel, a friend made me a mixed tape full of songs about home, about leaving and returning: "Homeward Bound" by Simon & Garfunkel, "She's Leaving Home" by the Beatles. I walk through the city listening to it on my Walkman, and I think of the life I had just a few months ago, the little house in the kibbutz, the boyfriend, the dog. I replay how I messed it all up, contemplate the many instances when I could have saved it if I'd tried. And some days it hurts so fucking much I think it might be possible to die of a broken heart after all.

WHEN IT GETS too hot to walk—the air trapped between the buildings, heavy and liquid—I learn that the F train will take me to Coney Island. When the train emerges from its tunnel, it feels like surfacing for air. The sky unfurls like an unclenching fist and is dappled with soft, perfectly shaped clouds. Families amble along the wooden promenade. The day smells like hot dogs and sugar. As I sit on the beach with my back to the amusement park, the roller coaster behind me creaks and rattles; children squeal with joy and terror. I kick off my shoes, fold my flared red corduroys up to my knees, and tread into the water. The cold ocean bites at my feet, choppy and dark, but I don't mind. Being by the water is a little bit like returning home. The waves hiss and swirl around my feet, and suddenly I am overwhelmed by a pang of loss, a searing sting of longing. As always, it comes out of nowhere. I miss my father. As if it hasn't been twelve years. Look how far you've traveled, I think, and still.

In August Gilad arrives from Israel with Nadav. They park their car down the street, a dusty 1969 Buick Century they bought in Queens for seven hundred dollars, no tape deck.

That first night, Gilad stays over. We lie in bed and I start crying and can't stop. He holds me. Neither of us speaks.

We go up the Empire State Building, take the ferry to Staten Island, sit between the Twin Towers and take pictures from the ground up. Sometimes we touch, lean into each other's bodies because we don't know how else to be together. Then other times, he hardens, becomes cross with me, irate.

Gilad has a relative in Brooklyn, an old Jewish lady with the kind of Brooklyn accent I've only heard in movies; she lives in a small apartment with floral couches and yellowing photos in frilly frames. She frowns when she sees me at the door with Gilad and Nadav. Inside, she serves us tea in gold-rimmed china. I'm on my best behavior, elbows off tables, *pleases* and *thank-yous*, but when I go to the bathroom, she leans over and whispers to Gilad, "Is she your girlfriend?" And when he says, "No . . . well, not anymore," she exhales a long sigh of relief and says, "Good."

"Why is that?" Gilad asks.

"She's very nice," the old woman hastens to say. "What is she, Yemeni?" And she gives him a knowing look. "Not for you."

Gilad and Nadav tell me that story later, on the drive back to Manhattan. They find it hilarious, that blatant, old-generation racism of some elderly Ashkenazi Jews, the kind who call Mizrahi

Jews like me shvartze chayes, "black animals" in Yiddish. I'm not laughing. I know how Gilad and I look to her: me, the girl from the Yemeni neighborhood east of Tel Aviv whose uneducated grandparents walked barefoot from Yemen to Israel, lived in poverty, had too many children; and Gilad, the blue-eyed kibbutznik whose pioneer family—salt of the earth!—all served in the air force. I wish we were still together just so I could prove her wrong. Then I wish I were back in India, where everyone looked like me.

In New York people think I'm Indian, Persian, Spanish, Turkish, Moroccan, Lebanese, Brazilian, Italian. They speak to me in all kinds of languages. I resist the temptation to pretend to be who they want me to be. I enjoy being claimed by so many nationalities; I like the idea of having a facial structure that is malleable, shifting, as though it makes me a citizen of the world. In my desperate wish to belong, I accept every invitation.

But after a while, it makes me feel untethered, adrift, as though I no longer know the most basic thing about myself. As though I belong nowhere.

Walking down Ninth Avenue one day, I hear someone call after me, "Yemeni! Yemeni!" and I turn to see a large man in a white galabiya outside a convenience store, waving with a large grin. I look behind me, and then hesitantly walk toward him.

"You're Yemeni!" he says. "I'm Yemeni too!"

I have never met a Yemeni outside of Israel, a Yemeni who wasn't Jewish. He invites me into his convenience store, gestures toward the stool, and hollers to his brother in the back to make coffee. I am surprised and proud for being recognized, feel validated and seen.

The brother emerges carrying a tin tray, three small cups with dark, sweet-smelling coffee. "You should come with us to Yemen," he says.

"I can't," I say. "I have an Israeli passport."

"Nonsense." He waves a hand. "We'll dress you up like a local woman. No one would know." And they burst out laughing.

WHEN GILAD AND Nadav leave for Canada, I ask to catch a ride. I've never been to Canada, and I have a high school friend in Montreal.

We drive to Connecticut, Rhode Island, Massachusetts, New Hampshire, Vermont, Montreal, Toronto. The three of us sneak into darkened campgrounds late at night, sleep in one tent, shoulder to shoulder, and slip out early morning so we don't have to pay the fees. Every few nights we splurge on a motel. We eat most of our breakfasts at Denny's, $2.99 for two strips of bacon, two greasy eggs, and two pancakes. It keeps us full until the evening. After a few days, I don't even feel nauseous.

Somewhere past Toronto, Gilad and I get into a huge fight. Perhaps I tried to get out of contributing for gas: the New York–based Hebrew paper I've been freelancing for still hasn't paid me, my Visa bill is racking up, my Israeli bank account is in overdraft, and aren't they traveling that way anyway?

Gilad says I am spoiled and entitled. He's been mean and cold for days now. In Toronto he told me that maybe our love wasn't so special, or else it wouldn't have ended with me falling for someone else. He said that his family (who once felt like my family) don't know we're traveling together, that they think he should stay away from me, that even Nadav, whom I still consider my friend, has expressed concerns about him getting hurt again. Then he and Nadav went on a double date with two Canadian girls on our last night in Toronto, leaving me to watch TV alone in our grim motel room.

Now, driving through a Canadian forest smudged by the first

colors of fall, he loses his temper and yells at me, which he has never done before. His composure—reminiscent of my father's—was a part of what drew me to him: a yin to my yang. At first, I am too stunned to respond, and then I scream, "Stop the car!" slam the door, and storm out. Marching down the side of the highway, I consider hitchhiking back to New York or Montreal, think of my backpack in the trunk. Gilad and Nadav stare at me through the windshield and finally they inch beside me. "Just get in," Gilad says, not apologizing. I walk a little farther before I slide, sulking, into the backseat and sit pressed against the door as though ready to bolt. It's all my fault. I'm the one who broke his heart and wrecked everything, so there's really no way he'll ever be apologizing. For anything. He has a free pass for a long time. Maybe for life. It enrages me. Because I wish for a redo but can't have it. Because I can never forgive myself for ruining the one good thing I had. Because sometimes, in moments of fleeting clarity, I can see that I gave in to fear. I didn't want to be caught unprepared again. I had to leave first.

They drop me off at the Greyhound station in Buffalo, where I board a bus back to Manhattan. They continue west, toward Vancouver.

ON ROSH HASHANAH, I am alone. Shira is in the Bahamas with her boyfriend. I smoke a cigarette and sip beer by a window washed with rain, overlooking the bleak concrete courtyard. When I call my family to wish them Shana Tova, the noise and commotion on the other end spill into my empty apartment, the echo bouncing from the walls.

"When are you coming home?" Ima yells. "And don't say in a couple of months! You've been saying that for six months already."

For the first time I answer honestly, "I don't know."

"Just come home," she says. "You don't sound happy."

I say nothing. I don't know how to tell her that some days, it feels like I might never be back. How to explain that losing Aba at an age when my identity was still entwined with his, when he was my homeland, made me feel exiled, displaced. How sometimes his absence pulsates in my body like a phantom limb or an excised organ. I want to tell her I am not done searching yet. I want to say being happy has nothing to do with it. But it's noisy in the background, and she seems distracted, and I still don't have the words.

I LEAVE NEW York when the leaves start to fall, pile crackly and colorful on the gray pavement, leaving skeletons for trees. I'm leaving because the imminent winter terrifies me and my money is running out, and because maybe it is time for a new dream. Shira is leaving too, heading back to Israel to start university. Chasing sunshine, I fly to Los Angeles, where I'll be staying with my high school friend Dorit, who has moved there, and hopefully find some under-the-table work to make money for my travels.

L.A. is rows of obscenely shaved palm trees, smoggy sunsets, a dry, warm smell that reminds me of Israeli summers. The California appeal is lost on me; I'm used to sunshine, palm trees, and beaches, and I haven't been away long enough to appreciate its resemblance to home. Also, I don't have a car. My friend Dorit has found God since we last saw each other, and in her house, everything is split into two: two sinks, two sets of cutlery, two sets of dishes in separate cupboards labeled DAIRY and MEAT. I marvel at her faith, the simplicity of following imposed guidelines.

I find a job at a hair salon on Beverly Boulevard, opposite CBS

Studios. My boss is a stout, sleek-haired Moroccan-Israeli with an inflated ego and a red convertible. He hates Muslims, gays, and blacks. Whenever one of his regulars comes in, aging women with puffy gray hair, he exclaims, "I'm in love with you! Do you know that I'm in love with you?"

As I shampoo the greasy receding hair of TV executives, massage flaky scalps, fold tinfoil for highlights, sweep piles of hair, I practice the things I will tell Gilad when I see him. Maybe it's not over; maybe I can still fix this. Then I worry he might not even call when he gets to L.A. on his travels. What if he doesn't want to see me? When I catch a glimpse of my reflection, I look away. It's hard to forgive yourself in a place full of mirrors.

When Gilad and Nadav roll into town, they drop by the hair salon and I have never been happier to see anybody. We hug hard. A few days later, I pack my stuff and leave with them. My boss doesn't pay me the money he owes me. I rack up more charges on my Visa. In desperation, I call my second-oldest brother, who transfers a few hundred dollars into my account, for the second time since I started my travels. "I am doing it because our father did the same for me," he says. "And you deserve to have someone bailing you out too." I will call him again from Nepal, a few months later, for my ticket home. But never again after that.

Gilad, Nadav, and I drive into the desert—Nevada, Utah, Arizona—like a scene from a road trip movie, an old American car cruising toward a hot, shimmering horizon; long hair flapping out open windows; dusty, tanned forearms leaning on the ledge. My chest swells, breathes in the dry, warm air. I am almost happy.

Somewhere between Vegas and the Grand Canyon, Gilad and I fall a little bit back in love, and it's like New York was to me, familiar but new, and not quite what I had hoped it would be. Too much has happened. It's too late to start over. In Utah one morning, the three of us wake up to our night breath frozen in crisp sheets on the inside of our tent. We drive south, chasing warmth again, down to Tijuana, where Gilad and I sip margaritas at roadside cafés and have sex in rooms infested with cockroaches.

IN SAN DIEGO, on our way to the famous zoo, the music on the radio stops and the announcer says, "Israeli prime minister Yitzhak Rabin was assassinated." Gilad swerves the car and parks it on the side of the road, and we sit and stare at the radio for answers. Outside, the day is sunny. People are walking, laughing, sipping coffee, like the world hasn't just changed forever. I fight the urge to jump out of the car and shake them.

We find a motel and I can hardly speak to the attendant when I ask for a room. She eyes me suspiciously, even after I say, clearly upset, "Sorry, our prime minister was just assassinated," thinking she should understand. I always found it curious, the way American characters on TV reacted to the assassination of JFK, as if they knew him personally, but now I can't stop crying. The assassin, we learn as the day progresses, was a fundamentalist right-wing Jew. He shot Rabin after a heartfelt speech he made at a peace rally in Tel Aviv. On CNN, we watch Rabin onstage singing "Shir LaShalom" ("A Song for Peace"), with singer Miri Aloni, and he looks happy, hopeful, almost childlike at that moment, a man with a dream. He smiles at his wife, letting her into the car a moment before he's shot. I know that the country I left is no more; Israel will never be the same after today. And for a moment, I think, I can't go back. Later, I watch young people lighting candles in the square outside city hall in Tel Aviv, forming circles on the pavement, and I long to be with them. This is a day Israelis will look back on, a moment we will forever retell, like trauma survivors. "Where were you when Rabin was killed?" people will ask and answer.

Nadav sits on one bed, Gilad and I on the other, legs stuffed under the floral bedcover, brushing against each other. Gilad squeezes my hand, and I lean my head on his shoulder, tears streaming. I feel bonded with him, not just by grief but by this memory, forever our answer to this question. It will always be him and me on the way to the San Diego Zoo, him and me on this hotel bed, watching CNN and holding each other on the day Rabin was assassinated.

THE CAR DIES in New Mexico. I'm driving a desert road late at night when it overheats, coughs, and clatters into silence. We sit in the silvered darkness and look at each other. We manage to crawl a few kilometers at a time, stopping to let the car cool in between, until we make it to El Paso in the morning. No one wants to buy the car, battered and wearied from the long trip, the paint chipped, the rear dented, so we leave it outside the Grey-hound station with the keys in the ignition, pry off the license plates as souvenirs, pose for photos on the roof, and board a bus to New Orleans. After a few days there, fueled by alcohol and pot and sporting long beaded necklaces, we head to Florida.

In Miami, Nadav decides to go back to Israel. He has no energy left in him for a backpacking trip. For a couple of weeks, it's just Gilad and me in the humid tropical heat. We spend those days making love desperately, feverishly, like when we first fell in love. Only now, it feels like the last time.

We say goodbye at a train station in Miami. Gilad is catching a train to the airport, from where he'll be flying off to Peru, and I'm heading back to a wintry New York the following day, and from there to India. We embrace on a bench trapped between two trains going in opposite directions.

Gilad looks at me for a long moment. "Do you want to come with me to South America?"

I hold my breath to listen for an answer. Then I whisper, "No," eyes brimming.

"It's okay to fall in love," he says before he leaves and my heart squeezes into a crumpled ball. I watch him board the train, the backpack strapped on his shoulders, and memorize his slender frame, his shaved head, his confident walk. I look for him through the windows, but the train moves too fast, the faces all a blur.

ON THE PLANE to Bombay, I sit next to a young Indian American woman who's going back with her family. I tell her it is my first time to Bombay. On my first trip to India, I traveled up north.

"Where will you be staying in Bombay?" she asks.

"I don't know."

"But we're arriving at 9:00 P.M.!"

"I'll be okay," I say, feigning confidence in the hope that it will stick. I have no place to stay, no guidebook to the south of India, no idea where I'm going next. My heart quickens whenever I let myself think of the future. I press Play on my Walkman, fast-forward until I find "Leaving on a Jet Plane" by Peter, Paul and Mary on my friend's mixed tape. I watch New York through the window getting smaller. Feel something, I tell myself. Hurry. Don't miss it. But then the clouds close over it like curtains, and the city is gone.

MISSING IN ACTION

THE NIGHT I MEET SOPHIE, I'm sitting on a rock in the jungle, grinding my teeth and clutching a water bottle.

"You have rolling papers?" she says. Her voice is raspy, her Italian accent as thick as mango juice. And she's beautiful; her hair, skin, and eyes are in matching shades of gold and sand. I reach for my bag, fish out a pack of rollies.

She grabs a couple of papers, turns as if about to leave, but then stops and looks at me. "You comfortable on this rock?"

"Very," I say. "Try it. But I warn you: you might never leave."

She climbs up and sits beside me, shifts her bottom until she finds an accommodating crevice. "You are right." She laughs.

"And it's higher up, so you have the best view from here," I say. "You can see the whole tree."

The rock is a few steps up the trail from an ancient banyan tree in the middle of the jungle in Goa. Under the canopy of the tree, people from all over the world recline on bamboo mats, spread over a wide flat area created by aerial roots. They smoke joints, pass chillum pipes, play didgeridoos and drums. Some of these people live here, sleep in hammocks and bathe in the spring. Others, like me, come to visit from rooms rented on the nearby beach. Beside the trunk, somebody has set up a temple to Shiva, and visitors place coconuts and incense as gifts to the sacred tree. Thick roots hang off the branches like beaded curtains, separating us from the surrounding forest.

Pauli, "the Wizard," sits cross-legged in the center, swaying to the drumbeat. When he showed up after midnight, someone hollered, "It's a party now!" Pauli is a Roma Austrian man in his late fifties, tall and scrawny, with pliable limbs, a scarred face, and twitchy eyes. He told me stories about the time he spent in prison in Europe, about his battle with drug addiction, about escaping from juvenile detention to the jungles of India at the age of thirteen with the help of his gangster father. People say he takes fifty drops of LSD at a time. Pauli concocts his own liquid LSD and shares it free of charge. Nobody knows or seems to care how he can afford to be so generous. We stand in a line and open our mouths as if we are kids in an impoverished country and he's giving us malaria pills. When he drops them in, he counts loudly to ensure that we get the dosage we asked for. I took two drops. I've been sitting on this rock ever since, grinding my teeth and trying to breathe away the panic; drinking gallons of water that go through me, my body an empty, hollow tube.

"I see you before." Sophie licks the adhesive strip on the paper, looking at me sideways. Strands of her blond hair fall on her face and she tucks them behind her ear. "Always you sit at the restaurant and write. What do you write?"

"Just stuff." I flick my lighter on and off. Lately, it's been mostly diary entries, something to keep me busy while traveling alone, which I've been doing intermittently for the past couple of years.

"In . . . how you say, ebreo?"

"Hebrew. Yes."

Sophie lights the joint and blows out smoke.

THE ART OF LEAVING • 99

"This is your work in Israel? Writing?"

I hesitate. "I freelance. Sometimes." I find it disorienting to talk about work right now. The truth is, I have been doing a lot less freelance journalism since I started traveling: waitressing is faster and better money. I hope she doesn't ask about my time in the Israeli army next, because that would be a total buzzkill. Most travelers I meet are fascinated by this topic, especially men, who seem aroused by the idea of a woman toting a gun. Traveling after the army is a rite of passage in Israel. After spending some of their best years confined to uniforms and bases, reduced to digits and ranks, forced into a rigid world of rules and orders, most young Israelis need to break loose. Among backpackers in Asia and South America, Israelis are known to be rowdy, loud, intense, with a reputation for partying the hardest, for doing the most drugs. I was no exception.

Most Israelis, though, return home after their trip and enroll in university. Find a job. Start a family. Settle down. I'm still going.

"You travel alone?" Sophie passes me the joint.

I nod. "You?"

"With my friends." She points at two long-haired girls in tie-dyed dresses who are sitting on the mats. "First time to India?"

"Third."

She beams. "Me too."

I hand Sophie the joint and jump off the rock. "All I do is drink and pee," I say. "It's crazy." I walk down the trail into the jungle and squat. Above me the branches sway and morph. The light of the full moon blinks in and out of vision, a broken fluorescent, painting everything an eerie blue.

Back at the rock, Sophie is already heating another piece of hash under the flame of the lighter, crumbling it into her palm.

"Here." I reach into my bikini top, pull out a small chunk of charas wrapped in Saran Wrap and covered in a film of sweat. "Mix some of mine. I brought a bunch from the mountains." Sophie grins.

The Israeli guy I've been flirting with all night walks over to us and hands me a chillum filled with charas. It's considered an honor to offer someone a chillum to light. He smiles at me. I blush into my lap, lock my hands over the smaller opening of the chillum to create a prism, and press my lips around it. He sparks a match and lights the mixture on the other end. I suck slowly, until the mix is fully lit, then take a long, steady drag, blowing out a mushroom of thick smoke. I pass the chillum to Sophie.

After he leaves, Sophie follows him with her gaze. "You like him?"

"Who? This guy? No."

"Sure?"

"It's not like that." I sip water. "Actually, I have a boyfriend." The words still taste funny in my mouth.

Sophie studies me for a moment. "He's in Israel? Your boyfriend?"

"Canada. We met in Diu three months ago and traveled together for a bit. He had to go back to work." I light a cigarette and try to summon Anand's face; his features appear smudged, a reflection floating on a dirty window. This has been happening a lot lately.

Sometime later Fabrizio comes to visit, offering bananas. He's part of an older crowd in their forties and fifties, mostly Europeans who come to this beach every winter for a few months, a group I've been drawn to because they are proof that you don't have to stop traveling to grow up. Most of them import stuff from India to sell back home. Fabrizio is a wiry, small man with a stubby ponytail. His features are close together, his body muscular and darkly tanned like a true southern Italian. By the time he walks up, Sophie and I are best friends; we sit close, arms brushing, lean our heads on each other's shoulders when we laugh.

"Fabrizio!" Sophie says. They kiss on both cheeks. "Welcome to our home." She spreads her arm in a sweeping gesture. "We have not moved in hours."

"Except to pee," I say. "I pee a lot."

He hops on. "Comfy." He looks around. "What if you need something?"

"Everything you wish comes to you," Sophie says. "People bring food and chai and chillums."

We sit on the rock until morning, laughing and smoking. The people under the tree call us the three monkeys. At dawn, the jungle wakes up all at once; birds start singing in unison, monkeys skip between branches. The morning overflows like a pot of boiled chai. We finally leave the rock, the tree, the jungle. Back to the beach.

THE NEXT DAY, Fabrizio and Sophie come to my room to pick me up on Fabrizio's Yamaha 100. My room is a small shed, steps from the water, with an exhausted ceiling fan. I jump off my hammock, drop my notebook in its sagging belly.

We eat breakfast at the Moonrise, one of several beach restaurants that line the shore, and smoke a few chillums before Fabrizio pulls out a strip of acid and breaks it into three pieces. We hop on the bike; I sit on the back and Sophie in the middle. Fabrizio has been coming to Goa for twenty years. He knows all the secret spots.

We drive inland. Everything is spray-painted a blurry green, broken by fragments of blue and tips of whitewashed churches. The sweet smell of cashew blossoms is almost overkill, like a beautiful woman doused in too much perfume. I lean on Sophie's back, warm and checkered with gold flecks of sand.

We're riding past state lines into Maharashtra, to a small lake fringed by crystals. The lake is a yawning crack in the earth, shaped like a blue eye. I position my camera on a rock to take a picture of us naked, smoking a chillum in the water. Fabrizio and Sophie collect crystals while I swim from one end to another. The water feels heavy and swimming takes effort. On the way home, the sunset surprises me. Has it been another day? We stop by a deserted beach to watch the sun, a fat tangerine rolling into the Arabian Sea, leaving streaks of juice over the sky. I take another photo. All three of us are wearing orange and yellow, our faces flushed red. We're smiling widely. Famiglia.

FROM THAT DAY on, the three of us are inseparable. In the mornings we sit at the Moonrise. On the table: empty plates with hardened streaks of egg yolk, smiley peels of orange and pineapple, coffee mugs, ashtrays overflowing with cigarette butts. We smoke chillums, then take acid and drive somewhere on Fabrizio's Yamaha 100. When we swim, Sophie yells, "Meter, please!"—she's from northern Italy, unused to seas, while I was raised on the shores of one—and I fill my lungs and sink underwater, arm above my head so she can see how deep we are. I keep my eyes open, watch her long legs kicking, treading water. Below the surface, her skin is a pale seashell green.

"WHAT DAY DO you think it is?" I ask Sophie one morning at the Moonrise. We've been high ever since we met. I haven't slept in two days and haven't showered in four, but I swam in the ocean and dipped in the lake, which must count for something. My sarong stinks of coconut oil, sweat, and fire.

Sophie looks at the beach. "Well, it's not Wednesday."

The beach is speckled with sarongs, crowded with bathers. Local vendors meander between them, their arms heavy with tie-dyed shirts and sandalwood necklaces. On Wednesdays, Goa's weekly flea market day, we have the beach all to ourselves. The backpackers and vendors all head to Anjuna, a ferry ride away, for a day of shopping and socializing. In the beginning we used to go too. Now that we've been here for a while, the novelty has worn off. We also have no money left to spend.

"It's definitely not Sunday," she says. On Sundays we wake up to the horrifying shrieks of the unfortunate pig that has been chosen for Sunday dinner's pork vindaloo.

"The real question"—Sophie smirks—"is what date?"

I laugh. "What month?"

I pull my chillum pipe out of its velvet case and stuff it with a mix of hash and tobacco. Sophie rips a square piece of fabric from the frayed sarong she's wearing around her hips, moistens it with water, and wraps it neatly over the mouth of the chillum. Both our sarongs are now ragged at the edges, and hers is starting to resemble a miniskirt. I hand the chillum to her and she cups her hands around it. I strike a match, and Sophie puffs in and out slowly, sucks in a stream of dense smoke, holds, and releases. We pass it back and forth until it's finished.

We sit and stare at the sea for a while. The noise from the beach is muffled, as if we're watching it through a glass wall. A family walks on the water's edge, a cutout silhouette against a shimmering silver background.

We decide it's laundry day. Sophie pulls two acid stamps from her wallet and hands me one. We put them on our tongues and head to the well with piles of tie-dyed shirts and worn-out sarongs. Sophie lowers the bucket into the well, and it hits the bottom with a splash. Her lean, tanned arms swell as she retrieves the bucket, reeling in the rope. I squat next to her and begin to scrub my tank tops with a bar of soap and a round stone. Sophie walks over and hugs me, her cheek cool on my shoulder blade; her small nipples poke my back through her shirt.

We hang the clothes on a string, framing my porch with tie-dyed curtains. We swing on the hammock together with our feet dangling off and our thighs sticking like Velcro. The afternoon sun filters through the fabric, casting bright colors on our faces and hands, rainbows on skin. Sophie points out parts of her face and I repeat, "La bocca, il naso, l'orecchio . . ." I've been learning quickly, especially the bad stuff: "Porco dio, porca Madonna, bastardo, vaffanculo." Sophie calls me "Pistolina," a silly teenager, a young one, because I'm only twenty-three. I like when she says that, even though she's only three years older than me.

ONE WEDNESDAY WE go visit an old friend of Fabrizio who lives in the flea market. During the rest of the week, the flea market is just a large, thinly planted coconut grove with a few houses scattered in between. Now it's packed with travelers, rows of vendors with their merchandise spread out on blankets, juice and fruit stands, craftsmen and tattoo artists, Rajasthani women selling mirror-studded skirts and silver jewelry.

Fabrizio's friend, an Italian man with a long beard and a white turban, doesn't speak much English. He offers us a second hit of acid. While the three of them sit in the yard and chat in Italian, I walk through his house; it's sparsely decorated, with pillows and mats on the floor. I see a woman out of the corner of my eye and turn quickly, almost expecting her to vanish. It's me, or at least someone related to me. Full-length mirrors are a rare luxury in India, so I haven't seen my body in six months. I look different, thinner, and I've never been so tanned, so Yemeni-looking. My curls are starting to dread. I twirl in front of the mirror, toss my hair.

Outside I grab Sophie's hand, and together we run from one end of the fence to the other and back, catch our breath and burst out laughing. We look over the bamboo fence at the flea market dying at sunset.

"Check it out," Sophie whispers, pointing at a shower built into the corner of the yard, enclosed by bamboo walls. A real shower. We've been bathing with a bucket for weeks now. "We should take a shower," she says.

"Totally." We stare at each other and drop our gazes to our feet. My cheeks tingle. "You go first," I say without looking at her.

"No, you."

I hesitate but eventually go in. When I peel off my sarong and bikini, I think of Sophie and my face flushes. I turn the water on and gasp, paralyzed by the cold, marveling at the sparkly threads cascading down. A square of cloudless sky hangs in lieu of a roof, made of the finest shade of blue. I close my eyes, give in to the sensation of water beating on my skin, running down my body, draping over me like a silk shawl.

IN THE MORNINGS, before I smoke, the day is blinding white, the sounds abrasive and loud; everything has sharp, prickly angles. I recognize this feeling from somewhere, and I don't like it. It reminds me of someone I used to be, that person who wore her emotions inside out. I take a swig of water to rinse out the toothpaste and spit into the bushes. I look into the small mirror I hung on the porch: my eyes are tired, my jaw tight, my skin khaki-gray. It all changes as soon as I smoke my first chillum. It baby-proofs the edges, tucks me in a warm, fuzzy blanket.

. . .

SOPHIE'S GIRLFRIENDS LEAVE. "Can I stay with you?" she asks. "I can't afford my own room." I'm getting pretty broke myself, so I say sure, flattered that she chose to stay, pleased to share a room with her. That night we talk until morning, smoking chillums on my bed, back and forth, back and forth, until there's nothing left to say. Sophie's hand searches for mine, touches my face, tracing my curves. I turn toward her, our naked legs interlace. Her lips are soft, her breath heavy and sweet: charas and pineapple.

"Tell me about your boyfriend," Sophie says later. She turns to her side, propped on her elbow. "What is he like?"

I light a Gold Flake and inhale. What *is* he like? It's been two months since I last saw Anand. Our time apart is now longer than our time together. It's been difficult to stay in touch: there's no phone line on the beach and he's been tree planting in remote areas in northern British Columbia. Sometimes I forget I have a boyfriend. It all seems so distant: our meeting on the beach in Gujarat, our instant falling in love, our brief time together roaming through central India. The locals we met along the way kept telling us we looked like Bollywood actors: they said he looked like Amitabh Bachchan and I looked like Tabu. I loved hearing that because in my dreams, we were Bollywood: star-crossed lovers from opposite ends of the world who found each other on a tropical beach and fell in love against all odds. I cried when he went back to Canada, spent the following days feeling morose and heartbroken. Was any of that real? Then why am I here with Sophie? I want to blame the acid, but of course, it's been my choice to go on this bender, as if physically escaping my life was not enough.

My letters become shorter. *How are you? I'm having a blast, love you.* And then I stop writing.

. . .

THE DAYS BLEND together, stuck like pages of a book left in the
rain. Sometimes it feels as though it's all been one long day, and
other times I think it's been years. People could be looking for
me; maybe they think I'm dead. Maybe I'm one of those Israeli
travelers whose parents call the embassy to report them, my picture on telephone poles in New Delhi, looking wholesome under
the word MISSING.

I haven't spoken to my mother in a month. I imagine her coming here to rescue me from the drug pit, and it immediately so-
bers me up. The last time I called, I laughed, and she said, "Why
are you laughing? Are you high?" It was as if she could see me.

"I have to go," I said.

"Don't do drugs," she said. "Have you read the article?"

A major newspaper in Israel had run a feature about Israelis
going to Goa after the army to blow off steam and coming back
delusional. One guy thought he was a dolphin. On the flight back,
he needed to be wetted constantly. He thought if they didn't wet
him, he'd die.

SITTING AT THE Moonrise, I watch the crazy guy down at the
beach. He walks along the shore, stops to speak to an imaginary
person or a coconut tree. He picks up a shell from the sand and
laughs at it. He has long hair, a potbelly, a blue Bermuda swim-
suit. He's not young. Nobody's sure where he's from. Fabrizio
thinks he's Swiss. Others say he's from Belgium.

"Do you think he was always insane, or did it happen to him
here?" I ask Sophie.

She looks at him. "Must be here. How else did he get on a
plane?"

The crazy guy faces the water, raising his arms slowly. In Hebrew, we say he has "exited his mind," which sounds more proactive than *losing* one's mind, something one might choose to do. Maybe this is what I'm doing here: taking a leave from my mind, my life, my boyfriend, my screwed-up country. Isn't living wildly, dangerously, and "in the moment" a good thing? Isn't that what being young and a writer is all about? But then other times, I wonder if the acid is just an excuse, if I'm sabotaging my relationship with Anand the same way I did with Gilad, if it all circles back to me being scared shitless. Then I glance at Sophie, and my heart swells with affection for her. Maybe we can love more than one person.

I can't tell what's real anymore.

That night, at a house party on the other side of Goa, I say no, I don't want LSD. I smoked too much charas and I feel heavy and too stoned. I pass out on a couch outside, and when I wake up, feeling better, I go find Pauli and knock on his back.

"Two drops, please."

"One, two . . . three." Pauli winks at me.

"Pauli!" I punch him in the arm and he laughs. I never take three. Oh well. It's done. By the time I peak, most people are coming down. It's intense, as if I'm standing next to the bass speaker at a rock concert. Everything vibrates. Out on the patio, people's lit cigarettes swim in the dark like a rescue team in the jungle. I spend what seems like hours bent over my diary, writing madly. A guy sits next to me on the couch; he's covered in so much glitter he looks like a spaceman. He says his name is Normal and I laugh. "Not normal," he says, irritated. "Normal! With an N!" I laugh too hard to answer.

Sophie comes to visit, all sparkles, as if she collided with a truckload of stars. She's so beautiful she takes my breath away, like some Italian actress in black-and-white movies. In the mirror in the bathroom, I contemplate the possibility that I might be Greek. I sort of look Greek. Lately, people have been speaking to me in Italian. Sophie calls me "Italiana." Yesterday, after swallowing seawater, I said, "Io bevuto acqua di mare." "Oh my God! You make sentence!" Sophie kissed me on the lips and people were watching.

I spend the rest of the party dancing as if my life depends on it. More dancing, less thinking, this is the answer. But then the music stops like a heart attack. Everywhere I look people are leaking onto cushions and couches, seeping into each other. They look old, wasted, sad, their makeup smeared, their colors faded. The party is over.

THE HOT SEASON has started. The beach is emptying out. Everybody's heading north. Even Pauli and his drops are gone, off to Japan. The fan in our room breaks down one night and we wake up, bodies glowing, swathed in wet sheets. I pick up an old newspaper rolling on the ground in town, and it says seven Israeli schoolgirls were killed by a Jordanian soldier. Last time I glanced at a newspaper, it had Israeli helicopters on the front page with the word DISASTER in large, black type. I should know better by now. I turn to the horoscope. It says that I should be less impulsive. I think I should stop chewing my nails. And my teeth—I've been grinding them so much I'm afraid they're going to fall out.

I'm so tired.

SOPHIE AND I both run out of money around the same time. We need to go home but the buses are on strike and we're stuck. The beach is finally empty of tourists and vendors. It's just us, the locals, and the core community of aging hippies. Some mornings we are the only table at the Moonrise; other restaurants have shut

down, preparing for monsoons. "Maybe we should just stay—
maybe it's a sign," I tell Sophie, and she laughs. But I am not kidding. Maybe I could be happy here, away from the "land that
devours its inhabitants," as the spies in the book of Numbers described Israel—as if loss was bound to geography, trapped inside
my country's fluctuating borders.

Eventually we find a ride to Pune with an older Portuguese
guy. Fabrizio gives us gifts when we leave: a porcupine's quill, a
mixing bowl for charas he carved from a coconut shell. We promise to write, go visit him in Sardinia. "I love you, little monkeys,"
he says. The three of us hug, standing together in a sweaty, teary
clump. On the way to Pune, the car swimming in pitch black, Sophie feels me up under the blanket.

WE SPEND A few days in Pune with old friends of Sophie's: Aurelia
and the two Marcos. They rent an apartment near the ashram,
and we all sleep in one big bed, a few mattresses thrown in a row.
Aurelia is a dreadlocked hippie who loves to walk around buck
naked, her pubic hair red and curly. "Ma ke cazzo voi?" Sophie
says to her and even I understand; it translates as "What the fuck
do you want?" but literally means "What cock do you want?" We
all laugh.

The trains to Delhi are full for at least a month and now I'm
stuck in Pune, broke and overwhelmed. Life here is full of errands
and itineraries and mosquitoes and the sound of trains. The mornings are too bright, the traffic too shrill. It's a little bit like home.
One afternoon, after smoking chillums all morning, I faint in a
convenience store. I lean on the doorframe and lower myself to
lie down on the dusty floor, blink to get my vision back.

"You stop smiling since we got here," Sophie says when I return. She stands behind me and wraps her arms around my chest. "Please smile. For me."

IN THE SHOWER one night, the electricity goes out. It's a windowless room shared by all the apartments in the building. The room falls into total darkness, and then it's lit psychedelic pink; a few rectangles in brilliant colors chase themselves in circles like a merry-go-round. I follow them, transfixed, and then get disoriented, my heart tapping against the inside of my chest. I reach for the door, and stumble. It's not there; there's more space than I thought. The walls have collapsed and I'm locked in a black-and-pink desert. The tapping in my heart goes into double time. A flashback. I haven't done acid in four days. The door is there, I tell myself. You're in the room. This isn't real. Then the electricity clicks back, shining fluorescent light over the cream tiles and my skin, covered in goosebumps and beads of water and sweat.

THE DAY BEFORE we go our separate ways—Sophie on a plane to Rome and me on the train to Delhi to fly home to Tel Aviv—I help Sophie and Aurelia wrap up pieces of hash they're going to swallow and smuggle back to Italy.

At night Sophie whispers into my nape, "Why do I love you so much?" We fall asleep hugging, two question marks. When we wake up, our heads are touching, our bodies face each other in a heart shape.

THE TWENTY-HOUR TRAIN to Delhi ends up taking days. There's been an accident. I smoke my last joint at a deserted train station in Maharashtra: infinite plains of yellow and no life in sight. We've stopped here for a few hours while they're figuring out a new route. We end up detouring through Bhopal. For three days I sleep and wake in the train. This train, this compartment, becomes my world, my buffer zone between Goa and Israel. Sometimes I wish it would keep going, never arrive.

At dinnertime, the passengers pull out tin containers from their bags and dip fingers and rotis into them. The compartment fills with the comforting smell of homemade cooking. I stare out the window. Since I finished my charas, I've lost my appetite. I'm also down to my last few rupees. The mother of the family that shares my compartment stares at me with narrowed eyes. For the rest of the journey, she offers pakoras, samosas, sweet ladoos. In the afternoons, I play cards with the grandmother, a beautiful woman with a silver braid and a white sari who reminds me of my own grandmother.

I smoke my Gold Flakes sitting on the steps of the train, listening to Janis Joplin on my Discman. The door is wide-open and the countryside speeds past me: fields of blood-red chilies, rice paddies, groves of coconut and date. Barefoot kids run alongside the train, waving and shouting. Pieces of saris flap between the window bars as the train snakes across the state of Madhya Pradesh. I write in my journal, make lists of things to do when I get home, plan cleanses, meditation, an exercise routine. But my list-making brain has difficulties restarting; it feels sluggish, like a car that's been parked for too long.

On the last night, I sit on the steps after everyone falls asleep, hear the snores of passengers, catch the pungent smell of a bidi cigarette smoked from an open window. I lean my head on the doorframe and stare at the black cellophane night. The train chugs away, its rhythm as soothing as the crashing of waves that I fell asleep to in Goa. Then I see luminous green stars dangling off the trees, flickering off and on like a chain of Christmas lights, a psychedelic connect-the-dots. For a moment, my heart stops. I close my eyes and open them, willing the green lights to disappear. They disengage from the tree and disperse as if someone blew into them, skip between the tree branches, swoop and swerve alongside the train. Fireflies. Not a flashback. This is the real thing. One firefly lands on my arm and breathes light into it. I hold my breath. I don't want to scare it away. I want this moment to last.

THE MARRYING KIND

I T'S MY WEDDING DAY, and I'm barefoot in a deep blue sari, hunched over a cigarette outside a North Vancouver home. The December day is cold and wet, and the snowy path had to be shoveled before guests arrived. I take a few urgent puffs, like a high school student in a bathroom stall, and flick the cigarette onto the pavement. I rub my henna-painted hands together and breathe into them to keep warm.

My new brother-in-law pokes his head out the door. "You okay?"

"Yeah," I say, forcing a smile. "Just getting some fresh air."

I'm not going back in. Not quite yet.

Inside the house, thirty-odd guests I just met are pretending to be my family. Looking at them through the steamy windows, I'm almost fooled. They could be my family: a bunch of olive- and brown-skinned people with dark hair and dark eyes. From where I'm standing, it's hard to tell that the women wear saris and that everybody looks more Indian than Israeli.

I look Indian too. I look Indian to Indians in Vancouver who have asked me for directions in Hindi, to the girl who yelled at me, "You fucking Punjabi!" when I didn't give her a cigarette on Commercial Drive. I even looked Indian in India, where the locals berated me for dressing like a Westerner and walking around with white boys.

I've never looked more Indian than I do today. My wrists are heavy with sparkling bangles, and I'm neatly tucked in six meters of shimmering blue silk embroidered with gold and red stones. Anand's cousins helped with the sari, wrapping it around me as if I were a gift with many layers, draping one end over the shoulder and stuffing the other into my skirt. I'm only wearing a thin line of eyeliner, and my fingernails are chewed down and unpainted. But my hands and feet (which are bare because I can't walk in heels and don't own a pair of dressy shoes) are covered in intricate amber-colored designs.

Anand's aunt hired an artist to draw on the henna the night before—a small, informal gathering that was attended by a few of Anand's female cousins. I thought about the henna ceremonies in my family—elaborate affairs, complete with live music, traditional dancing, and heaps of food—imagined my mother and my aunts carrying baskets with flowers and candles. If I chose to have a henna back home, I would have worn three different traditional outfits, donned ornate Yemeni silver jewelry, and placed a spectacular headgear, weighing twenty-two pounds, atop my head. But somehow, it never even occurred to me to have a Yemeni henna ceremony. Then again, it never occurred to me to have a party at all.

The door swings open, letting out warmth, broken conversation, and the smell of curry. My boyfriend—husband?—steps out and looks around suspiciously, as if expecting to see someone else. "What are you doing?"

"Nothing. I'm coming in."

I take one more look at the empty suburban street. It is frozen still: the snow-topped houses, the parked cars, the cotton ball bushes. My feet start to feel numb. If I'd had shoes on, I might have walked away, down the trail, up the slushy road. My bangles would have jingled as I strode off, and the free end of the sari would have fluttered behind me, a splash of blue against all this gray and white.

"Are you coming?" Anand is holding the door open.

WHEN WE MET, two years ago, on my third trip to India, I wasn't thinking marriage. I was twenty-three, sitting outside a bungalow on a remote beach when he walked by. He looked a bit like Jesus, skinny and brown, long-haired and unshaven, his features carved in long, dramatic strokes. He carried a guitar case and a small backpack slung over his shoulder. When we started talking, I discovered he was an Indo-Canadian from Vancouver who didn't speak a word of Hindi.

One night we shared a bottle of cheap whiskey around a beach bonfire and talked until everybody left and the fire died out. Within days, we were throwing around *I love you*s in both Hebrew and English. After two weeks, we called our families to announce our state of bliss. We wandered through India delirious and glossy-eyed, made love in guesthouses crawling with wildlife, throwing lemons at rats as they scurried across the ceiling beams, shooing monkeys that slunk into our room and rifled through our backpacks for food. We cooked meals outside straw huts, shared sleepers on overnight trains, licked acid stamps and swallowed ecstasy at parties on sandy beaches.

We separated at a crowded train station in Pune, a classic scene from a Bollywood movie: a woman holds on to her lover's hand, extended from between the metal bars of the train's window. They utter declarations of love and cry. They vow to meet again. The train conductor blows his whistle, and the train starts chugging away slowly. The woman runs alongside the train until she can't continue. The train disappears into a cloud of smoke.

Over the following year, we managed to maintain a transatlantic relationship. Back in my real life in Israel, as my time in Goa and my affair with Sophie began to ebb into the glimmer of memory, I made a conscious decision to recommit to Anand. I told him all about Sophie and reassured him that he had nothing to worry about. He said he understood, regarded it as harmless experimentation, and mentioned a woman he had gone on a date with while working up north. I didn't pry.

For a few months, I waited tables in Tel Aviv while he planted trees in northern British Columbia. We wrote each other long, sappy love letters, and sometimes, when he was out of the bush, we spoke on the phone. At the end of that summer, he joined me in Tel Aviv for a few months, and then we were off to India again. Then, back on that train platform, we replayed our teary goodbyes before returning each to our own home.

Finally, when I'd made enough money for a ticket, I flew to Canada to be with him, lugging a suitcase filled with Hebrew books and—because I was a delusional Levantine with no concept of Canadian winters—a bunch of tie-dyed tank tops and flimsy dresses I had bought in India. I was hoping to travel in B.C. for a while and then find a job. Maybe I'd stay for a year or two if I liked it. Who knows? I'd been living like a nomad for the past four years, so I wouldn't mind the change.

Vancouver was beautiful that summer, golden and warm, and the days long and languid. I'd never seen the sun set that late before. We found a one-bedroom apartment in the West End, facing English Bay and a daily display of sunsets, bought IKEA furniture and a foam mattress. An old American car. A set of Teflon pots. On warm nights, the air soaked with the salty ocean breeze, we could hear the water lapping the shore through our open windows.

Other times, I explored the city alone while Anand worked. Vancouver was like a cover girl on a glossy magazine: breathtaking, distant, cold. I walked through its sterile streets, its manicured parks, aware that this was a place my ancestors had never set foot in, a place laden with other people's history. I had no friends, knew of no Israelis who lived in the city, and unlike in New York and Los Angeles—the two other North American cities in which I had briefly dwelled—I never heard Hebrew on the street. Unspoken, my own Hebrew started to wither, feel beside the point, a linguistic island. At the same time, my adopted English was still clunky and unwieldy. I was discouraged by my failure to convey complex thoughts, annoyed by my inability to fight with my boyfriend in an eloquent way, embarrassed by my frequent mispronunciations and misunderstandings. As an immigrant, my identity was already under review, but as a writer whose sense of self was strongly tied to language, a part of me felt erased. I stopped writing altogether.

ONE NIGHT AFTER dinner, Anand and I started talking about the future. "I'm thinking maybe I could go to college here," I said. I had found a vocational program I liked, where I could study film and photography, discover new ways to tell stories that didn't require words.

Anand glanced at me carefully. He had done some research these past few days. Apparently, the only way I could stay in Canada, get a work permit, and apply for student loans was to get married.

I tensed up.

At twenty-five, I'd never planned on getting married; never understood why people bothered. Growing up, I didn't throw white scarves over my head for veils or gaze dreamily at wedding dresses in magazines. I blamed my father for my textbook fear of abandonment. But my tourist visa was running out and so was my money, so if I wanted to stay with Anand, I had to make a decision. Fast.

"I don't want to get married," I whined over the phone to my sister in Israel. "Why do I have to? It's not fair. Why does it even matter? It's just a stupid piece of paper anyway."

"If it's just a stupid piece of paper," my sister said, "what difference does it make?"

"OKAY," I TOLD Anand as we lay in bed that night.

He looked up from his book.

"Okay," I repeated. "If we absolutely *have to* get married, then I want it to be really small, just us. Nobody has to know. We're doing it for the papers. That's all. And"—I paused for emphasis—"there's going to be no husband-wife talk. You're my boyfriend. Not my husband. Is that clear?"

Anand grinned.

A FEW DAYS before the ceremony, Anand called his father to tell him about the wedding and inform him that he was not invited. In fact, nobody was. It was just a little thing we had to do to sort out the papers. I heard his father yelling on the other end (I could make out the words "customs," "tradition," and "community") and watched sweat beading on Anand's brow as he struggled to throw in a word. Finally, he slouched onto the couch and nodded into the phone, defeated.

"My dad is throwing a party," he said after he hung up, rubbing his temples. "Just close family members, nothing big."

Within days, his father had arranged a catering service, a cake, and a proper sari for me to wear. Fifty guests were invited, and my boyfriend's aunt volunteered her large North Vancouver home. He wanted us to have *real* wedding bands, replace the 150-rupee rings we had bought each other in India, but we refused; we liked ours, his shaped like an Om and mine like a flower with a moonstone in it. I called my mother in Israel and assured her that there was no need for her to borrow money to fly to Vancouver, that it was just a formality. My mother sighed but didn't push. I figured she was so relieved to see me married off that she chose to pretend it was the real deal, or at least hope it would turn into one.

ON THE MORNING of the wedding, I woke up at 3:00 A.M., flushed with sweat, remembering a visit I made to a fortune-teller in the mountains of Israel the year before, for an article I was working on. My friend Elsin and I had driven her beat-up VW bug two hours north of Tel Aviv and up precarious mountain roads to see her. It was a hot day and the car wasn't air-conditioned. The fortune-teller greeted us in jeans and a T-shirt, not quite the mystical character I had expected, and led us to her living room, which had no crystal balls or velvet curtains. Children's toys were scattered on the carpet. She opened my cards on a table marked with crescent-shaped stains left by coffee mugs and then leaned over to examine my palm. Her face lit up. "Good news!" she announced. "You're going to be married by twenty-five!"

I leaned back, laughed a long, healthy laugh, and explained to her that that was impossible, that I did not intend to ever marry.

"She really doesn't," Elsin affirmed. "She's not the marrying kind."

The fortune-teller smiled knowingly and said I must invite her to the wedding. "What a load of crap," I muttered, rolling my eyes, as we stepped out of her house and into the car.

I WOKE UP again at 9:00 A.M. with a jolt, heart racing as if I'd been running all night. It was gray outside. It took forever to put on my sari, and it ended up looking stupid: the front pleats were uneven, and the part that draped over my shoulder kept loosening up. I pinned the fabric to my blouse with safety pins. It would have to do until Anand's cousins could fix it later. Anand came out of the bathroom wearing his brother's suit. "It's too big," he groaned. A red dot adorned his cheek where he'd cut himself shaving. I swore he looked fine and helped him tie his hair in a neat ponytail. My maid of honor, a male friend of Anand's, showed up with a bottle of champagne, and I downed a glass with my morning coffee.

The wedding ceremony was held in our living room to a smaller audience: the only guests were my maid of honor and Anand's brother. A poster of a contemplative Bob Marley was our backdrop as the justice of the peace, a gray-haired lady I'd picked from the phone book, performed the ceremony. I'd picked her because I liked the sound of her name, and because she was a woman. In Israel, Jewish wedding ceremonies are performed by men, so having a choice was just one advantage to marrying out of faith. Not that either of us cared much about religion. Anand was an atheist and my spiritual affinity was the kind one picks up on travels to Southeast Asia, along with mass-produced Buddha statues and incense sticks.

The early morning glass of champagne had made me tipsy, and I giggled like a teenager at a school dance and avoided Anand's eyes. I felt silly repeating these clichéd English lines I'd heard a million times in movies; they didn't feel real.

We exchanged the same rings we had been wearing for the past year and a half. Then the woman said, "I now pronounce you husband and wife," and my stomach turned.

AT THE RECEPTION party at Anand's aunt's, Anand is holding the door open for me, looking at me narrowly. "Are you coming or what?"

I walk in. He follows.

Inside, the house is warm and smells of steamed rice, coriander, and perfume. The guests wander around, taking dozens of variations of the same photo, lining up by the buffet table to heap vegetable samosas and lamb curry on their plastic plates. Anand's friends form a row of white boys as they sit against the wall on their best behavior, clad in cheap suits, empty plates in their laps. There is no alcohol served, which I find peculiar and cruel. Anand's young cousins chase me around, admire my henna, and grab the free end of my sari. Finally, I escape to the bathroom, lean on the sink, and stare at my reflection.

"You're married," I say. "How does it feel?" My reflection stares back, as if pondering the question. The truth is I feel nothing, except for a dull pain over my right eyebrow, a remnant of a champagne-induced headache.

"You're married!" I persist. "You are someone's wife!" My reflection flinches. For a few seconds it's hard to breathe, as though a foot presses on my chest. I find Advil in the medicine cabinet and wash it down with tap water before stepping outside.

AFTER THE BUFFET, everyone gathers around for the ceremonial portion of the day. I enjoy the traditional rituals for the same reason I like wearing a sari: I see them as an anthropological experience, like some weddings I attended in my travels. Only now, I'm the one on display. I let my new family feed me Indian sweets and shower me with rice. Anand and I break little clay cups with our feet while the guests cheer. The custom is that whoever breaks the first cup will be the boss of the house. For the next three years, we will both remember breaking the cup first.

In the late afternoon a cake is brought out, a massive creamy thing with our names written on it in pink. At this point my cheeks ache from smiling and my eyeliner is wearing off, along with the effects of the Advil. The party reminds me of a distant cousin's bar mitzvah I was dragged to by my parents. I feel like pulling on my mother's sleeve and nagging, "Is it over yet? Can we go now?"

The guests cluster around, prepare their cameras, and wait for us to cut the cake, holding the knife together as we bend over the cake and feed it to each other as newlyweds do. This is the one ritual in the party that I recognize from my own family weddings, from movies and television. As I stand next to my boyfriend, my sari tightens, clinging to my skin, making it difficult to breathe. I feel nauseated just looking at the icing. Sliding two fingers between my petticoat and my skin to allow for air circulation, I am startled by the cold touch of sweat. I lean toward Anand and whisper, "I'm not cutting the cake."

He turns to me. "What? Why not?"

"Because I think it's stupid. That's why. I'm not doing it."

"It's no big deal. We're almost done."

"I'm not doing it. And I'm not feeding it to you or being fed either. Anybody who knows me even a little bit would know I hate this shit."

He doesn't tell me I'm being ridiculous. He sighs, shoulders slumped. His aunts are whispering into each other's ears. A murmur spreads around the guests, growing louder as moments pass.

Nobody is sure what's going on. But I won't budge. I have given up enough. I never wanted to get married in the first place. I never wanted a party, and now I want a drink and I can't have it, and I will not cut the fucking cake!

My boyfriend (as I'll call him for the next three years, never my husband) ends up cutting the cake with his brother, not quite the photo op the guests hoped for. I stand beside them and smile like a bride should, feeling as if I won one battle amidst many defeats.

A COUPLE OF days later, I pick up the wedding photos and browse through them rapidly, pausing only to admire my outfit or to discard the ones of myself I don't like. I'm posing beside strangers I cannot name, smiling the same smile in all of them. Except for one. In this picture, Anand leans over the cake with a knife, smiling goofily, as his brother pretends to fall over it. I'm standing in the shadow looking smug; the smile I thought I had mastered so skillfully appears frozen and forced. I feel that pressure in my chest again, but this time it stays. It's like someone has my heart in his fist.

I call my oldest brother in Tel Aviv that night and recount what forever will be known as "the cake story." I do it in a light, amused tone, as if it were some funny tale for dinner parties. I think I'm being clever and charming. I expect him to appreciate the hilarity, to share my distaste, knowing well enough that I'm better than those cake-cutting brides. But my brother isn't laughing.

"I don't get it. It was just a cake," he says. "What was the big deal?"

I'm quiet for a moment, while my mind races in search of an answer. Then I say, "Whatever," and change the subject.

I hang up the phone and look over at Anand. He's stretched out on the couch, switching channels on TV. He catches my gaze and smiles. From this angle, he looks like a different man, a handsome stranger, the kind of man you'd meet on a tropical island for a holiday fling.

My husband.

I feel that weight in my chest again, and this time I know: it's doubt. This won't last, it tells me. It's not the cake, it's you. You're going to screw it up. Can't you see? He likes the cake. He likes the husband-wife talk. He *is* the marrying kind.

"What?" Anand's smile turns to a frown. The moment is gone. I bully doubt into a dark corner, where it will remain for the next couple of years, long after we both know we are better apart, long after we recognize that our relationship has never lived up to its romantic beginning. But not yet. Not today. I need to believe in us for just a little longer. So I say, "Nothing," wear a big smile, and join him on the couch.

SOLDIERS

ALI AND I ARE PLAYING BACKGAMMON on a coffee-splattered table outside Café Roma on Commercial Drive in Vancouver. It's an unseasonably warm winter day, a blue-skied wonder in this city of gray and glass, the kind of day that makes foolish Middle Eastern people like us rejoice in global warming. I light a cigarette, sip my double espresso, and watch Ali. He's squinting at the board, brow furrowed. Then he makes his move, leans back in his seat, and drinks from his cranberry juice.

Bouncing the dice in my hand, I scan the board and size up the layout, taking note of Ali's vulnerable spots. I throw the dice, and after a brief consideration—nothing says amateur more than counting spaces—I go on the offensive, break a house, and take down Ali's soldier. I place his casualty on the bar in the middle of the board with a self-satisfied grin, blowing smoke to the side.

Ali stares at the board and frowns, his lazy eye slow to blink. "What are you doing?"

"Kicking your ass."

"You're not thinking. You can build a house."

"I know. I don't want a house."

"But you're leaving yourself open—"

"I know what I'm doing." I knock back the rest of my coffee. "Are you seriously telling me how to play backgammon?"

We've had this argument before. Ali loves to speak of Iraqi superiority when it comes to backgammon. After all, they played it on the banks of the Babylon River for thousands of years. I have little patience for his speech: I take backgammon seriously, and I'm good. It's one of many skills acquired in my years of traveling and lounging in coffee shops, skills I cannot list on any résumé, like rolling joints while driving, bargaining in bazaars, or getting by in foreign countries with hardly any money. I tell him about the tournament I won in India, my hours-long winning streak: a story I'm fond of because it makes me sound like a legend. They were all men too, lining up to play against me. One of them, a Turkish guy, kept coming back and losing until he stood up and yelled, "You're making me mad!"

Ali has heard the story before.

We both refer to the pieces as soldiers, don't know that in English they're named checkers or pieces, because in our respective languages, soldiers are what they're called. Ali and I were both soldiers once, in our own countries, both drafted shortly after the first Gulf War, after his country launched Scud missiles at mine, and mine—miraculously and uncharacteristically—resisted the urge to retaliate. But my service, as traumatic as it seemed at the time, was in an administrative base in Tel Aviv, steps from a busy street with trendy restaurants and beautiful people in fashionable clothes. Ali is lucky to be alive.

Ali's stories are always better than mine. I tell him about the summer it was so hot in my suburban town that when I stuck out my tongue, my gum started bubbling. He tells me of scorching Baghdadi summers, days so hot that you'd fill the tub with ice and it melted as soon as you got in.

Ali throws the dice and looks at the board. Again, he opts for the safest move, the conservative option. When it's my turn, I shake the dice, kiss my fist for good luck, and roll a double. I advance further, leaving my exposed soldier defenseless. Ali bites his tongue.

He wins the game. He's trying not to be smug about it. I hate losing. I tell him he plays boring and safe, that he plays to win, while I play for the love of the game. He laughs; he's heard that before too.

He walks me home through darkening streets. The sky turns the kind of brilliant cobalt blue that follows sunny days; a lighter shade of blue traces the edges of the mountains. The downtown's mirrored buildings glow with fading orange in the distance. When the temperature drops rapidly, I hug my leather jacket and gab about my travel plans. For a few days, I was set on Turkey. Then I remembered it's not actually warm this time of year, not beach warm. "I'm thinking Mexico," I say. At the Mexican restaurant where I work—hired because the Chinese owner thought I was Latin—people repeatedly ask me for their bill in broken Spanish. I've learned a few phrases.

We stop by the blue wooden gate outside my home. I grab Ali's hand. He doesn't pull away. His hands are always warm and mine are always cold. I tell people it's a sign of a warm heart, although it is more likely a sign that I should quit smoking. I tilt my head and look at him sideways. "Want to come in?"

"I can't."

I let go of his hand, resist a sigh. I don't say, "Call me." I know he won't.

HOME IS A basement suite off Commercial Drive that I've been sharing with two Egyptian sisters from Nova Scotia. Before I met

Leyla, I was wandering the streets of Vancouver searching for a reason to stay. I had just turned twenty-nine. Anand and I had broken up over a year earlier, and for the first few months, despite being broke and homeless, sleeping on friends' couches, and living off damaged vegetables and expired dairy products, I was the happiest I'd been in years. I walked the streets free and light—room in my lungs to breathe in the whole city. But then, the few friends I had in Vancouver all left for one reason or another, the rain came, and I remembered just how lonely I was. I missed home, but couldn't imagine going back to Israel to live. My last lengthy stay had been in 2001, during the second Intifada, and now, a year after my return, I was still startled by the sound of firecrackers on Halloween, still boarded buses scanning for threats. Every time I caught sight of news from Israel on a random TV screen or heard snippets on the radio, my muscles tightened. I took on extra shifts at the restaurant. I had planned to pack up my backpack and head somewhere warm as soon as I made enough money.

Then I met Leyla at a belly dancing class in the community center. She was the only one in class who hummed to the music, sang along with the lyrics, whose body, like my own, knew the dance moves by heart. That first night we had coffee after class and talked about politics, about the wars between my country and that of her family, the history of bloodshed and hatred that bonded us. We hung out again the following week, and the next. We fell into friendship like some people fall in love, quickly, deeply, as though we recognized in each other something of ourselves. When my lease ran out, Leyla and her sister, Rana, offered their couch.

On Commercial Drive, Leyla and I became a fixture. Whenever I went to Café Napoli without her, the barista asked, "Where's your wife?" When we walked down the street arm in arm, Leyla with the colorful hijab framing her face, the Algerian men outside Abruzzo Café jerked their chins toward me, whispering in Arabic, "Hiya Yahoodia." *She's Jewish.* What they were saying was, "See those two Arabic-looking girls? They are not what they seem." What they were saying was, "What are these two doing walking arm in arm?" I translated for Leyla, whose Arabic was not as good as mine, and we both glared. Secretly we were pleased with the attention, with the confusion we caused, with complicating their notions of Jews and Muslims, Israelis and Egyptians.

Leyla introduced me to her friends. Ibrahim was a joker with a curly head of hair and a taste for fashion, a gifted painter who'd studied art at the University of Baghdad; Firaz, quieter, more thoughtful, also an Iraqi immigrant, worked in computers. My new friendships felt easy, a slice of home replanted in this foreign land. Our kitchens smelled the same; our music used the same scales, the same beat. Their language was the language of my grandparents, who had emigrated from Yemen to Israel in the 1930s—a language I resisted studying in school, learning to associate it with the enemy rather than with my own heritage. In my first year in Vancouver, I heard Arabic spoken on the bus once and immediately tensed. Then I looked back and saw two young students—a boy and a girl—chatting in the backseat. It was the first time I came face-to-face with my own prejudice, my own deep-seated fear. I had no idea how ingrained it was.

In finding Leyla and her friends, I began to discover something in me that had lain dormant: the Yemeni identity I had rejected as a child growing up in a country that suppressed Mizrahi traditions and educated in a school system that concentrated on European Ashkenazi history and literature.

In Vancouver, I didn't feel a part of the Jewish community—mainly Canadian and Ashkenazi. Most people I met in the city had never encountered a Yemeni Jew, didn't know what to make of me. To Canadians, Jewish meant delis and lox and matzo ball soup, as exotic to me as a *Seinfeld* episode. At parties, upon finding out I was Jewish, people asked if I spoke Yiddish. Others looked at me inquisitively. "But you look like an Arab," they said.

I began thinking of myself as an Arab Jew, finding the term wonderfully romantic and contentious, surprised by how easily it rolled off my tongue. I became consumed by my Middle Easternness, infatuated with my Arabness. On the bus to work, I read *History of the Modern Middle East* by William L. Cleveland, highlighter in hand, listening to the legendary Arabic singers Fairuz and Umm Kulthum on my headphones, dreaming of traveling to the Middle East with my yet-to-be-acquired Canadian passport, taking courses at Cairo University, learning to belly dance from the famed Nagwa Fouad and Mona Said.

Ali was Firaz's new roommate. A recent immigrant from Iraq, he was the most conservative of the bunch; he didn't smoke, didn't drink—not for religious reasons, he insisted when I pressed one night, in a drunken attempt to flirt. He just didn't like to lose control. He dressed like my accountant uncle—a Lacoste shirt tucked into acid-wash jeans. His hair was receding and he sported a mustache before it was fashionable to do so. But he had a beautiful, strong profile, broad shoulders, and a manly, confident walk. He had a dimple in one cheek, and a lazy eye I found irresistible. His accent was subtle, sexy, and every now and then, a guttural *K* slipped into his English, like the *Q* at the end of *Iraq*, a sound alien to most Canadians, impossible to pronounce, but I knew it from Iraqi friends' parents or grandparents in Israel. And his hands—

they were big and dry and warm. Whenever he touched me, which he rarely did, and always so briefly that I thought I'd imagined it, they applied pressure, meaning.

Leyla gave me a sideways glance whenever I talked about Ali. "I know you miss home," she said. "And he may look like it, but he's not it."

Leyla is scary smart. Sometimes it is intimidating, other times infuriating. At twenty-three she had already lived in half a dozen countries. She became an observant Muslim of her own volition on a trip to Africa; her secular Egyptian parents hadn't raised her that way. I couldn't understand her choice to become religious, but I admired her resolve. We talked about everything, questioned everything, including the hijab, including God, including my commitment issues and my inexplicable attraction to Ali.

"You have nothing in common," she said. Ali didn't read. His favorite movie was *Analyze This*. He made no sense in my world.

Still, we had the army. We had backgammon. We had summers and heat and food and music and language. To Leyla I said, "I know. It's physical, okay? It's not like I want him to be my boyfriend." Then, cheekily: "Think of it as my contribution to world peace." Leyla rolled her eyes, not dignifying my quip with a response.

THE FIRST TIME Ali and I hung out alone was at a peace march. George W. Bush had just announced his plan for invading Iraq, and worry about the impending war was palpable. Our Iraqi friends were especially concerned; their families still lived there. We all met downtown and marched in the rain, yelling, "What do we want? Peace! When do we want it? Now!" We were invigorated by the energy of the crowd, buoyed by the sounds of our voices becoming one with the mass.

By then Leyla and I had gotten together with Ali, Ibrahim, and

Firaz a few times, mostly at bars and a couple of art openings, and Ali and I had spent some time chatting, or I did, uttering drunken nonsense I later regretted. At the peace rally Ali and I lost the group and found shelter from the rain in the lobby of an office building, where we finally had a serious, sober conversation. I took pictures of him that day. In one photograph, he stands in front of the Vancouver Art Gallery like a tourist, stiff in his high-rise jeans and old-fashioned leather jacket. He had asked me to take that one. Another is a close-up shot of his Roman profile, looking away with a half-smile, appearing shy, self-conscious.

ONE EVENING LEYLA and I go to the apartment Ali shares with Firaz in the suburb of Burnaby, to watch *The Prince of Egypt*. We end up staying late, after the trains stop running, so Firaz and Ali laid out mattresses on the floor. Leyla and Firaz fall asleep beside us, but Ali and I stay up talking in whispers. We speak of our troubled homelands, share stories from our days as reluctant soldiers, from our time sitting in shelters, listening to bombs or missiles falling, wearing gas masks. I tell him that my first suitor had arrived at our house with a gas mask during the first Gulf War. "Thanks a lot for that, by the way," I say. Ali laughs so hard he can't talk.

Night sneaks in through a crack in the window, the smell of dry, cool air, of no rain. We rest our heads on the pillows and Ali starts singing, softly, in Arabic. I close my eyes and give in to the honeyed sound of the throaty, familiar syllables. I fall asleep to it as though it were the sweetest lullaby.

In the middle of the night, we cling to each other, and Ali strokes my body with large, warm hands. A storm begins brewing in my belly. Then it all ends before it starts. "Go to sleep," he says, when I turn to him.

"Why?"

"It's better that way."

I wake up in the morning wondering if I had dreamed it all.

"Why don't you ever call me?" I ask him the next time we meet. After the night I stayed over, he disappeared. Weeks went by. The one time we were all supposed to get together, he canceled last minute, leaving a message on Ibrahim's phone.

We are sitting on the swings at Grandview Park. Our friends are at Bukowski's, now our regular bar on Commercial Drive. When I stepped outside for a smoke, I asked Ali to join me, then grabbed him by the hand and brought him here, to the park. It's my spot. I have been coming here at night since summer. I'd smoke a joint, swing as high as I could, and watch the city lights flicker in the distance. Sometimes an arctic wind would sneak under layer after layer of clothing, stabbing me with ice needles, and I'd be seized by a sweet pang of loneliness, the thrill of anonymity. I'd look around with surprise that I was here, of all places. Half a world away from home. Alone. Free.

"You left that morning without saying goodbye," he says. He does not look at me.

"I left a note. I had to go to work."

"You should have woken me up."

We swing side by side, until we tire and slow down. I grab the rope of his swing and pull myself closer to him. I can smell his cologne: fresh, sharp.

"So . . . Mexico," Ali says, out of nowhere.

"Oh no. I changed my mind," I say. "I think I should go east. Thailand, maybe. It makes more sense."

"Of course." He stands up, brushes off his jeans. "Shall we go back?"

Disappointment sours my mouth.

That night, on the phone from Israel, my sister calls me a heart-less bitch for leading Ali on. She does that in the nicest of ways. It's 4:00 A.M. Vancouver time; on the other end I hear traffic, the hum of midday Tel Aviv. Earlier that day a suicide attack had killed eleven civilians on a bus in Jerusalem. Hamas had taken responsi-bility. But my sister never mentions such things and I never ask. Our time to speak is too precious to waste on bad news. I sit on the bench outside the apartment door, lean my head against the wooden panels, and chain-smoke.

"Do you think that maybe he likes you?" she says. "Maybe he doesn't show it in the way you're used to. He's from a different culture."

She's right, of course. Ali is unlike any guy I've ever met. It's like he is from a different generation altogether. The East Van hippie boys are so much easier.

"Just be careful," she says.

When I wake up the next morning, I am overcome by hang-over and remorse. I regret the stupid things I say when I'm drunk, feel sorry for coming on too strong, for playing with his heart. I tell myself to let Ali go, move on.

That weekend, Leyla and I go dancing at a Middle Eastern night at the Anza Club, an event hall in the Mount Pleasant neigh-borhood. A guy in white pants, hair smoothed by too much gel, zeros in on me. He tells me he's from Lebanon. He is movie-star handsome and he knows it, dancing around me, singing to me with animated facial expressions, hand mocking his beating heart. The whole thing is over-the-top. Still, when he asks, I give him my phone number just to see his reaction. He stares at my name on the note with a frown, abandoning the theatrics.

"Where are you from?"

"Israel," I say and watch the smile fade from his face.

. . .

SOMETIME AT THE end of that fall, Leyla takes off her hijab. One day I come home and her curls, tightly wound, are free. She's always been stunning. Now she is luminous.

We spend Christmas together, a few Muslims, one Jewish girl, and Rana's boyfriend, who is Anglo-Canadian. We cook turkey with all the fixings.

Leyla steals sips from my wineglass. She has borrowed my low-neck blouse, my dangly earrings and tight jeans. At some point in the night, she stands at the doorway smoking my cigarettes, blows smoke to the side, and announces, "Look at me, I'm Ayelet." Everyone laughs.

Ali and I are cordial. I don't touch him. I don't flirt.

After dinner, the boys teach us a traditional Iraqi game called Mheibis. Rana volunteers her ring and Leyla one of her silk scarves. The game is generally played in two teams, but the boys modify the rules to accommodate a smaller group. One player walks by and covertly slips the ring into someone's hand. Another player has to find the ring while the rest of us exercise our best poker faces. It is a game of deception and trickery, of careful observation. Psychological warfare. The player in charge of finding the ring can interrogate, manipulate, or intimidate in order to expose the ring bearer. When it is Ali's turn to hide the ring, he stops by me and looks me in the eye long enough for me to miss a beat. His hand grabs my hand under the cloth. He does not slip the ring into it. I do my best to mask my relief; I am a terrible liar. My face tells the truth even when my words don't.

On New Year's Eve we go to Bukowski's and some drunken girl asks us if we are all one family. "No, we're just all Arabs," Leyla says. We look at each other and smile. We do look a little bit like family. When it's midnight, we hug and kiss each other on the cheek. Ali's lips just barely miss mine.

In January, Palestinian suicide bombers explode in Tel Aviv's central bus station, killing twenty-three. My family doesn't call. Leyla and I march from Library Square to the Vancouver Art Gallery to protest the planned invasion of Iraq with thousands of people chanting "Stop the war" and "Drop sanctions, not bombs." Protesters form a drum circle on the steps of the art gallery. We listen to a lecture about the UN sanctions against Iraq at Simon Fraser University. We attend a candlelit vigil. It feels good to be a part of a movement, to be engaged in something positive, proactive, when back home everything is such a disaster. It makes me feel a little less helpless.

When we go out at night, Leyla starts ordering her own drinks. At home, she smokes my pot. The two of us get rowdy at Super Valu while shopping for Nutella. We stumble back home from the bar singing our hearts out. One day, stoned, we look at *The Province*'s cover page in a newsstand and see a picture from a peace rally we attended the day before. Leyla leans in and squints at the wide-angle photo of the crowd. "Look!" she gasps. We are right in the middle of the photo, two tiny figures, mouths open in mid-chant, chins raised, expressions focused, earnest. We bend over laughing, tears in our eyes. I glance at the photo again; I love seeing the two of us captured on film, our friendship, our intentions, eternalized.

I don't see Ali for a while.

LEYLA STARTS DATING a friend I introduced to her. A woman.

"You know you're going to hell, right?" Ibrahim tells me. Everyone laughs.

"They're calling me the Jewish devil," I complain to Leyla. "They say it's all my fault. The hijab. The drinking."

Leyla gives me a look. "Well, you did break my prayer stone."

"That was an accident!"

She holds back a smile.

One night, we lie together in her bed, talking. We've been sharing body products and laundry detergent and bedsheets for so long that we even smell the same, the way siblings and lovers do. Leyla lies on her side, studying me. "What would you do if you stayed?"

I stiffen, immediately feeling like the air is sucked out of the room. "I don't know."

"What about writing?"

"What about it?"

"Maybe you could take a program or something."

I stare out the window. It has been so long since I've written anything that I've begun to feel that the dream is dead. Maybe writing isn't my calling, after all. And besides, I have no money for school and I couldn't possibly write in English, so what's the point? "It's not that simple," I say.

"Sometimes I think you don't really want to go," Leyla says.

"What? Why?"

"You haven't given notice at work. And you don't have a ticket, or a plan."

But I have to go. Leaving is the only thing I know how to do. That seemed to be the one stable thing in my life, the ritual of picking up, throwing out or giving away the little I have, packing and taking off. That was what home had become for me. But then I think of leaving Leyla and my heart crumbles. It's a familiar ache. It's how I feel every time I leave Israel. My family.

Leyla lies on her back, looks at the ceiling. "There must be something so limiting and lonely about needing to be free all the time."

WHEN I TELL my friends that I've decided to go to Montreal, they burst into laughter. "Montreal, at this time of year? Are you nuts?"

But I've never experienced a real winter and I'm curious. Besides, tickets from Montreal to Asia are dirt cheap.

It has started to rain, finally, after weeks of atypically dry weather, and I welcome it with gratitude, like something bottled has been released. I inhale the fresh smell of wet earth, admire streaks of lights reflecting on the pavement.

Leyla is falling in love, and I hardly see her. As with everything she does, she is passionate, committed. I wonder how it feels to know something with such certainty, to believe in it with all you have, even when you fear it may not last. I can't even commit to a brand of cigarettes. I haven't seen our friends for a while: perhaps they're busy; perhaps Leyla was the glue that kept us together. After a few days the novelty of the rain wears off and it's another Vancouver winter: gloomy, wet to the bone.

I take my citizenship test, buy a one-way ticket to Montreal, and prepare to move my stuff into storage: twelve boxes, a backpack full of clothes, one rolled mattress, a duvet in a garbage bag.

One day on the bus, a couple of weeks before I leave, a man sits next to me smelling of Ali's cologne, and I suddenly ache for his warm hands, his winking eye, his guttural *K*. That evening I call Ali and invite him to the birthday party of a friend, an Algerian girl I had met at belly dancing class. I don't know why. Maybe it's because Leyla has been sleeping at her girlfriend's and I miss the sound of her key in the door, miss when she was my wife. Maybe it's because I'm leaving soon; what harm can it do now?

At the party, my friends—most of them immigrants

themselves—don't know what to make of Ali, of us. He stands out in his outdated attire, in his frozen smile—the smile I recognize from my first years in Canada, the smile I used to plaster on when I couldn't follow the speed of conversation, didn't get the joke, the cultural reference. He looks like he did in the picture I captured on the steps of the art gallery. When he passes up on the joint, he hands it to me, holding it out from his body, pinched between two fingers, like it is something both delicate and repulsive. I laugh out of tune with my friends, aware of his gaze, my discomfort exacerbated by the down-pull of the pot. On the way home he looks at me. "You shouldn't smoke so much pot," he says. He sneaks a warm hand into my cold one and my heart freezes.

I WIN OUR last backgammon game. It's a spectacular, satisfying win. Ali is graceful about it. He leans back, his gaze lingering on me, so full of warmth and affection that his sharply drawn face softens at the edges. I urgently reset the board and avoid his eyes.

Rain starts up on the way back home, fat, warm drops. We stand outside the house, saying goodbye. I'm about to give Ali a hug when he leans over and kisses me. At first, I'm startled, but then I kiss him back and wrap my arms around him, let him lean me against the side of the house, let his hands travel under my clothes, onto my belly, my rib cage, the small of my back. He pulls away for a moment. "Let's go in," I say.

He steps away. "No."

"Why not?"

He hesitates, looks up at the rain. "You're leaving." He chews on the inside of his lip. "If I go in, I'll get more attached, and it will just hurt more."

We stand in the rain, wet, starting to shiver. The moment is gone. He plants a soft kiss on my lips, a period at the end of a sentence. Then he tucks his hands into his pockets and looks at me askance, shaking his head and chuckling.

"What?"

"You know, you play backgammon like you live your life."

I raise my eyebrows.

"You play aggressively, you constantly take risks, you don't want to build houses. You leave yourself open all over the place, and when things get dicey, you run away."

I smile as if he has said something funny. I smile because I can't think of anything to say.

*　*　*

THIS IS WHERE this story ends, or the version of it that I wrote years ago, soon after Ali and I said our goodbyes. This is where my memory chose to check out: Ali makes this insightful observation, which makes me feel seen, which makes me realize that perhaps I hadn't given him enough credit, and we part, never to see each other again. But reading through my diaries reveals a different ending. A part of the story I purposely forgot. It turns out I had reshaped the story into one I could live with, omitting the parts that made me look like a jerk.

Toward the end of my army service, after all those transfers and reassignments, I was stationed at a unit that worked to ensure safety in training. We dealt with accidents, with moments of inattention and thoughtlessness, with "friendly fire," that careless and cynical phrase with its playful alliteration, not just an oxymoron but a crime of language, really. The lack of intent never mattered. Soldiers were hurt. If anything, it was all the more infuriating because it could have been prevented.

So this is how our story really ends.

A few days before my trip to Montreal, I have my goodbye party at the smoking room at Mona's Lebanese Cuisine, an establishment I love for its food and music and energy, and where I will end up working for six years after I return from traveling, immersing myself in the Arabic community, becoming a part of the family that runs the place, feeling, finally, at home in the city.

That night, my friends and I smoke narghiles and drink arak, the room thick with apple-flavored smoke and anise. Ali and I sit in the corner like a couple, his hand around my shoulder.

After the party, on the steps of my home, Ali tells me—a stone in his throat—that he has fallen for me, and my crush on him deflates as though pricked by a pin. For the next few days, as I get ready to leave, he is clingy, desperate. He calls, asks to accompany me on my final errands. He inquires about my plans for the future, when I will be back in Canada, and where I see myself in, say, two years, and I tell him I don't know. I have no plans. Surely he knows that about me by now? I resent having to deal with this on my last few days in Vancouver. I say things like "I am not looking for a boyfriend," and "I like you but not in that way." It is all too little, too late. He's not hearing me. In his world, my flirting, my attention, can only mean one thing. Women don't act this way unless they have serious intentions. I wish I had listened to my sister, to Leyla. I wish I could redo everything, and this time be good, be compassionate, be thoughtful. I can't shake the feeling that I liked the idea of Ali more than I liked Ali, that my contribution to world peace had little to do with the world and more to do with my need for instant gratification. My need for a good story.

He insists on taking me to the airport. By the gate, we hug. "I will miss you," he says.

I gaze at my feet. "Don't."

"I will anyway."

. . .

I WILL EMAIL Ali from Montreal, then Bangkok. I will be in a small fishing village on an island in the South China Sea when the U.S. invades Iraq. I will message Ali from an internet café with no walls in the middle of a jungle, the smell of fish and salt permeating the humid air. He'll tell me he's heading back to Iraq for a while, to be with his family. I will cry and wonder if maybe I have feelings for him after all.

A few weeks later, I will leave Thailand and fly to Israel, already infatuated with someone else. The memory of Ali will make me feel foolish and contrite; I won't be able to recall the attraction. When I return from my travels the next fall, Ali will be gone. Our friends will tell me that he never liked the rain. He moved to Spain, then the U.S. For a while, our friends will keep me updated, until they too lose touch.

Sometimes he will pop up as a potential friend on Facebook. My heart will clench at the sight of his picture, his name. I will remember him. I will lower my eyes. Then I'll refresh the page and he'll be gone.

KEROSENE: A LOVE STORY

DRANK KEROSENE.

I dropped the bottle, folded over, stuck a finger down my throat. My hair fell to the sides of my face, the shells I'd braided into it bouncing against my cheeks, cool and dry. The liquid tasted grimy, like a gas station. Like a disease. Sleek and oily, a flammable raw egg. It coated the inside of my mouth, tingly, sharp. Broken glass and jelly.

I'm going to die.

I looked up, scanned the market for Raz. Where was he? Thai housewives with canvas bags curled their lips at me. Vendors pointed and whispered. Nothing came out. The poison was absorbing into my insides, itchy, ants crawling inside my skin.

I'm going to die.

I tried vomiting again. Flush it out. Quick! Reverse the spell. The plastic bottle rolled by my feet, a gleaming film around its neck, oily fingerprints on the label. The clear substance sparkled, seductive, deceiving, little stars catching the sun.

Is this what dying feels like? I had spent most of my life fearing other people's deaths, not my own. It was that cavalier attitude toward my mortality, that youthful, blissful shortsightedness, that had enabled me to live as recklessly as I did. Was I really going to die on a Thai island before I turned thirty? How was it possible? My death—so trivial, so stupid. I thought about my mother in Israel, my family sitting shiva; pictured my friends in Vancouver gathering in someone's house, wiping away tears. "She thought it was water. She was really thirsty."

I shoved my finger deeper, my ring scratching the roof of my mouth.

"Hey, what's going on?" Raz placed a hand on my shoulder. Finally.

"I drank kerosene."

He chuckled. "Why would you do that?"

I gave him a hard look. "I thought it was water."

Raz examined the bottle of fuel he had bought earlier for fire juggling, now two-thirds full, then took my hand, led me to an empty lot behind the stalls—garbage piled in heaps, streams of dark, greasy water—and left me leaning against a rock. Two barefoot kids watched as I tried to vomit; one of them whispered into his friend's ear and they both laughed, then scurried away. Without the canopy of trees and tarps, the sun was strong and white, burning another layer of tan onto my skin. My feet, covered in severe eczema, throbbed with renewed intensity.

Not dead yet.

"Here." He came back holding a bottle of water. "Drink this."

Some time passed and I still couldn't throw up, but I wasn't dying either. My body felt wasted and dirty—hard-drugs dirty, hangover dirty.

"Let's go home." He wiped the sweat off my face.

"Shouldn't I go to a hospital?"

"Nah. People drink kerosene all the time."

"No, they don't."

"People do. I read it somewhere."

I stared at him. I couldn't tell if he was being serious. Half the time I couldn't tell what was going on in his head.

"Your body is strong. It will fight the poison."

My eyes stung. I rubbed them with the heels of my hands.

"Believe it," he said. "Think good thoughts."

I wanted to believe it, wanted so badly to subscribe to Raz's magical thinking. I took a lungful of air, as if it could dilute the poison. The children squealed, chasing a rolling tire. "Okay," I said.

He beamed. "Yeah?"

"Yeah." I nodded. "Let's go."

I followed him back into the market, gazing down at the blemished asphalt, a blur of flip-flopped feet parting. I climbed onto the backseat of the bike, adjusted my sarong, wrapped diagonally across my chest and tied at my neck like a halter-top dress, and tucked its flapping ends under my thighs. Behind me, the market, the scene of my near-death, diminished as we drove away.

"You know," I said at the intersection, "for a minute there, I thought I was going to die."

He turned and gave me a funny look. "Seriously? This is how you behave when you think you're dying?"

I nodded.

"Wow. That was impressive. You were totally calm."

I leaned against his bare, freckled back, proud as if I'd been praised by my father. His skin smelled of cheap cigarettes and sea salt, smoked fish.

BY THE TIME we arrived at the dock, the boat back to the beach had already left, slicing the South China Sea's darkening waters, black like oil. The next boat was leaving in half an hour. Raz went to buy water, and I rested my head against a wooden table, fighting intense waves of nausea. A guy we'd known from the beach asked if I was all right. He winced when I told him what happened. "I don't know what to do," I said.

He jerked his chin toward Raz. "Aren't you with him?"

I nodded.

"Then ask him what to do." He lowered his voice. "He's a bit crazy . . . but he *knows* things."

*　*　*

THE DAY WE met, the sky cracked open like an eggshell and raindrops the size of pebbles pelted our beach. When the rain stopped, the sea flattened like a sheet snapped over a bed. I walked over to see Tamar and Shai, an Israeli couple I had befriended a few weeks ago, my bare feet sinking into the wet, cool sand. Tamar was out on her porch, wringing the soaked hammock.

"What's wrong?" she said.

I sat down and started crying. "I don't know. Everything."

"Don't be silly," Tamar said. "It's probably PMS."

"I've been crying all week." I sniffled. "And my feet are killing me." I pressed on my inflamed feet with both hands, trying not to scratch. They looked like raw meat. I had caught people staring at them in disgust. Some asked if I had burnt them. My family doctor in Vancouver had prescribed a steroid cream. A doctor in Bangkok had given me injections. Nothing worked. If anything, it had been getting steadily worse; back in Canada, it was only on my toes. Now it was all over my feet, pulsating, itching, aching, driving me crazy.

A dreadlocked homeopath I saw in Montreal had suggested eczema is often stress-related. My skin's flaring up was in fact "a call to reflect and reevaluate my life." The thought of reevaluating my life made me more stressed. Trying not to scratch and failing, over and over again, made me feel spineless and weak.

"I think I'm having a midlife crisis," I told Tamar.

Tamar laughed. "I'm pretty sure you don't get midlife crises at twenty-nine."

"I'll be thirty in three months," I said. "Thirty!"

I had arrived on the beach a few weeks earlier from Canada, where I'd been living for the past five years. I had a one-way ticket from Bangkok to Israel, no money, no job, and no prospects. My temporary home was a bamboo bungalow on a secluded beach, accessible only by a long-tail boat—a motorized, canoe-like watercraft that traveled daily from the nearest village—or a life-threatening bike ride through mountainous jungle roads. It was the kind of place where backpackers went to unwind from the hardships of travel, hang their hammocks, and stay awhile. People came and went, but a core of us—Tamar and Shai, me, and a few others—would remain for the entire winter, pretending it was home. We prepared communal dinners over a bonfire, followed by jam sessions that lasted well into the night. Some of us spun fire, using poi—balls of wicking material attached to chains—or a long staff dipped in kerosene on both ends. We drank local whiskey mixed with Coke from a bucket, and by the third or fourth round, began making absurd plans for the future: we would move together to Tel Aviv or Barcelona, rent an apartment building by the beach, open a restaurant, start a band.

I was still sitting on Tamar's porch when I saw Raz coming down from the mountain, emerging from the shadows of the trees. First, his purple sarong, draped around his head like a turban, flashed in and out of sight, then him, shirtless, with a backpack and a drum: a fit but otherwise average-looking guy with a lithe gait, receding hairline, and dark eyes, small as grapes.

Tamar gasped. "Didn't I just say we needed a drum for our

jams?" A tall man with a guitar case and a blond girl with a fluorescent backpack trailed behind Raz.

"Welcome to the beach!" Tamar opened her arms in a theatrical gesture.

I made eyes at the handsome boy with the guitar: British accent, blue eyes, and a long torso. Just my type. The blonde stood a few steps behind. Raz told us in a mix of Hebrew and English that they had been walking the jungle from the village that morning and got caught in the rain.

He grabbed my Discman from the floor and asked, "Hey, can I borrow this?"

I frowned. "Um, no."

"Okay." He put it down.

"This is one of the most expensive things I own," I said.

He eyed me with genuine interest. "Really?"

"This, and my SLR camera. And I just met you, so no, you can't borrow it."

"Okay."

"You mean the most expensive thing you have on the beach?" the British guy said.

"No." I laughed. "In life."

"It's true," Tamar said. "She doesn't even have shoes."

Raz chuckled, intrigued. "No shoes?"

"I lost my flip-flops last week. It's no big deal."

Raz glanced at my feet. I crossed my legs, tucked my reddened feet under my knees. "Who needs shoes?" I said.

After they left I told Tamar, "Where does he get off? Asking me for my Discman five minutes after we met? I hate how some Israelis think you're family the minute they meet you."

"I don't know," she said. "I like him. There's something about him."

. . .

Over the following days, I learned he was almost twenty-one, half Israeli, half American, a scuba instructor who traveled with next to nothing. Chris, the tall, handsome guy, was a henna artist from London. Kelly, the blonde—also British—shared a room with Raz but never mingled with the rest of us. I ignored Raz and flirted with Chris, tried to charm him with my wit, impress him with my travel stories.

Raz I found infuriating. One day he came out of the water and grabbed my towel from the clothesline outside my bungalow.

"Hey!" I snatched it from his hands. "I just washed it."

He grinned. It seemed like his response to everything.

Another day he came by my porch with a Frisbee. "Want to play?"

I looked up from my book. "Where did you get it?"

"I borrowed it from your neighbors' porch."

"You can't do that."

He twirled the Frisbee on one finger.

I flipped a page and muttered, "You need to be reeducated."

"Reeducated." He laughed, slapping his thigh. "Good one. You're funny."

In the afternoons, I lounged on cushions at the open-air restaurant, nursing a fruit shake for hours, listening to music, and reading. The restaurant, built on stilts and nestled between the trees, was a cooler, breezier place to lounge on hot days. One afternoon, Raz sat beside me.

"What are you listening to?"

"Arabic pop," I said.

"Do you have any Cat Stevens?"

I shook my head no.

"I feel like listening to 'Peace Train.' "

"Maybe someone has it. Ask around."

"You're right." His eyes grew round. "Let's go find it!"

His enthusiasm was contagious.

We spent the next twenty minutes asking everybody on the beach for a Cat Stevens CD. I was just about to give up when I saw Raz sprinting across the sand, waving a case.

We sat with our legs dangling off the restaurant's railing, sharing my earbuds. At the chorus we joined in. The waiters frowned at our attempts to harmonize. Then Raz jumped to his feet. "I'm going to pick fruit off the trees. Want to come?" I did.

WE STARTED HANGING out together, collecting shells, picking fruit, going for swims. Raz rented a bike one day and showed up at my doorstep. I hopped on, held on to his waist. "Where are we going?" I yelled as the bike cut through the dense jungle.

"To look for a bald man with a snorkel and a mask."

"What?"

"Long story." He pulled to the side of the road, next to a curry stall, and bought two plastic bags filled bright yellow. We canted our heads back and drank the curry, then fished out the drumstick with our hands. Raz ran across the road and returned with a water bottle he'd found in the ditch, shrunken and warped by the heat. He held it over my hands while I washed the yellow away.

"So, a man with a snorkel, huh?" I said as we got back on the bike.

"You ask too many questions," he said.

SOON, HE BROUGHT an extra hammock left by some departing backpackers and tied it next to mine so we could swing in tandem. Afternoons melted into evenings as we talked about our lives, our pasts, our heartaches. Unlike most Israelis I met on the beach and in my travels, Raz shifted between two identities, two languages, as did I. We discovered both of our fathers died when we were young. We both owned next to nothing. We loved the sea, spent most of our lives near it, enjoyed scuba diving and swimming. Raz's relationship in Israel had ended recently: it was one of the reasons he had come on this trip. I'd been officially single for a year and a half, but my relationship with Anand had died long before that.

"So you and Kelly—?" I asked about the blonde.

"It's not a love story," he said without elaborating.

He taught me how to hit the drum, tie knots, make necklaces out of shells, crack coconuts, build a tent from sarongs and sticks. We crawled underneath it and lay on the sand, staring at the pieces of starry sky that peeked between the fabric.

"So what do you want to do?" he asked. "You don't want to be a waitress forever, right? What do you *love* doing?"

I pulled on a flower garland I had hung as decoration. "I don't know," I lied. "I don't even know where I want to live."

"Well, what do you like better, Tel Aviv or Vancouver?"

"I don't know." I put my hands on my face. "I like them both."

"So that's your problem? You're happy everywhere."

I had never thought of it that way. I leaned my head back and looked at the bungalows behind us, the candles flickering from their porches. By the water, a man dipped a staff in kerosene and struck a match. The staff lit up and erased the silhouette, the brightness turning everything around it black.

We were silent for a while, arms touching. The music from the restaurant boomed behind us and the fire spinner drew orange twirls across the inky sky. I was afraid to move, feeling the heat from Raz's body radiating beside mine. Though he'd been physi-

cally affectionate with me, his touch always felt dialed down, neu-
tralized. I couldn't quite read his signals. Feeling brave at that
moment, I said, "Can I kiss you?" He said, "Sure," so I did, leaning
over his sandy, warm chest. He kissed me back but didn't part his
lips, so the moment fizzled like an unfinished sentence. I lay back,
face hot, and gazed at the patterns on the tie-dyed sarong. I licked
my lips, tasting salt.

Long after he fell asleep, I brushed the sand off my sarong and
lumbered back to my bungalow. In the middle of the night, I
woke up to pee and found Raz curled inside my hammock. I
touched his shoulder. He rubbed his eyes. "Can I come in?"

I nodded.

Inside, he undressed, slipped into my bed, and hugged me.

I TAUGHT HIM things, too. Like how to swim mermaid-style. After
swimming out far enough, we removed our swimsuits and fas-
tened them on our wrists. Once, I explained to him how to wash
his plastic bowl in the absence of dish soap, using water and sand
to cut through the oil. I was proud that I had shown him something useful. Most of the time, I taught him the kinds of things
that couldn't make a person happy or help him survive: facts, history, geography, the meaning of long Latin words.

He tried to teach me how to be still, how to not spew words
senselessly, carelessly. I always talked, covering up for awkward
silences or any silence, not being able to tell them apart. Sometimes I could see people's interest waning, their eyes wandering,
but I went on talking, trying to fix the uneasiness with more
words.

"Words have power," he said. "Don't waste them."

He watched me from the bed as I pulled a dwindling pile of
bahts from my backpack. "Stop counting your money," he said.

"I need to know how much I have left."

"Why?"

"So I know how long I can stay."

"You don't need money to stay. There are ways."

The vague, New Agey things he said used to irritate me to no end. Now I paused, fingertips tapping. I put the stack back. If I didn't know how much I had, perhaps I could make it last longer. I stopped checking the calendar too. My flight was in less than a month.

Another day, parked on the side of the road, we watched the sunset from a cliff top. The sea was streaked with swirls of red and purple, drizzled like fruit syrup on a dessert plate. "What a great photo," I sighed. "I wish I'd brought my camera." He looked at me in a paternal way, this man who was nine years my junior. "You start a lot of sentences with 'I wish . . .' or 'It's too bad . . .'" he said. "Why spend so much time counting what you've missed?"

His wisdom always came as a surprise, like the brilliant musings of a child. Other times he was ambiguous, muddled; his language raw, inarticulate, exasperating for someone like me, who strived for linguistic precision. He liked making up words, mixing Hebrew and English, or using certain words because he liked how they sounded, words like *bamboozled*, which sent him into fits of laughter. Then, out of nowhere, he'd come up with a precise, startling insight, and I'd feel naked in front of an unforgiving mirror in a fluorescent-lit room.

"WHAT'S GOING ON between you two?" Tamar asked. We were sitting with Lucy, a fellow Vancouverite, on Tamar's porch. Raz was climbing up a coconut tree, as agile and fast as a monkey.

"It's all so romantic." Lucy gazed up at him dreamily. "You're so lucky."

Raz and I ate all our meals together, showered together, slept in the same bed. I took to prancing around in his trademark purple sarong. I knew people talked.

"We're just friends," I said.

"I'd take romance over sex any day," Lucy said, giving me a knowing look. She'd been sleeping with Chris. I felt a flicker of jealousy when I first found out.

Tamar followed Raz with her gaze. "There's something about him," she said. "Don't laugh. Sometimes I think he's enlightened."

"Watch out! Coconuts!" Raz yelled. A couple of nuts fell on the sand with a dull thud.

I cupped my hand above my eyes. He grinned and shook his behind at us, making monkey sounds.

ONE AFTERNOON, WHILE I was swinging in a hammock outside Raz's bungalow, Kelly came by to pick up her stuff. She avoided my eyes when she spoke, said she'd moved to the other side of the beach. She fiddled with the strap of her backpack, which had left red lines on her pale shoulders. I scrutinized her. She wasn't very pretty—a little mousy, in fact—yet he'd slept with her and not with me.

"You're weird," I said to Raz after she left. We were lying on his bed looking at the mosquito netting; the candlelight drew erratic shadows on the ceiling.

"Yeah?" He was amused. "Why?"

"Well, you won't sleep with me, for one."

He laughed. "So any guy who doesn't want to sleep with you is weird?"

"Well, no." I lay on my side. "But you sleep in the same bed with me, naked."

The energy in the room had shifted. Raz went still, staring hard at the ceiling. "No sex, no ego," he finally said.

I frowned. "What does that mean?"

"It means what it means."

I turned onto my back. My feet flared up with a sudden throbbing, pulsating like open wounds. Outside, a gecko croaked with a surprised inflection.

THE NEXT NIGHT, a newcomer joined our group at the bonfire. Nir was a beautiful Israeli man with mocha skin and a shaved head. He looked about my age. Over the fire, he snuck glances at me. Raz was off somewhere else. I never knew where he went. Sometimes, while we hung out on my porch, he'd take off without a word, smiling as he walked away. Every time he left, I felt a pinch of loss, wishing he'd stay, wanting more. "He's giving me a taste of my own medicine," I told Tamar. In Vancouver, I rarely informed Anand of my whereabouts, never called to tell him I would be late or give him an idea of when I'd return. So fiercely attached to my autonomy was I that I refused to surrender any of my liberties in the name of common decency. When friends asked about it, I shrugged. I was a free woman. He was a free man. Just because we were a couple didn't mean he needed to keep tabs. If I wasn't home, then I must be somewhere else.

"The bungalows are full," Nir, the new guy, said. "Guess I'm sleeping on the beach tonight."

"You can sleep in my hammock," I offered.

Tamar looked at me with an approving half-smile. She'd been warning me about becoming too emotionally involved with Raz. "You know I love him," she said. "But he's not your man. He's too young."

That night I hung out with Nir on my porch. He brought over

THE ART OF LEAVING · 157

beer from the restaurant. I lit candles and stuck them in sliced water bottles filled with sand. I went through my story again, how my travels had brought me to Vancouver, how I was at a crossroads. It was refreshing to chat with someone who didn't judge how much I talked. Someone who wasn't impervious to my charm. Someone who wanted to sleep with me.

"Maybe I could just stay here." I leaned back on my palms. "Work at the restaurant."

He laughed, took a swig of beer, and then turned to look at me. "Oh. You're serious."

"Maybe." I peeled the label off the bottle.

"You can't stay here."

"Why not?"

"Wouldn't you get bored?"

"I don't think so."

"You should go back to Israel."

I looked sideways at him. "Yeah?"

"Definitely." He nodded with mock authority.

It was getting late. I guzzled the rest of my beer and stood up. "Why don't you just sleep in my bed?"

In bed, I tucked the mosquito net under the mattress, said good night, and turned my back to him.

The next afternoon, Raz found me at the restaurant. Nir had snuck out early in the morning to search for a bungalow and I hadn't seen him since. Raz and I went swimming far, past the reef, where the water was dark blue. "The new guy slept in your bed last night," Raz said.

"So?" I searched his face for jealousy.

"So nothing."

"Nothing happened."

"He seems nice." He dove in, feet flapping like a mermaid's tail.

• • •

THAT NIGHT, I caught Nir studying me across the fire, following my gaze following Raz. I turned to look at the water. He picked up a guitar. "This song is for you."

"Pour moi?" I put my hand on my heart.

His voice was surprisingly soft. "You don't know what you want," he sang in Hebrew. Raz watched my reaction. I prodded at the fire with a stick, hoping the glow covered up the crimson in my cheeks. Raz grabbed the poi, poured kerosene on the balls, which burst into flames. His face lit up in intervals as he twirled the poi in figure eights around his hips, over his head, across his chest.

Later, as we swung in our matching hammocks, I said to Raz, "How come you're so young and so wise, and I'm so old and so stupid?"

"Don't be silly." He pried the cigarette out of my fingers and took a drag. "You're not old."

ON MY LAST day, Raz jumped out of bed and started dancing naked around my room. He was always energetic in the morning, as if every day was something extraordinary, the only day we'd ever have. "What should we do today? We can do anything."

I stared glumly at the bamboo wall. "I want to stay."

"Then stay."

"I have no money."

"Money shmoney," he said. "We'll figure it out."

We rode his bike to town. I called the airline and changed my ticket. Then, sitting on the bench outside the 7-Eleven, we devised a new regime. For breakfast, we'd buy a box of cereal and condensed milk. For lunch: plain rice with sweet chili sauce. We'd share a plate of curry for dinner, drink water from bottles people left behind at the restaurant, snack on fruit off trees.

"I'll move in with you," he said. "We'll be bums together."

Local teens loitered next to us, smoking. They eyed our dirty bare feet and laughed. I loved that he'd stopped wearing flip-flops out of solidarity.

In moments like this, I thought: Maybe this could actually work.

On the way back, Raz played tour guide; he loved doing that, calling out everything he saw as if it were wondrous and strange, "Dogs! Goats! Coconut trees! Bananas! A family on a bike! Rice fields, crazy-looking tree, a curry stall. Hungry yet?"

I held my camera out to the side and snapped shots. The pictures captured the blur of motion and parts of us: bare feet, shell necklaces around our necks, hair blown by wind, mouths open in laughter.

He made a stop at a secret waterfall he knew about, and I unwrapped my sarong and jumped in, the water breaking over my head in small streams, tumbling down my body. I caught him checking me out and my heart flipped. But then he ran in and joined me, spraying me with water.

Afterward, we sat drying in the sun. We didn't speak for a long time. I was becoming better at it. He stared at me. When I looked back, he dropped his gaze. "What?" I said.

"You're beautiful." His voice cracked.

We continued to sit together without speaking, but it was no longer a comfortable silence. The space between us felt tense, a sarong between two sticks.

"How are you?" he asked, softly.

I unclenched my jaw. "Fine."

"And the ego?"

"I don't know. How's yours?"

He laughed.

Riding back to the beach, I draped my arms around his chest, buried my face in the nape of his neck. At the stop sign, he took my hand, brought it to his lips, and kissed it.

* * *

THE NIGHT THAT I didn't die, I sat on the beach and watched the phosphorescence dancing on the waves, lighting them up like glow sticks at a full moon party. The kerosene had left a nasty tang in my mouth that cut through the taste of dinner, a constant reminder.

Life is short, I thought, and other clichés people think when they're faced with death. For a split second, my future snapped open like a Chinese fan. I could change my life. I could do anything. I could cure myself of the eczema, the indecisiveness, the heartache, the writer's block. I could be happy.

I walked into the water and swam through the dark silky sheets. Floating on my back and watching the stars, I tried to undo my love for Raz, force it out, the way I was willing away the poison. Reverse the spell. Quick! But it was too late. I was in love with him. It was as ridiculous as thinking that this could be home or that I could go on living without shoes, but it was the truth.

When I arrived at the bungalow, Raz was in the hammock, listening to my Mizrahi music CDs on my Discman. I sat next to him. He removed the earbuds.

"Tamar thinks I'm in love with you," I said in English, though we usually spoke Hebrew. English provided a buffer, the words carried less weight.

"And what do you think?"

My voice trembled. "I think she's right."

He pulled me inside the hammock, into his arms. "I love you too."

A gecko clucked on the roof, a gentle knocking sound.

"I lied," I said. "I know what I want to do."

"Yeah?" In the darkness, his pupils disappeared.

"I want to write."

"What kind of stuff?"

"I don't know. Stories."

"Read me something."

"No." I squirmed.

He wouldn't give up, so I reluctantly opened my notebook and read him something I wrote in Montreal, in Hebrew. It was not entirely finished and I wasn't even sure if it was a story, but I was so pleased to have written anything at all. It was a moonless night, the generator already off, so the darkness consumed everything around us, the bungalows, the trees, all swallowed whole by shadows, hijacked by the night. When I finished, he jumped off the porch and shouted, "That's it. No more fucking around. You write!"

THE NIGHT BEFORE I left, we sat on the beach with our friends, sharing a bucket of whiskey. I had managed to stretch my funds for a few more weeks, but now I had none left. I didn't even have enough for a hotel in Bangkok, but I figured someone would let me crash in their room. I passed around my notebook and everybody wrote dedications, scrawled down email addresses and phone numbers, promised to visit.

"I need shoes for the plane," I said. "They won't let me fly barefoot."

"The bastards," Chris said and everyone laughed.

"What are you going to do?" Lucy asked.

I stood up. "I'm going to find them."

"But you lost them ages ago."

"I know." I looked at Raz for reassurance and he smiled. "They went missing from the front steps of the restaurant. They were black, size ten. I bet if I went right now . . ."

"But you looked, like, a million times," someone said.

I went anyway. There was one pair of flip-flops on the front steps, black, size ten. I slipped my feet in. They fit perfectly.

ON THE WAY to the ferry, Raz made a stop at the market. He ran around choosing gifts for me and then presented them with the same sense of marvel he used to describe everything we saw on our bike rides. A silver travel mug! Crayons! A magnifying glass! Glittery pens!

The ferry was already boarding when we arrived. I sniffed his neck when we hugged: smoke, salt, coconut.

Only on the boat, as the island became a distant green speck, did I remember: that same day, twenty years earlier, my father had died. It was a few months before Raz was born.

AFTER I ARRIVED in Israel, the skin on my feet started falling off. Maybe it was a late reaction to the kerosene, maybe it was a response to an emotional stress I couldn't identify and fix, or maybe I was shedding the old me, like a snake, making room for new growth. I cried in the tub, scrubbing my wounds with a homeopathic soap, missing him.

He wrote me letters, said he loved me, missed me, told me about an affair with a Danish girl he met in Malaysia, about land for sale in Indonesia where we could start a commune. "We'll get chickens and cows," he wrote. His letters, like his speech, were barely coherent. He loved using *sea* instead of *see*. "I sea things more clearly now," he wrote. Then he started writing about faith. About God.

I wasn't in Israel when he came back from his travels. I'd met someone in Vancouver, fallen in love again. We wrote each other less and less.

The last email he sent me, after I had written him about Sean, my new boyfriend, said, "I'm disappointed that a Jewish girl ended up with a gentile." I was heartbroken. I liked him better when he was a secular hippie prophet who climbed trees.

※　※　※

A FEW YEARS later, Sean and I were strolling on Dizengoff Street in Tel Aviv, looking for a sunny patio, when I noticed a religious man in a black suit and a fedora on the corner, offering passersby the use of tefillin. The tefillin—leather boxes filled with scrolls and attached to leather straps that observant Jewish men wrap around their arms and heads during prayers—lay on a table in front of him. My heart stopped and then opened, like a cuckoo clock door. It was Raz: his dark fiery eyes, his red beard now long and curly. He looked at me and his face brightened.

"I can't believe it," I said. "It's been . . . what? Five, six years?"

"Something like that." His smile hadn't changed, still sunny and childlike. I fought an urge to hug him, wondered if I was allowed to shake his hand. I introduced him to Sean. "He knows all about you," I said.

"Really?" His eyebrows arched. "You talked about me?"

"Of course."

"It's good to finally meet you." Sean shook his hand.

I tucked my hands in my pockets, looked at the street, then back at him. We both smiled.

"You want candles?" he said. "For Shabbat?"

"Sure," I said, though I didn't, really.

"One? Or did you want two?"

"Sure," I said.

He handed me a plastic bag with two candles. Later, I read in the attached pamphlet that a single woman lights one and a married woman lights two. Was that his way of asking?

"You want to lay tefillin?" he asked Sean in English, and then asked me in Hebrew, "Jewish?"

"No," I said.

"What's that? A belt?" Sean studied the tefillin. "You Israelis are obsessed with belts."

Raz burst into a generous laugh. I laughed too, glad to see he hadn't lost his sense of humor.

"You seem happy," I said.

"Baruch HaShem." He raised his chin. *God bless.*

I moved a strand of hair from my lips and shifted my weight. "You know, I thought I'd never see you again."

"Don't say that." He broke into a grin. "We're all going to meet soon. Redemption day is coming!"

My smile froze. Some guy came to use the tefillin and I said goodbye and walked away.

"You okay?" Sean put his arm around my shoulder.

I nodded. I wished I had said more, told him that I was happy now too, that I was writing; asked if he remembered our bike rides, our swims, if he ever missed those days. If he ever thought about me.

I glanced over my shoulder to look at him one last time. He was wrapping tefillin over the man's arm, his hand moving in circles, continually, expertly, as though it was spinning poi.

NOT FOR THE FAINT-HEARTED

MY GRANDMOTHER SITS in her front yard watching the street, stoic in her tinted glasses, silver curls poking out from her flower-printed headscarf. Michal Street, a dirt road leading to the local synagogue, is under the spell of siesta. The small, plain houses appear deserted, their shutters closed to keep the daylight out. Sedated street cats saunter along the bushy hedges in search of shade, and laundry is hanging limply on saggy clotheslines. Behind chain-link fences, chickens cluck, bobbing their heads.

It's April and cool for the season, the breeze a thin, silky scarf. The sky is the color of white linen that was accidentally laundered with a blue sock. My mother pushes the rusty metal gate, which loudly squeaks its discontent.

My grandmother squints up at me. It's been two years since we last saw each other. In this time, she's aged and shrunken, while I've gained weight, my skin darkened from a winter spent on a Thai beach. If she has an opinion on my disheveled appearance, my blistered, flip-flopped feet, my near-dreaded hair or the shells I have weaved into it, she keeps it to herself.

My aunt, on the other hand, walks out of the house and gulps when she sees me. "What happened to you? You look like burnt toast!"

My mother laughs.

"Thanks," I say. "That's nice."

I bend to hug Savta, bury my face in the crease of her shoulder. She smells, as always, of fenugreek and cilantro and Nivea Creme. "How are you, Savta?"

She dismisses me with a hand, as if swatting a fly. "Yofi," she mutters. *Beautiful* in Hebrew. And then, "Hara." *Shit* in Arabic.

MY GRANDMOTHER HAS lived in this house, with a slab of cracked concrete for a garden, for sixty years. When my grandparents arrived from Yemen in 1935, they joined a few Yemeni families to establish a new village east of Petah Tikva, across the highway from the Arabic village of Fajja and amidst citrus orchards and swamps.

For the first few years, the family lived in a Yemeni-style mud hut my grandfather had erected on their lot, using sun-dried mud bricks mixed with straw, as was customary in Yemen. He didn't know then how much it rained in Israel, how muggy the air by the sea could get, so humid it's like breathing water. Still, the hut withstood the damp climate and remained standing long after the family moved into the two-bedroom concrete bungalow my grandfather built beside it. As a kid, I used to sneak into the hut with my cousins: I remember the cool, earthy smell of it, the brown film left on my hand when I touched the walls.

Evelyn, my grandmother's Filipina caretaker, emerges from the kitchen carrying a tray with tweezers, cotton balls, and candy-pink nail polish. "Savta," she says in her oddly accented Hebrew, flavored with Tagalog and Yemeni she's picked up from my grandmother. "Ready to get pretty?"

Savta's face lights up. "I'm so lucky," she says. "I thank God for bringing me a nice girl to paint my nails and pluck my hairs."

. . .

BACK AT MY mother's house, I settle into my childhood room. The mural of the New York skyline I painted at fifteen is looking sad, faded, with early mold blooming on its sky. I drape a sarong over the window to cover the broken slats and hang a mobile I made in Thailand on a rusty nail: a small crooked branch with shells and beads dangling on a fishing wire. I remember collecting those shells with Raz—feet wet, body salty and bronzed and free— and I deeply, achingly miss him and the uncomplicated life I led on that beach.

Back home, life is all complications. The second Intifada has been raging for two and a half years. Suicide bombers explode in buses, cafés, and restaurants. The tension is relentless, like an omnipresent hum. I try not to watch the news, not to read the papers, but "the situation"—the bland euphemism Israelis use for the conflict—is everywhere, a barbed wire wound through everyday life. Every decision you make, to meet a friend for coffee, to take a specific route home, might be fatal. We walk down city streets staring at each other; we gulp our cappuccinos and inhale our lunches, eyes glued to the front door. We never sit by large windows, never doze off on buses. We cut short conversations with acquaintances on the street, don't lounge on benches or stop to smell flowers, because a moving target is harder to hit. It's exhausting.

From the back of the closet, I retrieve my mixing bowl, carved out of a coconut shell from Goa, and a long bamboo bong a Nepalese sadhu baba made me a few years ago. The bong gurgles as I slowly light the mixture of grass and tobacco. I blow the thick smoke out the window. The world slows down a notch.

In the late afternoon, I go for a walk in my neighborhood, barefoot, as though I could absorb the earth's grounding energy through the worn asphalt. In a park by my house, I run my hand over the bark of trees, sit on the grass and place my palm flat on the ground. But even the city is glaring at me, rolling her eyes, grunting, "Get a job."

It's only been a week and already I feel like I'm suffocating, already contemplating an exit strategy: I could go work in Tokyo or Berlin. I just need to make enough money for my ticket out. I roll another joint and pretend that my convictions aren't beginning to falter, that my newly acquired beach Zen isn't slipping away like a wet fish from my hands. The smoke clouds the looks of judgment and frustration from family and friends. It helps me retain my fleeting sense of peace for just a moment longer.

I FIND A job as a waitress at a restaurant on a Tel Aviv beach: rows of low wooden tables and bright yellow chairs wedged in the sand. My mother's house in Petah Tikva is only thirteen kilometers away, and I figure I can crash on friends' couches if I miss the last bus. I have done that before. In the mid-nineties, I waited tables just south of here at Banana Beach, a Tel Aviv institution then in its first days. I was twenty-three and hopeful, as was the country. Buses didn't explode and tourists flocked the seawall. It was one of the best summers of my life. I am delighted for the opportunity to relive those days, to trudge barefoot in the sand, swim in the dark sea during lulls between rushes. I am comfortable working nights and sleeping till the afternoon, at home on the edges, places where I can almost fall: where the land meets the sea; on the margins of days.

During shifts, my co-workers and I furtively smoke joints and guzzle shots, and at the end of the night we go for drinks. If we finish late, we go for breakfast, sit on patios and watch, bleary and astonished, as the city awakens to another hectic day, a jarring transition from the short-lived stillness of dawn. We watch people hurrying to their office jobs all bright and alert and coffeed-up, with their suits and uniforms, earphones and travel mugs, and we pity their boring structured lives. We will never be like this, we think.

My co-workers—all of them younger—see me as someone who has sidestepped the conventional trajectory, who presents an alternative to the traditional model of living. They call me "the Turtle," for I always carry my home with me, never know where I'll be crashing at the end of the night. The name pleases me.

After a few shifts, I begin forgetting to arrange for places to stay. Or I start to feel like an inconvenience to my friends, slinking in in the middle of the night to claim their couches. I detect a hint of impatience in their eyes, a frustration with my newly returned hippie ways, with what they must see as a refusal to grow up. "You don't have any money, do you?" my friend Omer asks with a fatherly sigh when I visit. He pulls his wallet from the back pocket of his jeans and hands me a stack of folded twenties.

With nowhere to go, I wander the night streets, or I sit on the beach with my backpack and a bag of pot. Sometimes, one of my young co-workers joins me, usually a boy. Nothing ever happens, but the tension is enough to keep me up until the sun soars from behind the weathered buildings of Tel Aviv, the city fleetingly blushing like a young, timid girl, and the buses to Petah Tikva start running.

* * *

Savta is over ninety years old. No one knows her exact age because in Yemen dates weren't recorded, birthdays weren't celebrated. When I'm with her, I can't help but be mindful of the looming end, the impermanence of things. But she is also a reminder of my beginning, of a past I sometimes forget while in Canada, where I've been living alone, unfettered and unanchored.

Savta's name is Esther, like the biblical Jewish queen, wife of the Persian king Ahasuerus. It suits her: her raised chin, her natural gift for drama, the size of her clan. Except it is not her name at all, but a Hebraized name given to her upon arriving in Israel, not by the authorities—the practice of renaming immigrants would not begin until the founding of Israel in 1948—but by her cousin, who had been in Palestine since the early twentieth century and was versed in the ways of the place. She told Savta that she must have a Hebrew name to be initiated into this new society. That new name was the harbinger of a new era, but it also represented an erasure of Savta's past, her culture and her language, an act of silencing done in the name of assimilation.

She was born Salha (a name her family and friends would continue to use her entire life) moments before her twin sister, Saida, in Haidan a-Sham, a northern Yemeni village flanked by steep mountains that were freckled with caves. Her childhood was marked with tragedy and abandonment. Her father died when she was two, and shortly after that, her mother left her and her twin sister in Yemen and walked to Israel with a new husband. Nobody could explain to me why she left. Perhaps nobody knew. The twins stayed with family in the village, where girls were married off at a prepubescent age and bore many children; where Jewish men worked as artisans, had many wives, and died of unnamed epidemics.

In the family, we called her Savta. Hebrew for "grandmother."

Growing up, hanging out with Savta was not my idea of a good time. We had no common language: she barely understood my modern Hebrew, while I struggled to follow her heavily accented one. Her wit and wry sense of humor were lost on me. In elementary school, I weaved elaborate fantasies in which my grandmother was a European pioneer who'd paved roads and planted trees in the land of Israel, and my grandfather was a partisan in the concentration camps in Poland. I envied my classmates whose grandmothers took them to matinées and cafés in Tel Aviv, where they sat with their puffed hair and tailored skirts, speaking Yiddish as they sipped their filtered coffee, leaving lipstick stamps on the edge of their cups. My grandmother didn't watch movies and I couldn't imagine her lounging at a café. Savta drank her coffee with hawayij, a Yemeni mixture of herbs that tinted the coffee a rusty shade and floated on the surface like leaves in a pond. Even as a child, I knew you couldn't find hawayij in Tel Aviv cafés.

In one yellowed picture from my childhood, I am dressed in authentic Yemeni clothing: an embroidered tunic with red-and-yellow stitching and a hood, a row of silver coins arranged over my bangs. This was the extent of my interest in my heritage: a Purim costume passed around by my cousins, just like the Dutch girl outfit I had worn the year before or the Japanese kimono I donned the year after.

By the time I graduated from high school, I could discuss the Zionist movement and their immigration to Israel in detail, but I knew next to nothing about my own heritage, which, along with other Mizrahi narratives, was only briefly covered in our history textbooks. In literature class, I was rarely taught work by Mizrahi authors, or by Palestinian authors for that matter, as though our country was a European enclave accidentally dropped into the heart of the Middle East, as though 20 percent of Israeli citizens weren't Palestinian Arabs, and Mizrahi Jews who came from Arab lands didn't make up half the Jewish population.

. . .

TODAY, I BROUGHT a video camera to Savta's house. My family is used to me endlessly documenting, snapping shots with the old single-lens K1000 I had bought on Granville Street in Vancouver during my photography studies. But the video camera is a new toy. I borrowed it from my friend Elsin to videotape a family party and I enjoy fooling around with it. I pan over the old photos by my grandmother's raised bed: my two handsome uncles as young men, flashing the charming family grin; a smiling granddaughter in a ponytail. The camera settles on my grandmother. She sits between my mother and my aunt Rivka, staring at me, blinking slowly.

"Yafa," I say to her, the feminine form of *beautiful* in Hebrew. She snorts.

"How do you say beautiful in Yemeni?"

"Halya," my mother answers.

"That's Hatma's daughter's name," Rivka says. "You know who Hatma was? Your grandfather's wife."

"His first wife?"

Savta scoffs, unimpressed. "Yes. She was first."

Once, in a drawer in my mother's bedside table, I found a Palestine Immigrant Certificate for Saleh Mahdoon, my grandfather, issued by the Jewish Agency for Palestine in Aden, a port city in the south of Yemen, on December 14, 1934. The picture showed my grandfather and his two wives, one on each side, black-and-white ghosts, cheeks sunken from hunger: my grandmother and her tsara, the biblical word for a sister-wife, also translated as "trouble." In Israel, my grandmother, for whom the first wife was more trouble than sister, quickly discerned that polygamy wasn't practiced among the local Jews. "It's me or her," she told my grandfather, and then took two-year-old Rivka with her and left.

My grandfather followed her soon after. The first wife never forgave my grandmother this transgression, and forbade her daughter, Halya, my mother's half-sister, from seeing her siblings. Even after the first wife had passed, the daughter continued to reject her half-siblings' efforts to reconcile, carried on the inheritance of hurt and indignation until the end of her days.

"And then he married you?" I ask my grandmother.

"Then he married another one. Then me."

"So he had three wives? Wow. I didn't know that." I look at my mother accusingly. There is so much she hasn't told us. We didn't even know about my mother's estranged half-sister until my brother happened to run into her son in the army and he explained the family relations. "I'm sure I mentioned her," my mom said when my brother confronted her. "Didn't I?"

"The second wife's brother got jealous," Savta says, "because his father loved your grandfather very much. So the brother did ish'here on your grandfather. He drugged him."

I glance at my mother, who translates the Arabic word: "A spell."

"Wait, what?" I move the camera so I can look at Savta eye to eye. "The second wife's brother tried to kill Saba? What happened then?"

"His father-in-law saved him. He gave him oil to drink. Bottle after bottle."

My mother arches her eyebrows. "I've never heard this story."

Rivka shakes her head. "Me neither."

My grandmother's stories always came about accidentally, reluctantly, always a slip of the tongue. Stories to her were luxuries, like dreams and regrets. Perhaps she believed, like many immigrants, that to become a true Israeli, she had to leave the past behind, along with the stories that encompassed it. Or maybe it was her children who rejected her stories; like many first-generation sabras—native-born Israelis—they wished to disassociate themselves from their parents' diasporic history, assert their differences, and stake a claim for their own distinct identity.

"After that, your grandfather couldn't stay there," Savta says. "He moved away with Hatma and then he married me. You know how long the second wife waited for him? Waiting, hoping. Maybe he'll come back for her. Until she realized: en samara."

No use.

I picture this woman, standing on curvy dunes I borrow from Aladdin, searching the horizon for my grandfather. I file this romantic snapshot in my imaginary family album, the one I carry with me in place of actual photographs.

"Savta," I say, "I want to hear more stories. If I come by, will you tell me?"

She frowns, waves her hand. "Maybe. If I'm in the mood."

*   *   *

ELSIN CALLS ME as I am getting ready for work one day. She's sobbing and her words are disjointed. When they finally come together, they make no sense. "My father is dead," she says.

I cancel work and head over. When she sees me, she bursts into tears in my arms. "He tried to rob a bank," she says. "My father tried to rob a bank."

"Of course he did," I say. "What did you think? That he was going to die of an overdose? He had to make a spectacular exit."

I make her laugh, for just a moment. Then we both cry.

Elsin has been one of my closest friends since we met in the army. Back then, she was a hipster and I thought she was so much cooler than I ever was, and beautiful in a heroin-chic kind of way: skinny, pixie cut, high cheekbones, dark rings around her eyes.

That was before I learned that her father hailed from one of the roughest neighborhoods in Tel Aviv, that heroin was an addiction that afflicted her family, and that the only reason she appeared cool was because, like me, she spent time working at it, trying to be less Yemeni, less Mizrahi, more Tel Avivi. It was a journey we each had to take on our own, but we arrived at the same place. We are both here now, still best friends. More than friends: sisters.

For the next few weeks, I watch Elsin sink deeper and deeper into grief. A couple of times I sleep over, clean, and fill the fridge with food. We watch TV together, sprawled on her couch without speaking. We drink Turkish coffee sweetened with heaps of sugar and chain-smoke. Until one day she says, "Why don't you just stay here?"

"I can't afford rent," I say.

"I don't care about rent. You need a place and I need company."

So I move in, bring a few clothes and some toiletries. In the kiosk by her house, I buy a small bottle of water and a glass tube, burn a small hole in the plastic with my lit cigarette to insert the tube. Voilà. I have created a bong.

The apartment is on Herzl Street, a congested narrow street in the heart of Florentin, an industrial area turned hip in south Tel Aviv, filled with galleries and bars and tradesmen shops. The city slithers through the shutters, rattling the windows and glassware with the din of traffic and construction, demanding attention. An air-conditioning unit mounted on the living-room wall hums noisily.

I come home from the restaurant any time between 4:00 A.M. and 9:00 A.M. Still buzzing from work and the early morning espressos, I shower off the sand, the sweat, the beer and hummus stains, then recline in front of the TV, drinking beer and feeding the bong. Sometimes I write terrible poetry, but that's okay, because it's better than not writing at all. In rare moments of clarity, I suspect that pot doesn't lend itself, at least not in my case, to very good writing. It blunts my emotions too much, keeps them at bay. When I read old diaries, I'm astounded by the intensity of my moods. I never feel that much anymore, which I suppose is the trade-off for not falling apart.

Eventually, I crash on the couch in the living room. When Elsin wakes up for work, we trade places and I collapse onto her mattress for a few more hours. It's the kind of friendship we have, the two of us: we share pillows and sheets and dead fathers. Both our fathers died between Pesach and Lag BaOmer. Both were poets, Yemeni, poor, too young.

When I wake up for work in the late afternoon, my back is sore and my thighs are raw from constant chafing, the sand impressed into my skin. Behind the closed shutters, the city's drone is already starting to recede, the workday nearly coming to an end. "How's Canada?" my sister asks jokingly on the phone one day, because I've been in Tel Aviv for weeks yet she hardly sees me, our days and nights are at odds. As though there are still time zones and oceans between us. As though I'm not even here.

And on one of those days, indistinguishable from those surrounding it, I turn thirty, and nothing happens. Nothing changes.

* * *

ONE NIGHT I volunteer to watch Savta while Evelyn is out with friends. My mother was delighted when I offered, pleased by the close relationship that is developing between us. We sip mint tea in her front yard, the old concrete dyed orange by waning daylight. Savta stares straight ahead, blemished hands crossed in her lap. Every now and then, she sighs heavily, slaps her thigh, and wobbles her head, engaged in her own private conversation. Above us, a naked lightbulb sways, inviting mosquitoes to come die in its alluring glow.

"Savta, are you ignoring me?"

She sips her tea noisily.

"Why are you hanega?"

This gets her attention. She squints at me, cloudy eyes dotted silver. *Hanega* is a Yemeni word that describes the elaborate display of annoyance and indignation one might show a person who offended or displeased them. It is a word my mother and aunts use often, but this is the first time she hears me say it. I can tell she's trying not to smile.

A few days ago, on my way to see her, I passed a small bungalow on Michal Street with a FOR RENT sign in its window. On the way back, I stopped by it again. The outside was bare and painted an unattractive brown. It had a small front porch with room for a hammock, and a ledge where one could place planters for flowers and herbs.

The truth was, the appeal of my peripatetic lifestyle was starting to wear thin. For nearly a decade, I traveled as though my life might go stagnant without perpetual motion, moving fast and often because—as in the Intifada—it was safer to keep going than to stand still. I was tired of starting again, tired of apartments with no furniture. I found myself yearning for a set of fluffy pillows, a chest of drawers I'd pick in an antique store, walls that I'd paint myself after choosing colors from paint strips. Sometimes, I wondered what my life would have been like if I had chosen to stay, if I had pursued the journalism career I once had, if I had lived close to my family. If I hadn't been so terrified of staying in one place.

Lingering by that little house, I tried to conceive what settling down here would feel like. There was nothing waiting for me in

Canada anymore but a few boxes scattered in storage places. What if home didn't have to be as complicated as I made it to be? What if I belonged here? In this neighborhood?

When I was twenty-three, I brought a friend from Banana Beach, a lovely Ashkenazi girl from Haifa, to Sha'ariya. I had just returned from my first trip to India and saw the place in a new light, found it charming and quaint. We smoked a joint on a park bench at sundown, watched Yemeni kids with kippahs and side curls playing basketball and old women on benches, speaking animatedly in Yemeni to each other. "It feels like we're in the seventies," my friend whispered, wide-eyed.

Despite growing up within walking distance of Sha'ariya, I sometimes felt the same way, as though time stood still here, as though nothing had ever changed and nothing ever would. Most houses had been there since the neighborhood's inception, their plain style reflecting the dearth, austerity, and simplicity of those early days.

In 1949, a year after Israel was founded, fifty thousand Yemeni immigrants arrived in planes on the famous Operation on the Wings of Eagles, which many people erroneously call Operation Magic Carpet as it satisfies their exotic notions of Yemenis arriving from Arabia on flying rugs. Many new Yemeni immigrants settled in Sha'ariya, and eventually, the neighborhood was annexed by the city of Petah Tikva: stores opened, some main roads were paved, buses started running. A synagogue was built. A small movie theater.

And still, while the city around it grew more modern, sprouting apartment buildings and shopping malls and multiplex theaters, Sha'ariya always remained behind, overlooked, a relic from the past.

This distance between two places in such proximity mirrored

the insurmountable gulf that spread between my grandmother and me. Only two generations apart, our lives were so fundamentally different. As a child, I couldn't fathom what her life in Yemen had been like. My grandmother must have found me as alien and peculiar as I did her: a fast-talking, freakishly tall girl (as Yemenis were known to be petite) who wore jeans and tank tops, exposed her hair, and didn't worry she might get too dark in the sun. I was mouthy, defiant, disrespectful to my elders—qualities that would have undoubtedly gotten me in serious trouble had we remained in Yemen. Once, when I was twelve (the age she was when she had been married off), I made a big scene refusing to wash the dishes with the women after dinner, stomped my feet and demanded that my brothers help too. My grandmother stared at my mother in disbelief while my mother shrugged as though she had nothing to do with my education.

I grab my camera. The light is perfect. It's that hour before sunset when faces are washed with a radiant glow, wrinkles softened and smoothed.

"Bas," Savta says in Yemeni, her mother tongue. *Enough.*

"Lama?" I ask in Hebrew, my mother tongue.

"Lama, lama," she mimics. "What am I, a fashion model?" She bursts into laughter. I rush to take the photo but she moves and the picture turns out blurry.

* * *

SUMMER SHOVES THE short-lived spring out of its way, drapes over the city viscous and stifling. Whenever I'm away from it, I mythologize Israeli summer. I picture flowing dresses and lazy days by the seaside. Ice cream cones and open windows and kids running through sprinklers.

In reality, you don't want to be at the beach between noon and

four because you'll likely get heatstroke. In reality, you sweat all
the time, air conditioners hum day and night, a tireless, tedious
soundtrack to our lives, and everything is faded and fatigued in
the glare of sunlight. July and August in Tel Aviv are not for the
faint-hearted.

This may explain the increase in my fainting spells. They've
been happening, on and off, for years. Always from smoking too
much pot. Because: everything in excess. Because: fuck modera-
tion. Little deaths on a trail in Manali, a sidewalk in Tel Aviv, a
hotel room in Nepal. In Vancouver, in Mexico, in Thailand. On the
street, in the park, in bathrooms, in people's living rooms. Most
of my close friends have collected me from the floor at one point
or another.

Lately it's been getting worse. I get light-headed almost every
time I stand up, my vision darkening, usually for just an instant,
until the particles reunite to construct that lost image. But sometimes my vision doesn't return, my muscles dissolve into jelly, my
skin goes tingly, then numb. By now I can pinpoint the moment
right before the fall, blindly trace the nearest wall and lower myself onto the concrete, the tile floor, softening the landing with a
controlled descent. Most times it only takes a few moments before it's over.

Secretly, a part of me enjoys the romance of the swooning her-
oine, relishes the loss of body, the checking out, as though my
fainting spells are some mystic journey I get to embark on, a por-
tal to a private universe that is all my own, like fiction, an access
to this place of temporary death. But like Tel Aviv summers, the
fabled story I tell of my blackouts is grander than life. In reality, I
haven't written fiction in ages and there is nothing on the other
side but a sleep-like stupor. In reality, I sometimes miscalculate
and crumble on the floor, hit my head, bruise myself.

"Everything seems to be fine." An apathetic doctor glosses over my blood test results. "Except for a little bit of low blood sugar." He studies me, adjusting his glasses. "Do you do drugs?"

"No," I say hastily. Pot isn't really drugs, is it? It's been a while since I've done anything else. Besides, I'm not going to tell someone like him. He's seen hundreds of me: another stoner in Tel Aviv is not a story. Life is stressful here. A few weeks ago, a bomb went off at my friend Omer's workplace on his day off; another blew up on a bus I frequently take. And just yesterday, twenty-three people died in a Palestinian suicide attack in Jerusalem. Some days I get off buses for no apparent reason, following misguided gut feelings. When a bus pulls up next to a car I'm in, I pray for the traffic light to change and the instrument of death to drive away. He must know that. Maybe he smokes too. What else are you supposed to do?

* * *

Today, Savta is not in the mood. She scowls at the lens pointing at her face, her answers curt. When I ask her about the trip to Israel, she says, "We walked. It was long."

"How long?"

She jerks her chin. "Long."

"Years?"

"No, not years."

"Months?"

"Yes."

"Two months or six months?"

"I don't know. I was very sick." She sighs somberly. "I was suffering."

"What did you have?"

"I was sick all the years. Even today."

"Today you're old. But then you were young."

"Then also I had many problems."

"Like what?"

"Sick, sick." She raises her voice. "Sometimes this, sometimes that. But the kids were okay, thank God. I gave birth okay, thank God, and I took care of them, even though I was sick." She swats a fly. "Finished?"

We were around the same age when we left our homes and set out on a journey to a new country. But while my grandmother uprooted her life for the dream of a Promised Land, the home the Jews of Yemen believed they were destined for, the one place in which they could truly be free, I was an accidental immigrant. I did not relocate to Canada; I drifted there. And even then, I was unable to fully settle, continued to seesaw, one foot here and one foot there, spending months at a time in Israel and taking off traveling in between.

I titled my bank account during those years of travel "the wandering Jew fund." And indeed, there is something deeply Jewish about that somber, nostalgic yearning for a place where one can feel at home. Of course, historically, that pining was pointed toward Israel, the same country I had chosen to leave.

She doesn't miss Yemen, Savta says, scoffing, when I ask. Why should she? In Yemen, Jews were not permitted to carry weapons or ride horses, and their homes had to be shorter than their Muslim neighbors' homes. Girls in Yemen weren't allowed to study or pray, couldn't read or write, and were subject to the authority of men: their fathers, brothers, or husbands. In Yemen, she was an orphan in the times of the draconian Orphans' Decree—one of the collective traumas that shaped Jewish Yemeni history—and lived in fear of being confiscated by the authorities and converted to Islam. The practice, which was temporarily abolished during wives and many children, their lack of table manners and superstitious beliefs in demons and spirits. Their traditions were undervalued and mocked. In his 1950 letter to Chief of Staff Yigael Yadin, Israel's first prime minister, David Ben-Gurion, referred to Yemeni immigrants as primitive, "unaware of their most basic hygienic needs . . . far from us two thousand years if not more." And in 1909, an essay on the front page of *HaTzvi* newspaper declared the Yemeni Jew, "a simple, natural laborer . . . without shame, without philosophy and without poetry . . . in a wild, barbaric state." That sentiment echoed a 1908 memo written by Dr. Jacob Thon, from the Palestine office of the World Zionist Organization, who said, "Because they are satisfied with little, these Jews can be compared to the Arabs and in this respect they can even compete with them . . . If we get Yemeni families to settle down in villages, we could also have the women and girls work as cleaners and maids, instead of dealing with the Arab help." As he had hoped, Yemeni women soon began working at Ashkenazi homes, and Savta, who worked as a maid and a laundress for many years, was no exception.

During the late forties and early fifties, the patronizing belief that Yemenis were unfit to parent and had more children than they could manage helped rationalize heinous crimes such as the systematic abduction and forced adoption of hundreds of immigrant children, most of them Yemeni (and the rest Mizrahi), from transit camps and hospitals. That devastating chapter in Israeli history—overlooked and unresolved—became known as the Yemenite Children Affair. Fortunately, my family, who had arrived prior to the large wave of immigration, was spared, but my uncle's wife, Adina, was nearly kidnapped by the same method that many of the other testimonials detailed. She was taken to a hospital for a common cold, and when her parents returned for her the following day, they were told she had died. No death certificate or body was shown. She was lucky. Her father refused to accept the verdict; he scoured the hospital until he found her alive and healthy, in a different room, and snatched her away. Most families never saw their children again.

I PICTURE MY grandmother arriving in Palestine, bewildered by this new place and its pale-skinned Jews, men without side curls holding hands with scarfless women in khaki shorts, and their language—staccato and strange. Hebrew? Yiddish? I think of my first time landing in North America, the language chewy and clunky in my mouth. Despite knowing English from school, I felt powerless and isolated, frustrated at not being able to express myself with the richness and precision I'd been accustomed to. Savta (unlike my grandfather, who knew Hebrew from prayer) had to learn Hebrew from scratch.

In Israel, Yemeni immigrants gained a reputation for being intrinsically naïve, demure, and "so nice!"—seemingly positive stereotypes that were in fact belittling, as if they were children or the nation's pets. But my grandmother wasn't nice; she was a strong, feisty woman who spoke her mind, "a feminist," my aunt once called her. She often scolded her twin sister, Saida, telling her to stand up for herself, to not let her husband control her. She walked away from a polygamous marriage that didn't suit her.

How did it feel to be so voiceless?

Many years later, I will find out about the "women's songs," a form of oral poetry that Jewish Yemeni women composed and sang in Arabic and performed in birth and henna ceremonies, while doing housework or craftwork. Through these poems, the women voiced their heartaches and sorrows: they lamented their lost youth, wept over their fate as child brides, pined for their parents' home, complained about a hostile first wife. The songs were memorized, constantly rewritten, and passed on from mother to daughter. It was their form of protest, a poetry of dissent. But that tradition was largely discontinued upon arrival in Israel. It never made it to my generation. Growing up, I never heard Savta sing, although my youngest uncle remembers her singing to him while doing her housework, her voice lovely and filled with deep sadness.

When I learn about that rich literary tradition I hadn't even known existed, hadn't known I belonged to, a tradition now on the verge of extinction, I will pay a Yemeni singer in Israel to teach me these songs, and the Yemeni words of my ancestors will roll out of my mouth effortlessly, as though they've been waiting for me to utter them all along. I will sing with my mother and my aunts, and they will look at me and each other, amazed that I know these songs, that I can pronounce the Yemeni words, and that I cared enough to learn, chose to be a part of them, and allowed them to be a part of me. And I will wish my grandmother were there to hear me speaking her language. I will wish she were there to join us in singing.

.   .   .

SUMMER DOESN'T END in Israel. It fades, falters, and then strikes again with renewed vigor. September comes and goes and it's still too hot. Work does not let up.

One evening I recognize Aviva, the editor of a women's magazine I worked for in my early twenties, and I am aware of the tray I am carrying, the piles of empty mugs and grimy ashtrays, the stained apron cinched around my waist, the fact that there is nowhere to hide. This woman took a chance on me when I was twenty, straight out of army service. I was their youngest writer, driven and prolific and bursting with potential. Now I'm thirty and already a has-been.

She stops, hand on her chest. "Ayelet?"

We hug. I'm sweaty and sandy and barefoot, and she carries a little purse and smells of perfume.

"So what are you doing right now?"

I look around and half-shrug. "Well, I'm making some money while I'm here."

"So you're here now!" Her face brightens. "Give us a call. We'd love to hear from you."

I smile and nod. I don't tell her that I might be leaving again soon, that I haven't written anything publishable in years.

At the end of the shift, my co-workers and I go for drinks. We are refugees of the night, all thirsty for something: love, attention, distraction. Tonight we party harder than usual. Sitting at a sidewalk table outside HaMinzar, everyone drinks too much, flirts with each other, makeup smeared, sand in our hair. The night is so dense, so brimming with sex and alcohol and possibilities, that it feels infinite, as though the day will never come. In the bathroom, my shift supervisor, smelling of whiskey and cigarettes, drags me into a stall and kisses me, and I push her gently away, stunned. Time to go.

Elsin is sleeping at her girlfriend's. Too inebriated to sleep, I smoke and write poetry, smoke and watch TV, and then I smoke some more. I get up and make it halfway to the kitchen when the darkness rushes in, like blinds drawn with a snap. By now, I know my way by heart, using my memory as a white cane. The blindness usually disperses by the time I get to the kitchen. This time, it doesn't. I turn to the wall unseeing, start lowering myself to the floor, but not quickly enough. I hit the floor hard. Then my body is doing something new: it is convulsing, arms and legs limply slapping the floor.

When I wake up, cold tiles under my cheek, I have no idea how long I've been lying there. The phone is too far and it's still night and I'm alone. I stay lying on the floor until the milky morning light pours in from the kitchen window. I listen to the city waking up, buses growling, radios blaring, alarms chirping from neighboring apartments. I concentrate on the feeling of the floor underneath me, the solidness of it under my body. There's comfort in that. I think: there's nowhere else to fall from here. I think: things need to change.

* * *

ON MY LAST visit to my grandmother, I set the camera on the bedside table so it frames the two of us on her bed. Savta is wearing a maroon cardigan, a heavy gold necklace. She seems more at ease speaking to me directly. This is the most engaged she's been since we started our interviews.

It's November—nearly seven months since I arrived in Israel—and it finally begins to feel like fall. Days are short and sunny; evenings are cool enough for a sweater. The restaurant starts closing earlier, the beach too cool and windy to draw customers at night. I've made enough money for a cheap ticket to the U.S. From there I will board a bus to Vancouver. I'm leaving next week.

I haven't smoked pot in a few weeks. It is the longest I've gone in eight years. The light of day is more blinding without the fog, the graininess in my vision gone. Sometimes my heart palpitates with fear. Sometimes I don't know what to do with my hands. I take deep, long, measured breaths instead of smoking. I'm still figuring it out.

"Saba went away," Savta tells me. "Faraway place. After some time, I hear the Arabs talking. They said he is sick. Smallpox. Then one day Saba came near our house and called my aunt, the one who raised me, because my mother—she left me when I was two!" She spits and mumbles a string of curses in Arabic.

"Saba called my aunt, 'Ama, ya ama! ta'ali!' *Auntie, auntie. Come here!* He didn't want to come in, because smallpox is very contagious. When she came, he said, 'Tell Salha to meet me by the tree tomorrow, outside the village. I will do vaccination from the pus in my wounds.' The next day I came to meet him by the tree and he cut me with a knife here." She slit her wrist with a finger. "And then he put pus from his wounds on my cut and tied it up."

"With a bandage?"

"Bandage." She snorts. "With cloth. We had no bandage. And believe me, after eight days I had some smallpox wounds, but only a little bit and that's it. His vaccine worked. I was fine."

"Why did Saba go away?"

"To sell in the souk. He made jewelry. For ears, for fingers. Silver, that Yemeni women wear. Whatever you want. In Israel? No. Here, he looked for job like anyone. Worked in orchards. Sometimes they kicked him out from there. Go home! You don't know how to work!"

"Why?"

"Because he didn't know how to work!"

We both laugh. So much for a natural laborer. Her eyes water. She lifts her glasses and wipes them with a handkerchief.

In the kitchen, I boil water for Savta's tea and look out the small window at the row of forgotten dresses that sway on the clothesline like ghosts. I remember standing there as a child after Friday night dinners, looking in, watching my aunts and female cousins all crammed into the tiny room and feeling like an outsider. Their vitality still emanates from the walls like the smell of old spices, clinging to the cabinets, the chipped countertop, the porcelain sink that is veined with gray scratches.

Now I long to be in the room with them and listen. I want to ask questions. I want to know everything, because the more I know, the more at home I feel in my own skin, because being here, immersed in my culture and my history, anchors me, brings me closer to an earlier version of myself, the one who stayed behind when I left. It links me to all the women who came before me and all the stories they never told.

My grandmother sips her tea, her glasses steaming.

"Savta, do you have any jewelry left from Saba?"

She shakes her head. "We didn't bring. You know how I dressed in Yemen? Like a queen, all my fingers rings, even my toes. On my neck. All silver." She reties her scarf. "So what was I saying? We got by, thank God."

I lean over and hug her. Unlike my mother, a champion hugger whose body is a physical extension of her love, my grandmother rarely initiates touch. She gazes at me for a long moment as if seeing me for the first time. "Do you love me?"

I'm startled. "Very much. What kind of a question is that?"

"Question!" She rests her arm on my leg. "What's that on your hand?"

"A bracelet."

She grabs my wrist—an excuse to touch—and looks closely. "What kind of bracelet?"

"A bracelet from gems. I made it. See? I'm like my grandfather."

"You be healthy. May you have a bracelet of gold."

She lets my wrist drop on her open palm and taps her other hand on it. She mumbles something in Yemeni.

"What does it mean?" I ask.

"May God give you a good husband," she says. "Insha'Allah."

God willing.

III.
RETURN

I, who had lived so much of my life looking elsewhere, was slowly coming to acknowledge that not-belonging, also, can be a kind of belonging. There are all sorts of nations on this earth. It is a lonelier citizenship, perhaps, but a vast one.

—ESI EDUGYAN, *Dreaming of Elsewhere*

TOUGH CHICK

Main offense: assault
Weapon used: physical force
Weapon status: real
Drugs/alcohol involved: yes

I LIKE CONSTABLE LOUIE. He has a reassuring smile and he looks me straight in the eye. When I see him standing at the door in his stiff uniform and chunky belt, the glint of polished metal on his chest, I don't think, Shit! The police! What did I do?

He's here bearing gifts. It took the police three months to put together a photographic lineup and three more days for me to figure out a place for us to meet—a tricky task, since I don't live in or hang out at the kind of places where cops are welcome. My East Vancouver apartment is out of the question. The landlord just cleared the last of his grow-op and the entire house reeks of weed. The owner of the coffee shop I frequent said flat out, "Well, you can't bring him here. We have customers who are affiliated, if you know what I mean." We end up meeting at Sean's studio apartment, on the top floor of a redbrick building on Commercial Drive. Constable Louie has been here once before, when he came to take my statement after the assault. Only this time, I tell him I live here, with Sean. For a moment, I savor the taste of that lie in my mouth.

I invite him in, babble about the weather; can you believe it's already January? Did you have a good Christmas? I have high hopes for this photo lineup. I've been telling everyone that I could identify those kids anywhere, that their faces are imprinted into my mind. But it's been three months since that Halloween night and I can't help but wonder. Every time I see a group of teenagers huddling outside a pizzeria, I think it's them. I lower my gaze and pick up my pace, my cellphone clutched in my sweaty palm, my finger hovering over the Send key, the 911 digits already dialed, ready to fire up.

On October 31 2004 at 5:00 PM the victim boarded Vancouver bus No. 20 going north on Commercial toward Downtown.

I SIT AT the bus stop, crammed between a skeletal bride and a young mother with Spider-Man in her lap, wishing I didn't have to go to work. It's Saturday night, the restaurant where I work is going to be packed, and they'll probably make me wear a stupid witch hat. I hate work and I hate Sean, the guy I've been sort of seeing these past few months. I can't stop replaying the fight we had the night before. In fact, I think I should end it. Better now, before we get too attached. Before someone gets hurt.

On the way to the bus stop, I ran into my friend Ivy.

"How's Sean?" she asked after we hugged.

I inhaled from my cigarette. "Sean's an asshole."

Ivy smiled with her mouth closed.

"I'm thinking of picking up another cute boy at work tonight," I said.

"Of course you are." She nodded at the sidewalk.

"What?"

She gave me a level look. "The only reason you want to hook up with someone else is to prove to yourself you're not attached to Sean."

I scoffed. "Yeah, okay. Whatever."

"And every time you say 'whatever,' what you're really saying is 'I love him.'"

"Anyway," I said, forcefully stubbing my cigarette butt with my boot, "I'm late for work."

SEAN AND I met at my regular Commercial Drive coffee shop in the spring. He was sitting at the only sidewalk table—a tall, exceptionally handsome man in a pair of worn-out jeans, his hair thick and his features rugged, bent over the *New York Times* crossword puzzle. We drank our Americanos, smoked our Belmonts, and chatted. He pronounced my name perfectly, which I found extraordinary. He worked on tugboats on the Salish Sea, he said, two weeks off, two weeks on. A perfect arrangement. Hadn't I just been asking the universe for a part-time boyfriend? When a gust of cool wind swept over the patio, I hugged my arms and said I was cold. "Why don't you pick up a stranger from the street and ask him to warm you up?" he said, and I shot back, "You're a stranger. You warm me up." He chuckled, then studied me for a moment. I couldn't see his eyes through the sunglasses. I wondered what color they were.

The following day, I ran into him at the café again, and that night we went to see a music show at the Marine Club, where we kissed in the smoking room. His eyes, I found, were blue. So blue they seemed to carry the sea in their spheres.

Over the next few weeks, we hung out casually, went out for

drinks or stayed in, sipping single-malt scotch and listening to music in his studio apartment. Sean had an impressive collection of old records and he played several instruments. He drove a 1966 baby-blue Valiant, wore fedoras, and used vintage suitcases for actual travel. His kitchen had several chef knives and a well-stocked spice cabinet with the labels all facing the right way. He was nothing like the guys I usually fell for: he took way too much space, had an opinion about everything, which he expressed loudly and often, and he flirted with everyone, charming waitresses and old ladies and service clerks. It infuriated me. I wasn't used to being with a man who drew that much attention. I also wasn't used to dating someone who didn't need me, who seemed to enjoy being by himself as much as I did.

Maybe we were too much alike. Like me, Sean had been single for a couple of years and was content. He was also a traveler, recently back from Central America, with his own arsenal of sordid affairs and drug-infused escapades. He loved the sea as much as I did, so much so that he made that passion into a career, which I found more romantic than I cared to admit: the idea of a man attuned to storms, at home with unpredictability and unknowing, a man who understood the meaning of clouds, who could decipher the tides and the winds.

And there was his passion for books. A few weeks after we started dating, I called him one afternoon and he yawned into the phone.

"Partying all night?" I asked.

"No," he said. "I was so into my book that I stayed up all night reading."

I liked him despite myself. Meanwhile, he never expressed any serious intentions. We weren't exclusive. It was going nowhere. It was time to call it quits.

. . .

COMMERCIAL DRIVE VIBRATES with pre-party energy. All around
the neighborhood, people prepare their performance pieces for
the Parade of Lost Souls, a Halloween tradition in East Van; mothers fill bowls with candies for trick-or-treat, place candles in the
hairy guts of carved pumpkins. The air tastes volatile, a mix of alcohol and exhaust fumes, like everything is about to burst.

Or maybe it's just me.

Halloween makes me uneasy. Where I come from, nobody
drapes sheets on trees to make them look like ghosts, digs pretend graves in backyards, or hangs skeletons from porches. In Israel, death is a serious matter.

The bus is late, and when it stops next to me, it releases a rude
flatulent noise. The driver ignores me when I say hi.

I sit by a smeared window, sticky with fingerprints, and stare
outside. I usually like bus rides, enjoy being in motion, delight in
the constant shuffling of cards as people board and get off. I've
had some of my best conversations on buses, sung "Stand by Me"
with the entire back section, and even shared a smoke with
strangers on a late-night ride that turned into a bit of a party.
Buses are modern-day traveling circuses. You never know what
you're going to get.

This time it's rowdy teenagers, wearied middle-aged men on
their commute home, and gruff elderly ladies. It's a bad mix. The
three teenagers—two girls and a boy—yell at a woman who gave
them a piece of her mind before stepping out. They swear at her,
waving arms through the open window. People glower in disap-
proval, mutter about today's youth. The ladies shuffle to the front,
complain to the bus driver. He stares blankly ahead. A mild headache settles over my eyebrows.

Exasperated, I blurt, "Why don't you just shut up?"

"Who said that?" One of the girls stands up and scans the bus.
"Me," I say.

She glares at me. I turn to look out the window at the rows of wooden houses, their roofs like jagged teeth, and the milky clouds that swim above them.

As they left the bus, one of the youths threw her super-sized McDonald's drink at the victim's face. The victim stood up and was struck in the face by one of the youths, knocking her to the floor. The victim stated that she was then hit repeatedly in the face and kicked in the upper body.

ON TUESDAY, A police officer follows up on the phone call made at the scene and comes to take my statement at Sean's apartment, where I've been staying for the past few days, recovering from the assault. "Constable Louie," he says, shaking my hand firmly. He's a short, stocky man whose self-assured bearing compensates for his boyish features and soft voice. We sit at Sean's kitchen table; I chain-smoke, fiddle with the lighter, and stare out the window. The sky is mucky and gray, an ashtray left on a rainy porch. Across the alley, a forgotten Halloween pumpkin bares its teeth on an apartment's windowsill. I tell the constable what led to the assault, up to the part where the girl threw her drink, and he scribbles it in his notebook. Then I pause.

"What happened next?"

"She smirked at me," I say.

He looks up from his notebook. "Smirked?"

"I mean, before she tossed the drink." It was a vicious sneer, like a pit bull about to attack, yet the thought of her hurting me never crossed my mind.

THE ART OF LEAVING · 199

"What happened then?"

"I stood up."

"And?"

"Um . . ." I shuffle in my seat, light another smoke.

"Take your time."

I inhale, concentrate, try to tap into myself on the floor of the bus. But I see nothing; a veil is hiding my view. How did I get there? What did I say to her when she tossed the drink in my face? What if I punched her? Maybe it never happened. Maybe I made it all up.

"I'm not sure. I think I said something."

"It's okay not to remember. You were in shock," Constable Louie says.

But I have such good memory. I always remember everything. How can I not remember?

The victim states that she can identify the assaulters.

OF COURSE I can describe them, I tell Constable Louie. They were the kind of teens you see all around East Van, rough around the edges, their jeans too low, too tight, or too baggy. They drag their feet, smoke, drink in the park, get into fights, and glare at pass-ersby. The one who tossed the drink had a tight ponytail that stretched her eyes into catty slits. The other one had red-streaked bangs that fell over her face, shrouding her drunken gaze. The boy was overweight and wore his clothes loose, gangster-style. His mouth hung open in a dumb expression, like a toddler with a stuffed-up nose.

"I should've just shut up," I tell Constable Louie.

"Don't even think that!" He gives me a sharp look. "It wasn't your fault."

. . .

I CALL THE witnesses after Constable Louie leaves, hoping they can help clear the fog. They both gave me their phone numbers before leaving the scene. Virginia begins to cry as soon as she hears my voice. I've been told by Jessica, the other witness, that Virginia was the only one who intervened, even with her grandson in a carrier on her back. She pressed hard on the girl's neck until she backed off, and then shoved her down the rear door and off the bus. The other teens followed. I've never experienced this kind of gratitude toward anyone. It's so huge I have no idea what to do with it; it doesn't fit anywhere and it's too heavy to carry around. "These kids are from my community," she says on the phone, sobbing. "It's so upsetting to me. And no one helped . . . It makes me think no one would have helped me." I thank her over and over again until my words are wrung out of meaning, become a shrunken, shriveled version of themselves.

I call Jessica. She is a petite twentysomething woman who kept screaming at the men on the bus to help. Afterward she stayed with me and held my hand. "I'm so sorry I couldn't do more," she said. "I'm so little, and I was scared."

"What did I do when she tossed the drink at my face?" I ask her. "I didn't, like, punch her, did I?"

"No, no . . . You got up and grabbed her shoulder."

"I grabbed her shoulder?"

"Yeah, and said, 'How dare you?' or something along these lines."

"Did I call her a bitch?"

Jessica giggles. "You might have."

Images of the assault start flashing in my head: choppy, like a comic strip.

"You were brave," Jessica says. "You fought back the entire time. Even on the floor, you kept kicking and punching. You grabbed their feet when they tried to kick you."

"I did?" I'm relieved. "Did I say anything at all?"

Jessica thinks. "Only once you screamed, 'Let go of my hair!'"

```
Hair color: black
Hairstyle: long
Complexion: medium
Ethnicity: Middle Eastern
```

HER DRINK SPLASHES in my face like a cold slap; cubes of ice sneak into my shirt, sticky streams of Coke snake down my chest. I raise my arms, dripping, and look down at myself. My clothes are soaked. My hair is wet. I flat-ironed it the night before for Halloween, my Morticia Addams look, and now it's starting to curl. It's ruined. The teens start pulling my hair from both sides and it hinders my view, a thick, swaying black curtain. Then it's hot, a sudden gush of engine air. I'm on the floor, blind. I don't hear Jessica's screams. I don't feel pain. I keep thinking any minute now, somebody is going to make it stop.

```
There were approximately 40 people on the bus.
```

FOUR YEARS LATER I'm at my desk, staring at a blinking cursor on my computer screen. I've decided to take another stab at writing about the assault. I've written dozens of variations of this story; none of them work. I scramble through my drawers for notes I wrote at the time and find Constable Louie's card, now creased and discolored. For a long time, I kept it in my wallet just in case, tucked between cards for doctors, masseuses, and florists. I turn it around, look at the incident number scribbled in pen, and an idea strikes me. What if I could read my police report?

I call Constable Louie and leave a message. I tell him I remember him with fondness. I can tell from his hesitant words on my voicemail that he doesn't remember me.

When my report is ready to pick up, I head to the police station at Main and Hastings. As I wait at the bus stop for the Number 20, a group of teenage girls walk by, laughing and shouting, bumping into each other, the air around them thick with cigarette smoke, perfume, and bubble gum. I look away, stare hard at the shop across the street. Four years and I'm still scared of teenagers. My friend Eufemia, to whom I admitted this, advised me to exercise love and compassion, smile when I feel fear. I force a smile. Think good thoughts, I tell myself. Love. Compassion. My smile is a twisted knot; my eyes are wide, unblinking. I must look like a freak. I almost expect one of them to snap at me, What are you looking at? And then she'd punch me.

The bus slides up next to me and the doors open with a soft whooshing sound. It's brand-spanking new, with blue cushioned seats. It looks nothing like the rusted old vehicle from four years ago.

On the bus ride home, I rip the envelope open and begin to read my report, excited to fill in the blanks so I can finally write them into my essay. "You're brave," Eufemia said to me the night before. "I admire you for doing this." I dismissed it with a laugh. It's been four years, after all! I flip through the pages, skim over the cryptic abbreviations, the clinical lingo. I find my description, filed under "Victim," my identity broken into a list of cold facts. As I read the accounts provided by the witnesses, my hands start shaking. The descriptions are worse than my recollections. I slouch into my seat, trying to hide my tears behind the report.

Suspect 2 struck the victim in the face with a closed fist, knocking her to the floor face down. Suspects 1 and 2 struck her with their fists and feet, while suspect 3 repeatedly kicked her upper body and head. The victim attempted to fight back but was restrained by suspect 1 stepping on her neck.

WHEN MY ASSAULTERS leave, the bus is so quiet I can hear the hum of traffic from Hastings Street; a distant cellphone rings, a woman lilts, "Hello?" From this angle on the floor, all I see is sky, and it's darker and bluer than I would expect, as if the bus has fallen into the ocean. My earlobes hurt; I touch them and find that my dangly silver earrings have been yanked out and are now tangled in my hair. My head throbs to the rhythm of my heart-beat. I look up and see everyone gawking at me. They look help-less and pathetic, with their eyes and mouths torn wide. I realize I'm the show; I'm the spectacle on the dirty floor. "You won't be-lieve what happened today on the Number 20," a woman will say to her husband over dinner while passing the mashed potatoes. "Some chick got roughed up on the bus," a man will say to his buddies at the bar, sipping his frosty pint.

They watch as I collect my things from under seats and stuff them into my purse. I look up and scream, "What the hell is wrong with all of you? How can you see a woman getting beaten up and not do anything?" They look away, shuffle urgently toward the doors.

I grab my purse. "I'm out of here."

"Don't go," Virginia pleads, her hand warm on mine. "Wait for the police."

I look at her. I can tell she's on my side. I throw myself onto a seat and start crying. I will the passengers to disappear, which they conveniently do.

One man says as he walks off, "Great, now we have to switch buses."

Jessica and Virginia stay with me, take turns rubbing my hand. The bus driver remains at his seat. He still hasn't spoken a word to me. I feel numb, like when I'm in bed with the flu and everything looks surreal and still and distant. And just when I think it can't get any weirder, I look up and see Sean. He pokes his head into the bus and asks the driver, "Are you leaving soon?" I stare at him for a moment, think I'm seeing things. Perhaps I have a concussion. This can't be real. This is like a B-grade Hollywood movie. Then I let out a gasp and run to him, forget I was ever mad at him, forget I wanted to break up. I have spent years training myself to unlearn the shit I was taught by fairy tales and romantic comedies. I didn't need to be saved by anybody, especially not a man. I could take care of myself. But now Sean's here and I feel safe and grateful. My cry escalates as I dash through the aisle and down the stairs. He opens his arms to catch me, like a safety net at the bottom of a skyscraper.

"How did you know she was here?" Jessica's eyes widen as I bury my face in his chest.

"Magic," Sean says.

THE POLICE NEVER come. The bus driver says he called but it's been a while and nobody is coming. It's a bit anticlimactic, no sirens whining down the street, no police cars parked on the curb, their lights blinking orange on the pavement. Jessica, Virginia, Sean, and I wait on the bench next to the stalled bus. Lights burn yellow holes in the dark buildings. My clothes are beginning to dry but I'm still shivering.

"Let's just go," I tell Sean.

"We should call an ambulance," Jessica says. "You can't just go."

"An ambulance?" I snort. "That's crazy. I'm fine."

Resulting in: minor injuries

SEAN FLAGS A taxi and takes me to the free clinic. The doctor I see helps me pull clumps of loosened hair from my head, checks for fractures and bleeding, grimaces at the bruises on my torso and arms, and examines my two black eyes, my Halloween Zorro mask.

"There were three of them, you say?" He shines a blinding beam into my eye.

"Well, I was in the Israeli army, y'know." I slip back into my tough-chick act. I've been playing this role for so long that it takes no effort. It stuck, the way my mother warned me my eyes would if I kept crossing them. Even as I sit in the examining room, a part of me can't believe I didn't win this fight.

"I wouldn't want to be the other guys." The doctor winks at me. And for a moment, my confidence is restored.

Resulting in: emotional trauma

TRAUMA SNEAKS UP on you the way water slides under a basement suite door before it floods. A couple of hours after the assault, I do a little belly dancing move for Sean and we drink whiskey at his house like every other night and laugh about the stupid fight we had the night before. "I'm sorry," he says. "I freaked out." "*I* freaked out!" I say. I enjoy hanging out with him on a Saturday night; I usually work on weekends. I feel like I'm playing hooky.

I ask him to take me to my favorite restaurant for food and martinis; I might as well get the most out of my night off. But it's the night of the Parade of Lost Souls and we sit by a window and watch skeletons and ghosts and witches, and there are people in the restaurant, chatter and music, and a waiter who keeps asking if everything is okay when nothing is. I'm glad I have my glasses on to blur the edges of my black eyes. I look down whenever someone meets my gaze.

I still think I'll be okay tomorrow.

The next morning, I wake up bawling like someone has just died. I don't want to wake Sean, so I slide out of his embrace and go cry in the shower. When he gets up, I suggest we go out for coffee. I figure I should be fine—the coffee shop is only two blocks away—but while waiting in line, I start to feel light-headed. My face is washed with sweat and everyone is staring, probably wondering why I'm wearing sunglasses indoors on a rainy day. "There's no air in here," I tell Sean, leaning into him. My heart is beating so fast it hurts. I think I'm going to faint. "Take me home," I say.

AFTER ONE WEEK at Sean's, I go back to my own place. "I'm afraid that if I stay too long, *you'll* beat me up," I tell Sean. We both laugh. We've only been dating for a few months and he probably needs his space. It's not like he's my boyfriend. Also, I'm not used to having someone else take care of me.

Sean walks me home. "You're sure you'll be okay?" he asks at the door. "I can stay."

"No, I'm fine." I turn to open the door and pause. "Oh, and thanks," I say and look him briefly in the eyes, "for everything."

I LIVE IN a tight community and word gets out fast. As I begin going out for groceries and errands, people coo at me on the street, tilt their faces, and ask in their most compassionate voices, "How are you?" I take to walking the alleys, staring at the sidewalks, screening my calls. Constable Louie calls a couple of times to check up on me. I never knew cops did that. It's November and it's raining nonstop, dripping from the drainpipes, tapping on the windows, dribbling like a runny nose. Everything is so gray I forget we have mountains. I watch TV for hours on end and it lights my apartment in cold, unfriendly blue, like the innards of a fridge. I cry while watching *Friends*. I'm not going back to work because I'm still hurting, and because I'm afraid I might throw food in people's faces. When they ask for more water, I'll empty it over their heads. This anger is bad for business.

When I do answer my phone, I put on a light tone. I've been making jokes from day one.

"Well, in my country, when you get on a bus, it could explode," I tell people. "Maybe getting beaten up isn't so bad."

It's funny because it's true. I realize this is what I've grown used to in Israel, that air of menace, the ever-present threat, the taste of my heart in my mouth. It's like I'm always waiting for something to happen, ready for a fight, wanting to wage war with the day, the world, or a person; as though a part of me longs for the risk, that shard of glass in the sand that catches your eye, a promise, an assurance that I am alive.

I repeat the joke while talking to a Lebanese friend. Our neighboring countries have been at war for generations, but we've been living outside long enough to know we're essentially the same people. When I talk about *my* home, he just hears "home." "Well, maybe so," he replies. "But at least back home, people would have helped you."

I sink into silence. He's right. Maybe it's the belief that our enemies are out to get us that makes us feel united, like a family, that makes strangers risk their safety to break up a fight, offer you money when you're short for the bus, share their food with you on a train ride simply because you're sitting next to them. I once broke up a brawl myself, in the beach restaurant where I was working, pulled one man off the other and stood between them with my tray as a shield. Walking back to my section, I was pleased with myself for saving the day. In fact, I think that's what compelled me to speak up when I did. Those teens terrorized the bus and I wanted to be the one to put an end to it.

Later that evening, I share this insight with Sean. We sit on the couch, take-out containers perched in our laps. "How arrogant is that?" I wave my fork. "I need to learn to shut up."

Sean shakes his head. "It sounds to me like you called an asshole an asshole," he says. "Don't ever stop doing that. That's why we all love you."

I note the royal "we." The use of the word "love." I stare down at my curry.

TRAUMA IS A bit like falling in love: as sneaky, astounding, and unstoppable. And I should know, because in my case, these two are sliding in parallel streams under my door. Sometimes I wonder what would have happened between us if Sean hadn't shown up on the bus, if he weren't there to catch me. I'm trying to hold on to my act, stay cool, but it's like Sean can see past my armor.

Sometimes I get so shy around him I can hardly look him in the eye. Everything in my body is telling me to make a run for it. This love business is trouble. It's like a huge revolving siren is flashing red above his head.

Under the Crime Victim Assistance Act, the victim is awarded 24 one-hour counseling sessions to assist her recovery from the psychological injury resulting from the offense.

AFTER A MONTH I convince myself that all it takes is a conscious decision to stop feeling sorry for myself and join the world. I don't even bother using the government-funded counseling I've been awarded, just pluck my eyebrows, put on some dangly earrings, and go out for drinks.

I manage to fool myself for about a week, until my favorite clothing store asks me to model in their upcoming show. I've never done anything like that before, so I'm flattered and excited. When the show is over, I'm high on adrenaline and hairspray, drinking with new friends: models, makeup artists, and designers. I drink a little too much.

Somebody talks about buses. Everybody has a story about a bus.

"I was assaulted on a bus," I say.

"What?" Everybody turns to look at me. "When?"

"Six weeks ago," I calculate. "Damn, it doesn't seem that long."

I plaster a thin smile on my lips; it's the same smile I have when I talk about my dead father, a smile that is meant to make people feel more at ease. It says: Don't be afraid of me. I'm just like you. Bad things happen to everyone. Let's have another drink!

"What happened?" asks Pat, one of the models and my new best friend. Her face is crumpled with concern. I didn't plan on talking about it, but now everyone is staring. I sip my beer. "Oh, I just opened my big mouth and some teenagers beat me up."

Pat puts a hand on her mouth. "You poor thing! That's awful! I'm so sorry that happened to you. Are you okay?"

"Well, yes," I say. I try to laugh but it comes out as a wheeze. "I mean, it's been six weeks." And then it happens. A dam collapses and I fold over crying, sobbing in my smart flapper dress and fake pearls, my high heels, my big hair, my makeup. I realize I don't know any of these people but I can't stop. I'm crying so hard that Pat hands me one napkin after another. Streams of mascara and glitter slide down my cheeks. Six weeks. What the hell is wrong with me? Shouldn't I be over it by now? I grab my stuff and run.

On January 29 2005 Constable Louie attended
the victim's residence. He presented the VPD
photographic lineup to the victim. The victim
chose suspect 1 in 49 seconds.

I SIT ACROSS from Constable Louie in Sean's softly lit kitchen. We ran out of small talk by the time we made it to the hall. Christmas was fine. The weather is cold. I stare at him as he opens his briefcase, my foot tapping on the leg of the table. He places a glossy sheet lined with photos in front of me and sets his timer. It's like a page ripped out of a yearbook, except none of the girls are smiling. Some of these photos are actual mug shots. I can feel Constable Louie watching me, and I'm aware that the seconds on his timer are adding up, quantifying my indecision. I chew on the inside of my lip, close my eyes and open them for a fresh look. I will look and suddenly see her. I will point and declare: That's her! I've been telling everyone I could recognize them anywhere, but it's been three months. I'm trying so hard that my shoulders are clenched into a knot.

"Maybe this one," I say, pointing at a girl who looks vaguely familiar, and immediately feel like I've failed. It's the wrong answer.

"This one?" He points at number one.

I nod with tight lips. I search for some recognition on his face. I want him to give me the right answer. But I'm the only one who knows.

"How sure are you?"

I stare at the sheet without blinking.

"In percentage," he says softly. "Don't rush."

"Sixty-five percent?" Hesitation tints my reply, curves it into a question. Then I think: What if it's not her after all? What if I'm responsible for getting an innocent girl into trouble? I hastily add, "Maybe sixty," and crush any credibility I had left, together with my hope for closure.

Constable Louie leaves the sheet in front of me a little longer, just in case I change my mind again.

"I'm sorry," I say. "I thought it would be easier."

"That's okay," he says, straight-faced, and collects his papers. My eyes follow the sheet until it's tucked in his briefcase. I want to stop him, ask for one more look. But I say nothing, slump in my chair and watch him zip his bag. He stands up to leave and suddenly I know: it's all over. This was my chance, and now it's gone. They'll never find them. They'll forget all about this and move on to bigger cases. I'll never see Constable Louie again. And as I walk him to the door, I feel a familiar sense of loss, a dull ache in my chest. He smiles when he says goodbye, says he'll call. It's like the end of a bad date. I close the door and lean against it, fight the itch in my nose that precedes tears.

Sean appears from the living room, a mix of question and concern in his eyes. I wave my hand in front of my face, as if to dry the tears before they come. "I'm okay," I say, not looking at him. "It's fine, really. I'm fine." But then I let him hold me anyway, allowing my body to soften into his. Maybe I don't need to win this fight. We stand there for a long time without saying a word.

HORNETS

'VE NEVER SEEN HORNETS BEFORE, so when I call Sean at his job on the tugboat, I say, "There are weird wasps in our bedroom, with long legs. They're freaky-looking."

"Those aren't wasps," Sean says. "They're hornets."

"Whatever. Hornets," I say.

By the next time we speak, I've forgotten what they're called. "These wasps are scary," I say. "I have to dodge them when I walk into our bedroom. Sometimes I run upstairs to grab something and flee."

Our East Vancouver bedroom is a large wooden loft shaped like the bow of a boat and perched on the exposed beams that once supported the living room's ceiling. It's a bitch to clean—when we moved in two years ago, I spent hours vacuuming up cobwebs and hammering in exposed nails—and when it rains heavily, it sometimes leaks, but it has a rustic and romantic feel, and two skylights with a view of the mountains, the sea, and the city.

OVER THE NEXT week, I wake up to loud buzzing every day. The August heat wave makes sleeping impossible unless I leave the skylights open overnight. I cover my head with the sheet, create a hole from the folds, and peer out. Two hornets—a couple, perhaps—hover around the peak of our ceiling. I wait until they fly off through the skylight, and then make a run for the bathroom.

WHEN SEAN COMES home for an unexpected afternoon's leave, we lie in bed and I spot a hornet sneaking in through the skylight. "There!" I point. "See? Wasps!"

Sean laughs. "I've told you a million times they're called hornets, and you keep calling them wasps."

"Hornets," I say, almost spitting it out. For some reason, I don't like the word. The *r* and *t* and *s* roll funny in my mouth, bumping against my tongue and teeth like grit that snuck into my greens. Some words in the English language just rub me the wrong way.

"Look." I point at the peak of our ceiling, where the boards angle up into a dark corner. "Do you think they're building a nest?" And I suddenly know: they are building a nest. Of course. Why didn't I think of it sooner? We're both quiet for a moment. We can hear the hornets buzzing madly.

"They're probably doing it in there," Sean says.

"What are we going to do?" I panic. We go downstairs and google hornets. The site we find recommends going in with a bottle of Raid, wearing hornet protective clothing and running shoes. We both find the thought unappealing. Besides, Sean is leaving in two hours, going back on the boat for another week, so that leaves me to deal with it.

"I wish I didn't have to go," he says as he stands by the door.

I scowl, but then quickly rearrange my face into a smile, say, "I'll be fine," and kiss him goodbye. No point in making him feel shitty about his work. I stand barefoot on the front steps and wave until the taxi turns a corner and I can't see him anymore.

. . .

THIS IS OFTEN how it goes. This is what it means to be a sailor's girlfriend. A day after we moved into this place—our first place together—he went back to work for two weeks, leaving me to unpack an entire house. He was gone when I had to scrape the decomposed corpse of a mouse off the dining-room floor, when our toilet flooded, when our cat didn't come home all night and I had to walk the streets calling his name and tapping a spoon against a can of Fancy Feast. He wasn't there the next morning, when I found out that our cat had been run over in a nearby alley, and when I sat crying at my desk.

"It's not so bad," I say when people ask. I tell them that I had asked the universe for a part-time boyfriend. I tell them that Sean's work schedule is a healthy arrangement, that the distance keeps the relationship fresh. I say, "I like my space," and, "It sure makes for exciting reunions!" Most times I mean it too. Other times, I talk out loud, just to hear my voice, and a faint echo bounces up against the rafters before wafting out of the skylight like smoke. Then the house falls quiet again, the fridge hums, the floorboards creak under my heavy feet.

My mother calls after Sean leaves. It's late in Israel. I can hear the night in her voice—the tugging of sleep. "Is he home?" she asks.

"He just left."

My mother sighs. "How will you ever get pregnant with that schedule?"

"Ima."

"You're thirty-five."

"I know."

"You do want kids, right?" It's the first time she asks me flat out. Now that my older sister has finally given birth, the pressure is on.

"I have to go," I say.

*   *   *

IN THE WEEKS leading up to my thirty-fifth birthday, I began having death dreams. The scenarios were varied and vivid, but in all of them I died. The loss felt so real that I'd wake up in tears. For days, I roamed the streets of my neighborhood burdened with grief, blind to the West Coast spring and its dazzling display of cherry blossoms. Never before had my fear of death presented itself in a manner that was so on point, so elementary. I turned inward, trying to unlock the meaning of the dreams. Maybe it was because I was getting close to my father's age when he passed away, or maybe I was just like everyone else, afraid of getting old.

Or maybe the dreams were a premonition. Maybe I was going to die.

"It's not such a bad thing, being aware of our mortality," my friend Gurjinder said. "It makes us live with more urgency."

Yes, I wanted to tell her with a dismissive hand gesture. I know. I invented that. Except it didn't feel like a good thing.

At the time, it didn't occur to me that the dreams might have nothing to do with death and everything to do with babies. Despite the pressing matter of my age, I still wasn't sure how I felt about procreating. My early thirties had seemed like an extension of my twenties: I was still a waitress, still broke, still working nights and sleeping in, still partying and smoking too much. There was no yearning in my guts, no visceral hankering. I hadn't cooed at babies on the street and at times was impatient and unkind to parents for taking over the sidewalk with their massive strollers, for asking for special treatment at the bank lineup. I didn't know what to do with babies—how to hold them, change them—and I was a terrible, absent aunt to my nephews and nieces, all born after I left for Canada. I barely managed to take care of cats and was an infamous plant killer (including, astoundingly, cacti). Obviously, I lacked a maternal instinct; it was an admission I shared with Sean early on in our relationship. We were in my kitchen, standing on two sides of a wooden counter. He stared at me for a while without speaking.

"What?" I said. "Not everyone has to have children."

"No," he said. "But I think it would be a shame if you didn't. You'd make a great mom."

I changed the subject, looking away, cheeks flushed.

I had spent years teaching myself to be self-sufficient, not committing to anything—homes, jobs, men, furniture—trapped inside my incessant pursuit of freedom, taking risks in anything but love. "A great relationship is only a little bit better than being alone," I had announced to anyone who'd listen. In our first few months together, I kept telling everyone Sean and I were casual; we were just having fun. Except sometimes it wasn't fun at all. Sometimes, I was waiting by the phone while feigning disinterest, walking by his favorite cafés and bars as if by chance (we lived in the same neighborhood, after all). Pretending not to care was exhausting; I was holding on to my façade so tight that my muscles ached. Sean, on his part, had not pursued me assertively, had given me all the space in the world, which is what I claimed I wanted, yes, but it also meant that the risk of heartbreak was greater, that he might not like me as much as I liked him.

After I was assaulted on that Vancouver bus, something changed between us; we softened toward each other, guards lowered, and began reevaluating the terms of our relationship. By then, we had been seeing each other for six months, a mark at which most casual relationships are bound to evolve or end, or so my friend Carlin had professed. A few weeks after the assault, he invited me to join him in Victoria, his hometown, for Christmas. I stammered when he asked, said I'd think about it, both pleased by the invitation and terrified by the gravity of it. "What is there to think about?" my sister—my go-to person for reality checks— asked on the phone from Israel. "I thought you liked this guy."

My friend Marie, less diplomatic, sighed loudly and blurted in her charming Québécois accent, "Come on, admit it. You're in love with him. And I hate to tell you, but everyone knows."

I snorted a laugh. "That's crazy. Why would I be in love with him?"

"No reason. Why is anybody in love with anybody?"

I called Carlin immediately. "Why didn't you tell me?"

"I thought you knew," she said.

The realization that I had been lying to myself for weeks began to sink in rapidly. After the initial stab of panic, lightness enveloped me, the relief of surrender.

In his parents' home in Victoria, surrounded by his family, plucked away from our familiar setting of Commercial Drive with its trendy cafés and flirty waitresses, I saw a new side to Sean. I saw a man who helped his mother in the kitchen when she got overwhelmed with dinner, who loved spending time with his elderly grandmother, who chased his nieces around the house, made them laugh, and carried them on his shoulders. A man who would make a great father one day.

IT TOOK US a while, but eventually, we both conceded. This was love—the glorious, loopy-making, full-of-clichés kind. When we were together, I felt beautiful and reckless and radiant and ready to take on the world. We couldn't keep our hands off each other, eliciting sighs and eye rolls from friends at parties and disgruntled strangers on the street. We barhopped on downtown streets glittering with rain and neon, crashed parties, and jumped into private pools at night. We got in our car and drove until we were suddenly at the Rockies or Seattle or California. Once, we upped and bought tickets to Mexico for the following day.

Sean introduced me to the rewards of stability, to perks I had previously perceived as luxury, and to the revolutionary notion that money could be used for something other than your basic needs while you save most of it for traveling. Before him I had never been to a spa, had never dolled up and gone to a posh restaurant, had never owned stilettos or a fancy cocktail dress. I was the kind of person who trimmed her own hair. My idea of splurging was a shopping spree at Value Village or buying the next round at the bar. My idea of a savings account was an envelope in my underwear drawer, where I stuffed my tips every night until they added up to my next plane ticket.

A few weeks into dating, Sean asked, "Didn't you say you were a writer?" and when I nodded, apprehensive, he said, "Oh, are you one of these writers who never writes?" For our one-year anniversary, he requested a story. Riddled with clichés and grammatical errors, it was the first story I wrote in English. After that, more followed, and Sean proofread and commented on all of them. When I took the leap and enrolled in a part-time writing program in Vancouver, he carefully suggested that I reduce my hectic schedule from six waitressing shifts a week to four. "I know you don't like to ask for help," he said. "But we'll be okay." At the end of that year, I won a literary contest and had my first essay published in a literary magazine. I couldn't have done it without him.

Our relationship opened me up to the liberties that lie within commitment, within the security of a nurturing, happy relationship, and released me from my encumbering need to be free at all costs. It was a discovery that echoed my journey into writing in English, my astounding realization that creative freedom could be unearthed within the constraints of a second language, a vastness within the limitations that gave space for invention and fantasy.

I wasn't ready to consider that one day I might find the same unexpected freedom within the confines of motherhood. Motherhood itself seemed inconceivable. I knew children changed everything. I had seen it happen. On my last visit to Israel, I spent a few months with my sister after she had given birth. My sister had been my best friend ever since I was old enough to bridge our seven-year gap; I looked up to her, admired her resilience in the face of her losses. She somehow managed to hold on to a childlike sense of wonder and enthusiasm most adults lose much earlier: she goofed around like a kid, frequently invented new words (I once dubbed her the reviver of the Hebrew language), and came up with funny observations about everything she saw. Upon meeting her, most of my friends became her friends too. But as a mother, she was anxious, overprotective. I watched her with my mother, witnessing a new bond forming between them that didn't include me. Maternity created a barrier between us, and the only way for me to break through it was to join her on the other side. But I needed more time. Four years into dating—partly due to his frequent absences—Sean and I were still in the honeymoon phase. I was terrified of losing what we had, terrified of losing everything: the writing career I had finally devoted myself to, my freedom, my nomadic lifestyle. Myself.

❦ ❦ ❦

AFTER SEAN GOES back to work, I sit at my desk to write. Looking out the window, I spot our neighbor and house manager, Little

Bernard, climbing up the stairs to his house. Bernard is not actually little. He's a Portuguese man with a thick gray beard and square glasses. He lives next door with his wife, Maria, who always wears an apron around her waist. We call him Little Bernard to distinguish him from Big Bernard, who is our landlord, and a burly guy. This name has stuck so well that when I call his house and Maria answers, I say, "May I speak to Little Bernard?" and instantly want to bury myself. Maria doesn't seem to notice, or maybe she's heard it before. She puts him on the phone.

Bernard and Maria's back deck faces ours, and I can see right down into their yard from my office window. I see Bernard gardening, hammering nails, and sawing wood, Maria hanging laundry, picking fruit off the plum tree, and playing with their grandchildren. Every Sunday, their kids climb up the stairs with their families for a weekly brunch. Watching them makes me think of home, of warm Mediterranean nights, of Friday dinners at my mother's, the house full of chatter, running feet, and the smells of cooking. Once I saw Bernard giving Maria a red rose from their garden. She wiped her hands on her apron before she took the rose and smelled it.

There's nothing Bernard cannot do. An electrician by trade, he has fixed our leaky pipes, our toilet, and our furnace. Bernard comes upstairs armed with a large knife and a flashlight. I haven't seen a single hornet all day, so I'm afraid he's going to think I'm crazy. He shines a beam into the nook and summons me over. I reluctantly agree to look, tilt my head and see what looks like a large gray cotton ball, a clump of moss stuck to the side of the rafter. I don't want to stay for the carnage, so I go to my office and close the door.

A few minutes later Bernard comes downstairs carrying my bedroom rug and gingerly unfolds it to show me three little mummies, baby hornets covered in white silk. A family. I cover my mouth.

"You're lucky it was only one couple," Bernard says. "Hornets aren't as bad as wasps. They don't multiply as fast."

"Oh my God." I look away. "You're a lifesaver. Thank you so much."

Back at my office I stare at the flickering cursor on my screen. Gazing outside past Bernard and Maria's backyard, past the Burnaby hills, blue and misty in the distance, I am filled with deep, inexplicable sadness. I lean my face into my hands, fingers pressing onto my eyelids. When I remove my hands, everything is blurry.

THE NEXT MORNING, I wake up to a frantic buzz in my ceiling. The mother is back. I imagine her flying into the nook, her confusion as she finds the empty nest. I bury my head under the sheet and press the fabric over my ears. "This sucks," I whisper to the pillow.

I contemplate sneaking downstairs to pee. Two days ago, as I hurried to get away from the hornets, I slipped on the pull-down staircase and toppled down a half-flight of stairs, landing with a loud thud. The wooden steps were polished and there were no handrails. This house is not a place for a baby, our landlord cautioned us when we moved in. That's why he and his wife moved out after their child was born. I snickered at his warning, which seemed irrelevant to our life at the time. It's a great house for parties, though, with a deck for smokers that offers a spectacular view to the mountains, a living room large enough to be transformed into a dance floor, and even a nook made for a DJ stand. Our house parties have become a legend.

· · ·

MY RECURRING DEATH dreams went on for a while before I figured them out. One day, a few weeks after my birthday, I just knew: the dreams were my body's way of telling me to procreate. The death, that sense of loss, signified the end of my life as I knew it, the passing of a self I had grown fond of. My body was succumbing to a primordial, physiological need, having a conversation with time and biology I wasn't privy to. For a few days I grieved, cried over the ordinariness of my uterus, resented my body for wanting a family when all I wanted was to party. But the dreams stopped. And the crying, eventually, stopped too. Maybe I didn't really want to party all that much—not anymore.

I GRAB MY phone from the bedside table and call Sean from the warm insides of my cocoon. "The mother is back," I say. "She's going to come after me and avenge her dead babies."

Sean laughs, inhales cigarette smoke.

"They were just a young couple," I say, feigning melodrama. "All they wanted was to build a home and raise their family in domestic bliss, and I ruined it."

Sean laughs again. The boat's radio chatters in the background. I trace the seam of the sheet with my finger.

"I wonder if the father will be coming next," I say.

"You know there's no actual father, right?" Sean says. "It's a matriarchal society. The male just comes and goes. He doesn't take part in building the nest or anything. I think he dies after mating."

"Great," I say. "That's really great."

It's getting too hot. I peel the sheet off my head and look around. The buzzing has stopped. The house is quiet and empty again. I can hear the bell ringing from the nearby school, the muffled squeals of children running out to play. I fling the sheet off my sweaty body, kick it until it falls in a heap on the floor.

"You okay?" Sean asks.

"I miss you," I say.

"I miss you too," he says. "Only six days to go."

"Yes," I say. "Only six more days to go."

YEMENI SOUP AND
OTHER RECIPES

UGAT SHMARIM

MY MOTHER PREPARES A CAKE that makes people forget. They forget their troubles, their diets, and their calorie count. They forget they only came by for a minute—they had other plans, places to go—and then they forget they promised themselves they would have only one slice.

Ugat shmarim—literally translated as "yeast cake"—looks like a braided Danish or a Jewish-style babka, European delicacies that made their way into Israeli cuisine and into my mother's Jewish Yemeni kitchen. Every Friday, before Shabbat, my mother mixes flour, eggs, sugar, lemon rind, and yeast. She throws in a package of margarine: that way the cake is parve, not dairy, and can be consumed after a meaty dinner. While the dough rises, she beats cocoa and sugar with margarine, vanilla, and egg white for the chocolate filling. She flattens the dough on a flour-dusted table, applies a generous helping of chocolate, and braids it into a strudel. For thirty minutes the house smells so sweet you want to devour the air. When the cake is done right, the inside is moist and dense, the top is crisp, glossy with brushed yolk, and every slice presents a chocolate swirl that makes you dizzy with desire.

Relatives and friends who ask for the recipe often come back scowling. "It didn't turn out like yours," they say. "What's the secret?" Secret, as in key ingredient. As in: What have you left out?

"Secret!" My mother scoffs. "You think I'd hide something from you?"

Whenever I fly back to Canada, I smuggle the contraband cake past customs agents, wrapped in foil and tucked between my socks. I eat some right away and freeze the rest for when I'm craving a taste of home. When I reheat it, the smell permeates my house, drapes over me like a comfort blanket. It pulls me back and away. It's a cake that makes me remember.

My Canadian friends who share it with me ask, "Do you know the recipe?"

"Oh no. I could *never* make it," I say. "It's way too complicated. I wouldn't know where to begin."

When I was nine, I found a cookbook in our house. *Children Cooking* had a bright yellow cover and pictures of children in chef hats, making smiley faces on toast with julienned red peppers for a mouth and sliced cucumbers for eyes. Their aprons were spotless and their kitchen immaculate. The recipes had names like Smiling Eggs, Moses in the Cradle, and Boat Sandwiches. During my mother's siesta, I decided to try my hand at a recipe, imagining how pleased she would be that I had made something for her for once. I chose chocolate balls dusted with coconut flakes: an Israeli staple dessert popular at children's birthday parties. My mother had never made it; for our birthdays, she baked intricate cakes with frosting, layered with filo, and topped with shaved chocolate. I found all the ingredients in her pantry, except for coconut flakes, and decided it would do.

I climbed on the counter to fetch a bowl, then hopped off, letting the cupboard door slam. "Sheket!" my mother yelled from her bedroom. I flinched. Every day between two and four, we tiptoed around the house, speaking in hushed voices. Sometimes I imagined her lying there, stiff and alert with her eyes closed; that would explain why she never seemed rested.

I crushed biscuits, mixed them with cocoa, sugar, milk, vanilla, and margarine. I dipped my finger in the bowl, amazed to discover I'd created something yummier than the sum of its parts, the way I had felt the first time I wrote words that joined into a sentence. I rolled the paste between my palms, forming muddy-looking balls.

I'd just finished the last ball and was admiring my creation when my mother walked in. She stood at the door in her gown, squinting. She ignored the plate heaped with chocolate balls on the table and headed straight to the counter. "What's this?" She grimaced at the splashes of milk. "And this?" She pointed at the dishes in the sink.

"I was going to clean it," I said.

She started wiping the counter in rapid, urgent motions.

"I wanted to surprise you."

She looked at me and sighed. My shirt was smeared with chocolate. I wasn't wearing an apron.

That day the line was drawn. I abandoned my cooking aspirations. For the next few years, my contribution in the kitchen was restricted to dish washing. Sometimes, my mother asked me to cut the tips off the okras, a tedious task I hated, since it coated my fingers with sticky little hairs and sent me into an itching frenzy.

. . .

I CALL MY mother from Toronto. It's Friday, dinnertime in Israel. She shouts orders as she speaks to me: "Turn off the oven. We're missing a glass. Why with your hands? Use a fork!"

"You're busy," I say.

"No, not busy. What is it?"

"I was just wondering . . . how come I never learned to cook growing up?"

"How come?" She raises her voice. "You weren't interested in cooking!"

I hear my sister in the background: "That's because you didn't want us in your kitchen."

"Not true!" My mother is practically yelling. "You never asked."

My family calls her to sit down, join them, stop hovering between the stove and the table. "The salad isn't dressed yet," she cries. "Stop picking!"

"Go." I swallow. "We'll talk later."

CHOPPED SALAD

MY MOTHER SERVES SALAD with lunch, dinner, and on Saturday mornings, with our traditional breakfast of jichnoon, a Yemeni Shabbat bread served with brown eggs. Tomatoes, cucumbers, and a few slivers of white onion, generously dressed with fresh lemon, olive oil, and rock salt. Like most of her recipes, it only sounds simple.

Every Thursday my mother drives to the shuk at the edge of our city, a labyrinth of intersecting alleys lined with produce stands. She marches up and down the market, fondling peaches, stroking avocados, and tasting grapes, carefully selecting the freshest cilantro, firmest tomatoes, and sweetest apples. Watermelons are the only gamble. Despite the shopkeepers' promises, you can't tell a sweet, juicy watermelon by the sound it makes when you knock on it.

She takes note of the best produce and its corresponding vendor, mapping it in her mind as if formulating a strategic battle plan, then returns to the winning vendors and buys kilos of everything, making a couple of runs to fill the trunk with baskets.

As a kid, I trailed behind—grimacing at the stench of rotten vegetables, the slippery bits of lettuce and smashed fruit, the slimy tread of my sneakers—while my mom haggled with the vendors. "Your parsley looks tired today." She crinkled her nose at one vendor. "Why so expensive?" she complained to another.

"Especially for you: five shekels." The vendor winked. "Because you're so beautiful."

She waved a bill, frowning. "Should you be talking to women like that? You're wearing a kippah."

MAKING THE SALAD was the one food preparation activity we were encouraged to engage in. We struggled to dice the vegetables as small as possible, competing for our mother's final approval. A coarsely chopped salad was referred to with contempt as an "elephant's salad"; a finely chopped salad earned the much sought-after label of "mice salad"; but none of us could do it as well as our mother, who was so skilled with the knife that she sliced the vegetables without using a cutting board. She cupped a tomato in her hand, and in a series of swift motions, slashed it up and down and side to side like an apron-wearing Jedi master. She then opened her palm as if releasing a dove to let the tiny pieces drop into the bowl. "I've never seen anybody do that," I told her when I grew to appreciate her rare talent. She smiled modestly. "I saw a French chef on TV do it once."

SCHNITZELS

EVERY DAY, when my father came home from his law office for siesta, we ate lunch as a family. I was delighted whenever my mom made schnitzels: this Austrian dish, brought to Israel by European Jews, was a national favorite, adopted into the mishmash national cuisine alongside shish kebab, couscous, and pizza. My mother modified the original recipe to make it her own. She never hammered the chicken breast, cutting it instead into long, fat strips. She added garlic to the beaten eggs, then dipped a chicken strip in, dredged it in breadcrumbs, and dropped it into hot oil until it was golden and crispy on the outside, moist and tender on the inside.

The one time my mother visited me in Vancouver, she walked through our kitchen, arms crossed, nodding like an art collector at a gallery. She ran her hand along our stove and our IKEA island, eyed the steel pans hanging on the wall.

"Do you have chicken breasts?" She gazed into my freezer. "Potatoes?"

Sean and I had planned elaborate meals to impress her, but she wouldn't have any of that. She was happiest when she could cook for us. I watched her sashay between the stove, the sink, the fridge, training her body for a new dance routine, marking her space. She was at home when she cooked. It didn't matter that she was half a world away from her comfort zone. Kitchens were pockets of solace in every house, a neutral territory, a gastronomic Switzerland.

· · ·

AFTER MY FATHER passed away, my young mother spent most of her days in the kitchen. She didn't speak much, rarely looked at us, but she cooked endlessly, with furious, careless motions. When she dug in the drawers for a pan, she'd bang the pots against each other in a high-pitched cacophony. She chopped vegetables with homicidal intent, and when she tossed schnitzels into the sizzling oil, it sounded like a scream. She disappeared into the kitchen, became one with the appliances. Food replaced her words; cooking became her currency.

When she wasn't cooking, she cleaned. I woke to the sounds of furniture dragged across the floor, rugs beaten, appliances wheeled. Cleaning was my mother's form of meditation; it was also the one thing she could control. Her world may have fallen apart, but at least she had clean surfaces, laundered clothes, food on the table.

Even when we couldn't afford brand-name jeans or pocket money, our fridge was always full. My mother found ways to prepare meals on a tight budget—simple recipes that called for basic ingredients. She calculated her garlic usage for a whole year and bought dozens of bulbs when they were cheap. She ground them all, filled jars with the pulp, and froze them: two rows lining the shelves of the freezer door like teeth. For a whole week, the smell of garlic floated through our house; it stuck to our clothes and hid in the toothpaste, clinging to our hair like campfire smoke.

My mother fed me, did my laundry, cleaned my room, but it wasn't enough. I followed her around as she worked, trying to engage her in conversation. When that failed, I found more effective ways to get her attention.

We fought about everything: my performance at school, my fashion sense, my messy room, my friends. I screamed that I hated her, stomped my feet, and slammed doors. She told me that I was ungrateful, that one day I'd have a daughter just like me. At the end of tenth grade, after my dedicated work at the teen magazine led to five failing grades, for which I was nearly expelled, my mother demanded that I focus on my studies and threatened to put restrictions on my job, which made me feel deeply wronged and misunderstood, a truly tortured artist. How dare she go after my writing? Our relationship became so strained that once she passed me by on the street and didn't even acknowledge me.

"The problem," my brother once said, "is that you're too much alike."

I snorted. "We're nothing alike."

I became a fickle eater. I hated cilantro, despised tomatoes, detested eggplants. I subsisted on hot dogs at the stand outside my high school, and burgers and fries at MacDavid, the kosher fast-food chain that predated McDonald's in Israel. Then I discovered restaurants, where I began conducting many of my interviews, charging the magazine with the expenses.

My family never went to restaurants. My mother thought paying for prepared food was foolish, considering her cooking was the best out there and came for free. For my mother, eating out meant us standing on the sidewalk in front of Falafel Nadav in downtown Petah Tikva, lit by a broken neon sign, and biting into our bursting pita pockets, bowing to keep tahini from dripping over our clothes.

Now I was ordering shrimp, calamari, cheeseburgers with bacon: things my kosher mother would never touch. Sometimes I even ordered schnitzel. Maybe it was the thin slices, the lack of garlic, or my guilt that soured it, but it was never as good as hers.

CHICKEN LIVERS

My FIRST APARTMENT IN TEL AVIV was a two-bedroom on Dizengoff Street—a major artery in the heart of the city—that I shared with my best friend, Elsin. It was in an old, graceless building streaked by rain, with dark, musty stairways and a backyard strewn with garbage.

My mother donated her entire selection of cleaning supplies, and Elsin and I scoured the apartment for two days straight. When we finished I walked barefoot on the tile floor, its touch as tantalizing as a chilled bottle of beer to a sweaty hand. My feet felt lighter, my head clearer. I never knew cleaning could feel so good. I never knew it was such hard work either; growing up, I'd been reluctant to help my mother with the housework.

"Wow." Elsin admired my work. "You should do this for money."

The next day I made a few handwritten ads: *A young, energetic housekeeper for hire.* I posted them on telephone poles and bulletin boards, my phone number hanging in detachable fringes. I was now, like my mother and grandmother before me, a housekeeper. In Israel's early days, most housekeepers were Yemeni women, working for Ashkenazi families. Back then the term *Yemeni* in its female form was synonymous with *maid.*

My first two homes were my two brothers' bachelor apartments. Over Friday dinner at my mother's, one of them mentioned to her, "Ayelet does an excellent cleaning job."

"She does?" My mother's face stretched in astonishment.

"Why is it so hard to believe?" I bit into a piece of challah.

FOR DINNER ELSIN and I made pasta with sauce out of jars, pizza on pita bread, tossed salads with store-bought dressing. One day

Elsin came home from her mother's with a tray of chicken livers and suggested we prepare them the following evening. Chicken liver was a staple food we had both grown up eating. My mother made it often, fried with caramelized onions. It was a cheap source of iron, one of the many ways my mother fed an entire family on a limited income.

The next evening I was late from work, and by the time I came home, Elsin had cooked her portion. I stared at the smooth-skinned livers in the bowl.

"I didn't know when you'd be coming," she said. "You just have to fry them."

I chopped onions and garlic and tossed them into an oily pan, leaning backward, away from the splattering oil. I added the livers, which sizzled loudly. "It's burning," I yelled.

"Lower the heat," Elsin answered from her room.

"There's almost no oil left."

"Add some more."

"Won't it splash all over me?"

"Should be fine."

When the livers began to brown, I gingerly flipped them onto their sides. After a few minutes, I hollered, "How do you know when it's ready?"

"I don't know," Elsin said. "Intuition?"

I stared at the pan. "Well, can you get your intuition over here and tell me if it's ready?"

Elsin walked into the kitchen and looked at me in a new way. "Oh my God. Who would have thought? You have a kitchen phobia."

My face reddened. "I just . . . I never really learned to cook."

She stirred the livers and then turned off the gas. "You know, it's never too late."

JICHNOON

I SRAELIS LIKE TO ASK EACH OTHER, "What's your background?" since most families are originally from somewhere else. Once they know your heritage, they can conjure the smell of your parents' kitchen: couscous or gefilte fish, rice or potatoes, spicy or bland. When Israelis discover that I'm Yemeni, their eyes often glaze in envy.

"Does your mother make jichnoon every Saturday?"

"Yes," I say.

"How about malawah?"

"Yes," I say. In fact, my mother prepares dough for malawah, flattens it between sheets of parchment paper, and stacks them in the freezer, so at any given time, I could throw one in a pan. I don't tell them that. It would just be cruel.

IN A COUNTRY riddled with cultural prejudice, the stereotypes associated with Yemenis over the years have ranged from romanticizing to fetishizing to patronizing. When they first arrived in Israel, Yemeni immigrants were considered savage and primitive. A fundraising film from the fifties, meant to highlight the work of Moetzet HaPoalot (Working Women's Council), said Yemeni women are "fruitful and multiply but they need proper instructions"—instructions given by Ashkenazi women, as the film demonstrated. Growing up, I was told Yemenis were "nice," "modest," "satisfied with little," and "such great singers and dancers!" These days, Yemenis are often the butt of racial jokes and the subject of mockery. But everyone seems to love our cuisine. Jichnoon and malawah have made it into the national comfort food hall of fame. Malawah is made of thin layers of puff pastry, like a crispy pancake. Jichnoon, Yemeni Shabbat bread, is rolled into croissant-like shapes, layered, and baked overnight in a special aluminum pot with a tightly sealed lid.

Friends invited for jichnoon on Saturday morning often look over the table and timidly ask for a fork and knife.

"You hear that?" we sneer. "She wants cutlery!" Taking pride in our hand-eating skill is our way of turning the prejudiced view of Yemenis as savages on its head.

A FEW YEARS ago, my cousin Yifat moved to Vancouver with her Canadian husband and rented the apartment downstairs from Sean and me. At that point I was no longer afraid of the kitchen. After I'd moved to Canada, away from my mother's watchful eye, and spent most of my days unemployed and alone, I began trying my hand at basic recipes I'd found on the internet. When my boyfriend and his friends complimented me on my cooking, I was encouraged to attempt more complex dishes. I became good at Indian and Thai curries, shopping at specialty stores for obscure ingredients and grinding fresh spices.

Soon after Yifat's arrival in the city, she invited us for a traditional Yemeni Shabbat breakfast. "It won't be as good as your mother's," she warned.

Late Friday night, the smell of jichnoon started creeping through the house, and by the time I woke up on Saturday, it hovered in our apartment, thick as fog. Downstairs, Yifat served brown eggs, tomatoes grated to a pulp, and spicy bisbas, a cilantro chutney-like condiment. I tore a piece of moist jichnoon and it emitted a swirl of steam. Sean grabbed an egg and examined it. "I always wondered, what makes the eggs go brown?"

"They're in the oven all night with the jichnoon." I laid a spoonful of bisbas on my plate.

"Do you cook them first?"

I hesitated. "I think?"

"How come you don't know that? I know how to make *my* mom's food."

"It's complicated," I said. "It takes a whole day—"

"You don't even know how to make bisbas. That can't be complicated."

"Seriously?" Yifat said. "You never made bisbas?"

"My mother never taught me," I protested.

"Why not?"

I shifted in my chair. "Maybe she didn't like sharing the spotlight."

Sean and my cousin exchanged glances.

"Maybe you should have asked," Sean said, yanking a piece of jichnoon and dipping it in tomato.

BISBAS

T HE FIRST TIME I TRIED BISBAS, it bit my tongue like a bee sting. My mouth turned hot and numb, and my eyes started watering. It tasted like danger. It didn't help that my mother sometimes threatened to put it in my mouth if I was bad.

Bisbas, a green paste made of cilantro and garlic and sprinkled with red chilies, was an essential condiment in our house, served with every meal and used the way one would use salsa or chutney. At twenty-two, after my first backpacking trip to India, I returned to Israel with a newfound appreciation for Yemeni cuisine, a fondness for fenugreek, cilantro, and turmeric, and a higher tolerance for spiciness. The first time I grabbed the jar of bisbas and spooned some onto my plate, my mother and sister paused from eating and stared at me. "What?" I said.

. . .

IT WAS A pale February in Israel when Sean and I arrived for a visit, hungry from the moment we stepped into my mother's house, ready to be fattened up. After Friday night dinner, Sean cornered my mother in her kitchen. "I'd like to learn how to make bisbas," he said.

"You do?" She laughed.

"You do?" I said, choking on the water I'd just sipped.

He looked at me. "You okay?"

The next day, my mother invited Sean into her kitchen. I was shocked by how easy it was. I tagged along, a few steps behind, still feeling like a trespasser. I hid behind my camera, snapping shots of my mother stuffing cilantro into a meat grinder with garlic, chilies, and cumin. When strings of green spewed from the other end, they smelled like freshly cut grass. Sean wrote notes while my mother explained every step with the meticulousness of a television chef. She then filled little jars with bisbas and froze them, putting a few aside to give away to her sister, her mother, her sons.

"Can I watch when you make tzli?" Sean said.

My mother beamed.

TZLI

MY MOTHER'S TZLI is her signature dish, the main event at Friday dinners. Over the years she tried replacing it with other recipes and was faced with overwhelming dissent from my siblings. The tzli (simply translated as "roast") is a five-ingredient wonder—chicken, potatoes, onions, oil, salt—yet somehow it makes the most satisfying, flavorful arrangement. Some days, when I miss home, it translates into a craving for my mother's tzli that nothing else can satisfy.

The first time I made tzli, the potatoes turned to mush and the chicken fell off the bone. The second time, the chicken and potatoes were tinted an unappealing yellow. Other times, I added too much water, burnt the onions. It seems so simple, yet I find it impossible to perfect. It's a recipe that makes me humble.

My mother cooks by intuition and memory, the way a musician plays an instrument without reading notes. She owns no measuring cups, no cookbooks. Her recipes call for a bit of this and a bit of that and the addition of spices according to taste. Sometimes they're just a list of ingredients you have to rearrange like an anagram.

"You're sure the tzli has only salt?" I asked her after my first failed attempt. "How does it get brown out of nothing?"

"It's the onions," she said. "You have to caramelize them, then add the chicken legs. Keep turning until they're brown on all sides. Add potatoes and water. Easy."

ONE FRIDAY MORNING, on a visit to Israel, I woke up to the smell of fried onions and stewed chicken tickling my nose. When I stepped into my mother's kitchen, I found all four burners at work: three covered pots and one plump eggplant laid in the blue flame. The kitchen table was covered with steaming Pyrex. At any given time, there was enough food in my mother's kitchen to feed a small village. Relatives and friends often showed up unannounced at lunchtime.

"There are only five of us tonight," my mother said. "We're having a small dinner."

A small Friday night dinner was still an elaborate affair: an assortment of appetizers—fried cauliflower, roasted yams with

rosemary, chopped salad doused with lemon and olive oil—
followed by tzli, Yemeni soup, and ugat shmarim for dessert.

The eggplant whistled, shriveled, and blackened, thin chim-
neys of smoke shooting from its cracks like lit cigarettes. My
mother poked the eggplant with a fork and it released a sigh. She
stripped off the flaky skin, letting the meaty guts spill onto a plate.
She cleaned up the burnt bits, mashed it with a fork, and added
tahini, lemon, salt, and a pinch of minced garlic from a jar.

"My eggplant salad never tastes like yours," I said.

"Do you burn the eggplant? You have to burn it until it's black."

"I have an electric stove."

"That's okay," she said. "Just put it on a pan. And use a fork. No
blender."

She seemed so eager to share her knowledge with me. Over the
past few months, she had been nothing but helpful, not at all
what I remembered or expected. As a child, I felt unwelcome in
her kitchen. I figured she didn't want to reveal her secrets because she needed to be indispensable. We all had our creative outlets: my siblings and I drew, painted, made music, and wrote.
Cooking was her gift, her genius; if she shared that with us—then
what would she have left?

Only years later, I realized I had been wrong. Like most adoles-
cents, I was self-absorbed and so engrossed in my own grief that I
couldn't comprehend the extent of both her tragedy and her tri-
umph. She had lost her husband at forty-one, was left with six
children to care for (which she had done swimmingly, despite the
dwindling financial resources and her broken heart). It wasn't so
much that she pushed us out of her kitchen as that she was holed
up in it. In a house full of kids, where she was always in demand,
the kitchen was her sanctuary, her shelter, and she had to guard

that territory jealously so she could keep going, so she could keep sane.

We were sitting at her kitchen table when I shared that insight with her, my mother rolling jichnoon with oily fingers. As I spoke, she nodded repeatedly, without speaking, her face open and grateful, her eyes gleaming.

YEMENI SOUP

A T THIRTY-FIVE, I learned how to make Yemeni soup.

It was winter in Vancouver, dreary and cold, and my naturopathic doctor advised me to eat more soups.

I never liked Yemeni soup as a child, hated how turmeric stained my fingers yellow, scowled at the wilted cilantro, despised hilba, a ground fenugreek paste that clouded the clear soup the way water fogged arak, the Middle Eastern anise liquor. Hilba emanated from your pores the following day, a tang Yemenis were often teased for. Whenever Yemeni soup was served at my grandmother's house, I sulked, refused to eat it, and left to play outside.

Yemeni soup was one of the dishes my mother had learned from her mother after she got married. It was a recipe my grandmother had been taught by the aunt who raised her in Yemen, a recipe that made it through the desert and across the sea, surviving for decades, never written down.

When my mother was a child, this soup constituted their weekly serving of meat. My grandmother gave the chicken wings to the girls so they could fly away, marry off, and the legs to the boys so they could form the foundation of the house.

. . .

FOR ONE WEEK in November, my mother and I met in Los Angeles, where my sister and her family were living at the time. "I'm making Yemeni soup," my mother said. "I even brought hawayij."

I opened the brown paper bag and sniffed it, the blend of spices instantly transporting me into her kitchen.

This time I got to watch as she prepared the soup, scribbling the steps on the back of a used envelope. We stood side by side, mother and daughter, shoulders touching, gazing into the pot, waiting for the water to boil. She added chicken drumsticks and thighs and dished the excess fat out with a spoon. She dropped in a full onion, which would later disintegrate into translucent rings, and chunks of tomato, peppers, potatoes, and carrots. She sliced garlic straight into the pot, and finally threw in an entire bouquet of cilantro. While she poured hawayij into the soup, I stirred the yellow into the water with a wooden spoon.

THE AROMA OF Yemeni soup lingers in my kitchen for days after I cook it. I grew up trying to shake this smell off me. Now it lives in my house, a permanent stamp on my walls, a pungent greeting that welcomes my guests. When the hawayij my mother had given me in Los Angeles was finished, I started making my own: grinding cardamom, cumin, turmeric, chilies, and coriander in a mortar and pestle, the way my grandmother and great-grandmother had done before me. When I stand by my electric stove and pour hawayij into the pot, I'm a Jewish Yemeni woman making soup. I forget I live in a cold and strange city, ten time zones away from my family. I'm home.

Ugat Shmarim

O NE WINTRY CANADIAN NIGHT I'm stunned by an intense craving for my mother's cake. I decide to call my mother for the recipe. I need to make it, this one time. I need to know how.

It's been two years since I last made it to Israel, a year since my mother and I met in Los Angeles. So much has changed: Sean and I moved to Toronto so I could attend an MFA program in creative writing, and after years of talking around the subject, we started trying for a baby. But Toronto is still not home, and this apartment in up-and-coming Parkdale still doesn't feel like a proper place for a family. In respites between writing, I spend hours toiling away in the kitchen, filling it up with the smells of my childhood in an effort to make the place feel homier, to make me more motherly, the only way I know how.

None of my siblings have ever dared to try making this cake. I always assumed it was too difficult. But today I'm feeling courageous, confident in my skills. I call my mother with the admission that we're more alike than I ever cared to admit. Cleaning gives me peace of mind; a full fridge makes me feel rich; when I'm in the kitchen, I don't like interruption; I cook by intuition, rarely following a recipe. If anyone can make this cake, I can.

My mother is already in bed but she's delighted that I want to make the cake, eager to pass on the recipe. "Don't get discouraged if it doesn't work the first time," she says. "It takes practice. Keep trying."

Writing down the recipe takes a while. Some of the ingredients, like a cube of yeast commonly used in Israel, are unavailable in Canada; others come in different packages, different sizes. And when my mother calls for four cups of flour, she doesn't mean standard cups. "You know the small glasses we have at home?"

"I think so."

"Your father wouldn't drink coffee in any other cup. You know the ones?"

My father passed away nearly three decades ago.

"What's the secret?" I say. "For the recipe?"

She laughs. "No secret."

I proudly tell her of my new invention, a vegan split pea soup. She tells me she made a Chinese recipe from TV. "Chinese!" she repeats in awe. I recommend the salmon cakes I found in an issue of Oprah's magazine. "I don't like *salomon*," she says, pronouncing it the way many Israelis do. We don't agree on everything. I find her beef too well-done. I use less oil in my cooking, choose ingredients that are natural, organic. She sneers at my decision to use chicken broth in my Yemeni soup rather than a bouillon cube.

We've been talking for almost an hour. She hasn't asked me about babies once, though I know she wants to.

Then I say, "Next time I'm in Israel, I'm going to watch you make jichnoon."

"It would be my pleasure." I can hear her smile.

THE SMELL OF cake lurks in the kitchen at first, nothing but a hint, then it brims over: warm, sweet, wholesome, homey. I feel as though I'm bathing in its silky aroma. "Do you smell it?" I clutch Sean's hand and whisper, afraid to disturb the moment. "I can't believe it's coming from my oven."

IF I FORGET YOU

I'S GOING TO BE YOUR LAST TIME in the house," my mother said, stirring a pot and wiping her hands on the checkered kitchen towel permanently draped over her shoulder. It was early morning in Israel, blue and cool, and everything was coated with the surreal haze that followed extended air travel, tinged with strangeness and fatigue, the inconceivability of being here, now.

"You say that every year." I stared into the fridge, comforted by the predictable display of layered Pyrex and fresh produce.

"No," she said. "This time we have a date."

Sean and I had just arrived for our annual escape from Canadian winter, a tradition we started after we had moved to Toronto, where his work on the lakes shut down through the season. Since I could do my writing and teaching from anywhere, we decided to spend the winter months in Israel, soak up sun, and enjoy time with family and friends. But this visit was different. In previous trips, Sean had boarded the plane with a guitar case while I lugged my heavy camera equipment. This time, we replaced these items with a stroller, a car seat, and a baby carrier. And, well, a seven-month-old baby. Our daughter was born two years after we decided to give this baby thing a real shot. It was her first visit to

Israel, her first time meeting many of her relatives. Her first—and apparently last—stay at my childhood home.

Carrying her up the cobblestoned path to the front door, I introduced her to my childhood landmarks. In the forgiving early morning light, suffused with nostalgia, the house appeared stately and handsome. It was easy to overlook the years of neglect: the cracks and scars and bruises, the patched-up holes in the roof, the untended lawn littered with weeds. I pointed at the giant palm tree that soared over the red-tile roof, the row of olive trees my father had planted in the back, one for each member of the family, until one of the trees inexplicably perished shortly after his death. On the north side of the house, a shallow pit yawned in the earth where the ancient lemon tree once stood. My mother used to reach out from the second-floor kitchen window to pluck plump fruit straight off the branches. How devastated I was the year I returned to see the tree gone, succumbed to sickness and uprooted, the first hint at the impermanence of our home.

My mother cooed at the baby and covered her with noisy kisses, and my daughter yielded to her, instantly recognizing my mother's body as a familiar, safe place to cling to. They had met once before, when my mother ceremoniously arrived in Toronto days after my daughter was born, overjoyed and relieved that I finally had become a mother after years of hesitating and procrastinating, and ready to impart all her knowledge to me. I had never made my mom happier. I was thirty-nine, the same age my mother had been when she had her sixth.

I placed my coffee mug on the window ledge and looked out. Our street began to wake up from its slumber: radio chattered from the neighbors' open windows, a baby cried, a phone pealed from a nearby house. Looking west, the city ascended into four- and five-story apartment buildings, lackluster rectangles in shades of beige with laundry lines slung under their windows, their roofs bristling with water heaters and antennas. Palm trees poked between the buildings like weeds in a cracked pavement. My mother joined me, and I leaned into her soft body and breathed her in: sugar, flour, citrus, too many spices to name, a hint of soap and laundry detergent. This was the household's signature fragrance. In a few days, that same blend would emanate from my own skin. Many years ago, while I was living in New York, my mother had sent me a bag of winter clothes through a friend traveling to the U.S., and as soon as I opened it, that smell burst out and flooded my lonely apartment, and I sat on the floor, holding the clothes to my nose, and cried.

In two months, right after we leave for Canada, the house would be bulldozed and an apartment building erected on its ruins, where my mom and her partner, Nissim, would gracefully retire. It was the right thing to do: selling the lot was my mother's retirement plan, and the house was falling apart anyway. But it didn't make it any easier. An act so violent, so final. An erasure of our past.

I WAS SEVEN years old when my parents started building their dream home. At the time, my family—father, mother, and six children—was living in a cramped three-bedroom apartment in downtown Petah Tikva. Our fifth-floor apartment had wood paneling in the hallway, orange Formica cupboards in the kitchen, and small terrazzo tiles for a floor—the kind that graced every Israeli home built in the mid-twentieth century. The windows were barred for safety, with wide ledges on which we fearlessly sat, legs swinging outside, watching the busy street below, and sometimes hurling down old toys just to watch them crash. An enclosed balcony was converted into an extra room for my oldest brother, with sheets draped over the sliding glass doors for privacy. In the afternoons we rode the slow, clattering elevator (which often got stuck) downstairs, drew hopscotch grids in chalk on the pavement, played catch or hide-and-seek with our neighbors, until the sun sank heavy and swollen behind the buildings, streetlights clicked on, and shutters rattled open—our mother calling us from the window for dinner.

My father was elated when he found cheap land for sale in Mahane Yehuda, a Yemeni neighborhood halfway between downtown and Sha'ariya. Mahane Yehuda—where he was born and raised for the first few years of his life—was a village once, founded by Yemeni immigrants in 1913, a jumble of sheds, huts, and small stone houses, dissected by dirt roads. Later, the city expanded around the village, swallowing it whole.

My father had been saving for this house his whole life. Sometimes, on the way back from the beach, he'd take the long way home and drive through the affluent suburb of Savyon, eye the rows of lavish villas and their sprawling lawns, and dream about the house he'd build for his family one day. Fortunately for my father, once construction began, several tradesmen—a carpenter, a window maker, an electrician—offered their services for free, returning favors for the many pro bono cases he had taken on throughout his career, which helped lower the overall cost.

During the year it was built, my father took us to the house every Saturday and we walked around the skeleton of it—all concrete and brick and poking metal wires. The windows were gaping mouths, and through them, the sun shone a dusty beam on my father. "Here"—he pointed—"is where the kitchen will be." His voice echoed as if he were in an empty theater.

The split-level house was inspired by a synagogue's floor plan: boys resided on the bottom floor, girls on the top. It was built to suit our family's needs, more specifically my mother's. Small hatches in each floor led to a laundry chute, so my mother wouldn't have to collect our dirty clothes from our rooms. Adjacent to the kitchen were a pantry and a laundry room with clotheslines extended outside its window and a large, square sink for hand-laundering in which many next-generation babies would later bath. My father also installed a shower in the garage, his grand gesture to my mother the neat freak, so when we came back from the beach on Saturdays, we could rinse off the sand before stepping on her pristine floors.

The first day in the house, we ran through it and reveled in its newness. We inhaled the aroma of fresh paint and sawdust, admired the sheen on the tile floors, the glare on the glass windows. After years of sharing small living quarters, we viewed the six-bedroom house as infinitely large, a boundless playground filled with cozy nooks and secret crawl spaces. When my cousins played hide-and-seek with me, they would run up and down the stairs until they were out of breath, and still they couldn't find me.

My father enjoyed the house he had built for less than a year before he suffered a heart attack. He was ill for a few months, and for a while, there was talk of installing a special lift. A contractor came by and drew marks on the wall where the elevator would launch. My father passed away before it was set up. The gashes on the wall, crudely carved and showing the gray, crumbly matter inside, remained there for years after he was gone.

In the months after my father's death, the house seemed grotesque, forsaken. We disappeared into our own grief, passed each other in the hallways like strangers. Whenever I was alone at home, I'd turn the lights on in every room, scared of the black pits that gaped past the doors, threatening to suck me in. At night I couldn't sleep, listening to the house creak and groan, to the whistle of the wind stirring leaves on the roof. Obsessed with death and the afterlife, I was convinced the dead were trying to communicate with me. During the days, spring showed off its new colors, and the smell of orange and almond blossoms nudged its way in through the wooden shutters, oblivious to our loss.

YEARS PASSED AND the house livened and filled up again, while the novelty of it settled into the comfortable, cozy familiarity of a home. We threw parties on the front lawn, even two weddings, and barbecues on the roof. On hot days, classmates would stop by on their way back from school, and I'd bring out the garden hose and spray us all with water. Some of our best friends had keys to the house and would come and go as they pleased, open the fridge and help themselves to food. Girlfriends and boyfriends often slept over, and cousins and uncles and aunts came by for coffee or lunch, or for jichnoon on Shabbat morning. Even during the first Gulf War, our home was brimming with people. Guests who happened to be visiting when the siren sounded joined us in the bomb shelter in the basement, including, once, a Canadian friend of my brother's who was visibly shaken by the sounds of explosions, his eyes wide behind the gas mask. Another time, my mother and her friends, fatalistic and immersed in their game of cards, couldn't be bothered with going to the shelter. A photo shows them playing cards around the kitchen table with their gas masks on.

Eventually, after our respective army services, my siblings and I started leaving. One by one. Room by room. We moved to a kibbutz, to Tel Aviv, to New York, to Amsterdam. We went traveling or on an exchange student program. But we always came back—between trips, between apartments, between boyfriends. We'd show up with our bags, our suitcases, our boxes, and stay awhile—

a few weeks, a few months, a year. Sometimes we'd bring our partners. Save for a few adjustments here and there, our rooms remained untouched in our absence. In my closet, I still had skimpy tie-dyed halter tops from Goa and dozens of scribbled notebooks and letters. Outside my window, the remaining olive trees had grown thicker and taller, heavy with green fruit that brushed the second-floor windows.

Our mother was always happy for the company, even after she met Nissim, who eventually moved in. By the time the two met, she had been a widow for twelve years. Twelve years of scoffing at the idea of meeting a man as though it were a joke. Nissim was a carpenter who refurbished old furniture in his dusty, cluttered shop in the flea market in Jaffa, where Tel Avivi hipsters came to purchase antiques and dine in one of the many restaurants that had opened since the place became trendy. He was also a widower, had also raised his young children on his own. My mother laughed frequently, began wearing lipstick and doing her hair. The two of them went dancing and took vacations in Eilat and Turkey. She was the happiest I had seen her since my childhood.

SEAN AND I settled into my old room and placed a well-used crib against the wall. I inspected the room with narrow eyes: the paint was peeling and the walls were cracked and flaking, swollen with moisture. Most of the wooden shutters were broken or missing slats, and windows were wedged in their tracks, crooked. The rickety sliding door frequently slipped out of its groove and flapped noisily on windy nights. Outlets hung on loose screws, the electric wires exposed. I plugged a radiator into the safest-looking outlet, stuffed a board in the back of the door to keep it from clattering, and draped a towel over the rattling window to block some of the wind that crept through the gaps.

The house had not been built for weather to begin with—too large and spacious to be properly heated or cooled—and the last thirty-odd years of disrepair had made it even less hospitable, the upkeep too expensive for a single mother of six to afford. What had once seemed like a luxurious villa was now a drafty, derelict concrete monster, invaded by wildlife. Cockroaches, ants, lizards, and mice were a common sight. Pigeons cooed on windowsills and crows crowded the roof. In the yard, packs of stray cats lazed in the sunshine and porcupines hid in bushes. Once, my mother found a black snake slinking on the kitchen floor. My youngest brother killed it with an ornamental machete, a gift from an uncle who had returned from South America.

On the coldest, wettest night of a spectacular Mediterranean storm that had flooded the desert and buried Jerusalem in snow, it started to rain in my baby's crib. We brought her into the bed with us and woke up to her coughing and sniffling, her little body feverish against ours. It was her first cold. To catch the rain, Sean and I placed one bucket in our room and three large pots in the living room, and spread towels on the kitchen floor—all of which needed to be replaced several times a day. We sat huddled in our coats by the radiator and could still see our breath.

Staying in the house for the first time as a mother, I began to resent it. It made my baby sick. The house was a hazard, a death trap. Then one day, we looked the other way for a moment, and our daughter toppled down a half-flight of stairs, miraculously unharmed. I blamed the house. The floors on which my baby wanted to crawl were covered in icy water, the bitter wind was whistling through the rattling slats, the outlets were precarious, the mold was blooming wildly on the walls.

"Maybe," I told my mother as she mopped rainwater into a

bucket, "it's nature's way of helping us let go of the house. So by the time they tear it down, we'll be thinking, Good riddance."

"Maybe," my mother said, unconvinced.

As demolition day approached, the rooms were cleared one by one, the decay more apparent in their bareness. Sean took on the living room, wrapping knickknacks and wineglasses in newspapers, while I volunteered to tackle the books. There were hordes of them. This was a house of eight avid readers and collectors, shoppers at used-book stores, forgetful borrowers, and compulsive gifters of books (many were inscribed from one family member to another). After we left home, Nissim amassed the remaining books and crafted a library of floor-to-ceiling bookshelves in one of the rooms. But there would be no space for them in my mother's new apartment. The library had to be dismantled and given away, destroyed, much like the house.

I divided the books into two piles: those I thought my siblings may want to look at first, and ones I figured we could give away. Nissim said he'd take them to his bookseller friend in the market. I started packing the unwanted books into boxes but it was taking forever and was heavy to transport, so Nissim came up with a better idea. He'd open the back of his work truck and fling the books from the second-floor window straight into it. I resisted at first. Like the demolition, it felt too harsh, too disrespectful. But there was so much more work to be done and I had no help and I was exhausted from sleepless nights with an infant, so I relented.

We hurled the books out the open window. I cringed as I watched them crash and pile in the back of his truck in disarray. Nissim drove off with them.

Over Friday dinner at the house, I told my siblings what we had done.

My oldest brother swallowed. "You did what?"

"I didn't give away everything," I said. "I left some for you guys to look at."

He pushed his chair back and hurried to look at the remaining books. I followed, watching as he rifled through the boxes urgently. "Where is the Young Technician series?"

"Um . . . I might have given those away."

"You threw away the Young Technician?" He looked up at me. "You shouldn't have done that. How could you know which books mattered to me? These were *my* childhood memories."

"I don't know. There were so many of them." My voice faltered. "I was just trying to help."

"They knew I was going to get rid of the books," my mother assured me as we cleaned up after dinner. "I've been telling them for months now that they should choose what they want to keep. You did nothing wrong. Everyone is just being emotional and sensitive right now."

"Could we maybe track down the books?" I asked Nissim as he was scouring the pots and pans.

He shook his head. "He only keeps them for a few days and then he throws them away."

"In the garbage?" My heart sank. "I wouldn't have done it if I knew." I had thought I was passing them on to a book aficionado, giving them new life. I couldn't shake the feeling that I had committed some crime against books, and even worse, that I had a part in erasing and bulldozing my siblings' memories.

That night, I found my mother standing by the entrance to my sister's room, staring into the void. "I can't stand the echo." She gave a mock shudder and shut the door. Then she eyed me, hesitant. "You know, he told me not to sell it."

"Who?"

"Your father. Before he died."

I felt a quick welling of anger at my father for saying such an irresponsible thing on his deathbed, but then I was flooded with regret and compassion. My poor young father. He knew he was dying. This house was his labor of love, an extension of him, his way to leave something behind, for us.

My mother's face crumbled. I'd been silent for too long.

"He meant don't sell it *then*," I said. "And you didn't. You stayed for thirty years and lived a full life in this house. We all did. Even your grandchildren. He would have wanted you to be comfortable in your old age."

My mother gave a tepid nod. I realized that to her, this was yet another goodbye to my father, a final farewell to the dream they once shared. I hoped that in the process of letting go, she could find space for forgiveness, absolve herself from the promises she couldn't keep.

THE DAY AFTER Nissim and my mother moved into a small temporary apartment in the neighborhood, my sister and I went to the house to say our goodbyes. We sat perched on the slanted tile roof facing the hills of Rosh HaAyin and looked out: the sandy path that led to my junior high school had been paved over a few years ago and lined with a row of slender palm trees. When we were growing up, the stream that had run along the path would overflow when it rained heavily, turning the dirt road into a mucky pond on which we used to sail paper boats. Back then our street was flanked with small, plain houses of older Yemeni residents and some newer villas, all lush with fruit trees and tended gardens. Many of these houses had been torn down in recent years, replaced by new apartment buildings that obstructed the view and swallowed the breeze.

Downstairs, I took pictures of my sister waving from the kitchen window to imaginary visitors, pretending to speak on the long-dead intercoms. There was something in that experience that was reminiscent of the trips we had taken there as children, when the house was under construction and we had to imagine it alive. But it was a heartbreaking comparison, as when old age evokes the helplessness of infanthood.

In my room, I uncapped the black marker I had brought with me and stared at the wall, stained by years of cigarette smoke. As a teenager, I had scribbled lines from poems and songs on my walls and once drew the Little Prince in watercolors by my bedside table. Being a fifth child, I was granted more autonomy than my older siblings. My mother had chosen her battles, and the walls of my room didn't seem to merit one. Now, I wrote "Childhood Room" in the center and drew associative memories and words around it in a circular motion, spreading wider until I covered the entire wall with black ink. Finally, I wrote, "How I always, always came back here."

On my way out, I unlatched the mezuzah from the house's main entrance. It was a beautiful and sturdy object, made of heavy metal, with a menorah, a Star of David, and what seemed to be an eye (against the evil eye, I presumed) etched on it. On top, a biblical quote was engraved: "If I forget you, Jerusalem, let my right hand be forgotten."

I took the mezuzah back to Canada and vowed one day to affix it to the doorframe in my own house—wherever that may be.

It has been sitting in my makeup drawer in Toronto ever since, waiting.

BY THE TIME Sean, our daughter, and I returned the following winter, the new apartment building was under way. Driving through the neighboring streets, I could see the bulky structure in place of the palm tree that once towered over everything. I averted my gaze, kept driving.

Nissim went to visit the construction site regularly with his tape measure, planning where to put the appliances and his refurbished furniture. He told me they had already laid the tile floors, and that on the large, west-facing balcony (one of the apartment's best features), they integrated tiles from the old house, which Nissim, in a thoughtful, moving tribute, had removed from the living-room floor before the demolition. "You should go see it," he said over dinner.

"I'll wait until they install the elevator," I said.

One evening, I went to see Aliza, the neighborhood hairdresser who had threaded my upper lip at sixteen after a boy I liked told me I had a mustache. When I got there, a few women were already waiting inside the small room, which reeked of hairspray. "Come back in half an hour," Aliza said.

Waiting outside the salon, I watched the evening descending over the main street of Mahane Yehuda, two short blocks one could drive through and miss in a blink. I inventoried the changes: The crammed seamstress shop was barred now. The little post office, where people had lined up on the sidewalk, fanning their faces with envelopes, was recently vacated—its seats piled out on the sidewalk. Benny the butcher, who rode a Vespa with a sidecar, had retired, his shop replaced by a kiosk with sidewalk tables where men sat smoking and filling out lottery forms. Everything had changed. Even Aliza—whose shop preserved its eighties decor, with the same accordion curtain separating it from her husband's barbershop and the same discolored posters featuring outdated hairstyles on the walls—was young and secular once, but now had her graying hair neatly tucked underneath a headscarf. The street was darkening, the winter sky above it bluish and brimming with stars, and the sidewalks bustled with people scrambling to finish their last-minute shopping. I glanced at my phone. I still had twenty-five minutes.

I didn't plan to walk there, but my feet guided me as though they had their own will, leading me onto the route I'd taken a million times, my way home from the bus stop, from the grocery store, from the newsstand with my stack of pop magazines, from the post office with packages from my European pen pals. I turned right into the lane named after my father, passed by the wooden benches inscribed with lovers' names, where rowdy teenagers would sit and smoke narghiles all night long, keeping us up. The building loomed above me, its blackened windows like excavated eyes. It was the end of the day and the site was fenced with corrugated iron sheeting to protect it from thieves and squatters. I walked along the perimeter of it, searching for something familiar. It was the same lot, after all, the same address. That tattered piece of sidewalk I was standing on, with the leveled curb that once led into our driveway, hadn't changed. The concrete fence between our house and Miriam's, whose roosters called every morning at dawn, was still there. Standing in front of our phantom gate, I began to feel a dizzying sense of disorientation. This was home, my body memory was pointed toward it, but I had nowhere to go. I couldn't even enter the site.

The day the house had been torn down, my sister called me in Toronto and the two of us beat ourselves up over the demolition as though we could have prevented it. Surely there was a better way, a better solution. It was a futile discussion and we knew it, but we couldn't stop, both of us sentimental to a fault and unprepared for the magnitude of feelings this loss had evoked. We wanted to turn back time and do it all differently. On the sidewalk in front of what was once our house, I felt the same furious, sense-less wish to go back in time and remove this building, reverse the outcome, write an alternate ending.

AT THE AGE of twenty-seven, after traveling extensively and mov-ing across the world, after searching for a suitable definition for home, one that I could live with, one that I could live in, I told my oldest brother with a sweeping hand gesture, "I have many homes."

Speaking to my oldest brother can be frightening. Eleven years my senior, he is a brilliant man, too sharp, too honest, his gaze too penetrating. He questions everything and he sees right through me. So when I told him how blessed I felt to have many homes, he stared at me deadpan and said, "Or none at all."

Growing up, I had often felt out of place in my own country, a feeling I couldn't comprehend or name until much later. It had to do with my father; grief shakes the foundations of your home, unsettles and banishes you. It might have also had something to do with the exclusion of my culture from so many facets of Israeli life, with not seeing myself in literature and in the media, with being taught in school a partial history about the inception of Is-rael that painted us as mere extras. Or perhaps that failed sense of belonging was an Israeli predicament, because how does one feel at home when home is unsafe, forever contested? When the fear of losing it is so entrenched in us it has become a part of our ethos?

As a roving twentysomething, I enjoyed toying with the idea of home as if it was a fluid negotiable term, a mental RV, a head-space. Home, I loved saying, was the ritual of packing and unpack-ing, arranging my books (because I always carried books, didn't travel light) on shelves in a Mexican cabana, a studio apartment in

Manhattan, or a hostel in Amsterdam. It was a train compartment in India or a ferry in Greece. It was a colorful woven rug I had bought in a market in Pushkar and carried everywhere with me, strapped to the top of my backpack. Wherever I spread that rug was home. Home became the liminal space in between—between identities, between cultures, between languages—and I was content claiming that space as my own, pleased to be different.

Even my immigration was halfhearted (a privilege, I now know, reserved for the young and fortunate). I moved to Canada following a man, with a backpack and a rug and no real plans of staying. For years, my affair with Canada remained as casual and noncommittal as my romantic entanglements. I owned next to nothing so I could pick up and leave at a moment's notice, lived in apartments furnished with milk crates I'd covered with sarongs, slept on foamy mattresses thrown on the floor. Home was transient, constantly shifting. Home, essentially, was the act of leaving—not a physical place, but the pattern of walking away from it.

I was so young and shortsighted then that I was oblivious to the repercussions these choices—or rather my refusal to make them, my debilitating indecisiveness—might have on my life later. Leaving, I discovered, did not cure my displacement, but rather reinforced it. I missed Israel the way I once longed for the world outside of it, mimicking my grandparents' yearning with a self-inflicted exile. I believed I could try other places on, the way one slips into outfits at a clothing store, and if none fit, I could always go back to my starting point as if nothing had happened. I thought everything at home would be waiting for me, unchanged.

"This is your home," my mother keeps telling me when I visit her new place. "Stop asking me for things." She is happy here, back on the fifth floor. The apartment is warm, spacious, new, and everything works. For my daughter, this will always be Savta's house, the scene of many joyful childhood memories. But I keep opening the wrong drawers and I still don't know where my mom keeps the towels or which switch to turn on in the bathroom. I have no history here; my height isn't carved on the decaying doorframes. My handprints aren't stamped inside nooks in which I had hidden as a child. My writing isn't scribbled over the walls.

My daughter, who's been a traveler since birth, having flown eleven times in the first year of her life, dragged by her parents to Israel and back, to her grandparents in Victoria, to writers' festivals and book tours, has begun to use the term "*home* home" to refer to our residence in Toronto, emphasizing the first "home" with a different inflection and a tip of her head, because when we're away, we might say we're going home whenever we return to our temporary sublet, my mother's house, or the hotel. It is her way of anchoring herself in this transient lifestyle that we have imposed on her. I realize I may have had many homes throughout my life, but I only ever had one true *home* home, and it was the security of that house that allowed me to leave over and over again, to drift and be flighty, because I knew I could always come back to it.

FOR THE FIRST few months after the house was gone, I was gripped by an urgent desire to own a place. I had never even considered it before. Buying a house meant putting down roots, staying in one place—a notion I had found terrifying and unsettling for most of my young adult life. Of course, I never could have afforded a house then. Now, older and more financially responsible, I was browsing real estate online with Sean and calculating mortgages, reading about up-and-coming neighborhoods, and looking up agents. Once we realized our chances of owning a house were slim, at least in the expensive cities we were considering (Toronto,

Vancouver, Tel Aviv—because we still couldn't decide), then I
wanted a metaphorical ownership. I wanted an answer to the
question I was often asked in interviews and in Q&As following
book events, a fair question considering my first book was titled
The Best Place on Earth and was peopled with transient, nomadic
characters searching for a place to call their own. "What is home
for you?" readers wanted to know. "What is the best place for
you?" And each time, I faltered, stammered.

Eventually, I came up with an answer. Home is where my family is, I say. Wherever Sean and my daughter are. The answer
seems to satisfy people. And it is true. But sometimes I worry that
instead of having Sean and my daughter ground me, I infect them
with my instability. I watch my daughter, who at three is already
learning how to leave, how to cope with goodbyes, how to shut
down to protect herself from heartache in the hours before departure, to cry over something else, something arbitrary.

SOMETIMES, IMAGES OF the demolition haunt me, as vivid and real
as memories. I see the bulldozers ramming into the brick fence
the way my sister once drove into it by accident, chipping the
fence and denting the bumper. I see the tire marks they leave on
the lawn as they slam into the front door like a blind, dumb animal. The olive trees are ripped one by one from their roots, their
olives raining down on the metal blade in futile retaliation. The
house collapses into itself, buried in a cloud of dust that hides the
sun like a sandstorm. Then nothing remains but a pile of rubble,
concrete, brick, and poking metal wires.

I tell myself the walls are just walls. Our past isn't folded into
them, our joys and sorrows aren't etched on the doorframes, our
tales have not stuck to the kitchen cupboards like turmeric and

nicotine. I remind myself we get to keep our memories and stories, take them with us wherever we go.

Perhaps this is my answer. Or at least another part to it, an extension to that metaphorical home where love resides. Home is collecting stories, writing them down, and retelling them. Home is writing, and it grounds, sustains, and nourishes me. Home is the page. The one place I always, always come back to.

UNRAVEL THE TANGLE

A FEW WEEKS AFTER MY FATHER'S DEATH, I snuck out during my mother's afternoon nap and walked to his law office in downtown Petah Tikva.

My father's office was on the ground floor of an aging two-story building, at the end of a cobblestoned trail, with his name still engraved on the metal sign outside. Inside, the room smelled faintly of smoke, and the dry, dusty midday heat pushed through the closed plastic shutters. Sitting in my father's worn swiveling chair, I ran my finger along his wooden desk, used the rubber stamp to imprint the words *Haim Tsabari, Advocate* on the skin of my hand, doodled on scrap papers with his pen. Then I began opening drawers, not sure what I was looking for.

In the bottom drawer, tucked between legal files, I found an old notebook filled with verse. I flipped through it. The poems were heavily punctuated, the Hebrew letters bejeweled with dots and lines, tears of ink. I took the notebook home and read through it, trying to decipher the archaic language as if it were a key to his identity. When I formed the words, whispering them into my pillow, they sounded mysterious, romantic, a secret language.

I kept the notebook under my mattress for days before handing it over to my mother. She passed it on to my father's friends, who decided to publish it in a book with Afikim, a small Yemeni-founded publishing house that had once printed a poem of my father's in their journal—his only prior publication. One of my father's friends asked if they could include some of my poems in the foreword. During the shiva I had walked in on him standing over my desk and reading through my poetry, his face the face of an adult who had been caught red-handed by a child. I had snatched my notebook from his hands and shut the door. I did not bring it up this time. I said yes.

This was not the way I had envisioned getting published. That promise my father had made me on his sickbed, just a few months before he died, ached like a burn wound that wouldn't heal over. *He* was going to publish my writing in a book. It was supposed to be his present for my tenth birthday.

My father's poetry book came out the following year: a slender paperback with a simple black cover, my father's name written on it in white. It had a smiling picture of him on the first page, looking square-shouldered and robust, followed by my two poems. It was the first time I'd seen my name in print: my poems, beside his, in the same book.

*   *   *

MY FATHER WAS the second of eight children, born in Mahane Yehuda in 1939 and raised in Sha'ariya, a neighborhood founded by Yemeni immigrants in the 1930s and tacked to the edge of our city like an afterthought. To the east, a narrow highway lined by cypress trees—a row of sharpened pencils—led to Ben Gurion Airport and all the places he couldn't yet go.

For the first nine years of his life, the country was still under British Mandate. At night, they would wake up to loud knocks and hide under their beds as the British soldiers came barging in, searching for concealed weapons. Other times, they would be startled by the sounds of inexplicable explosions. On warm days, the neighborhood kids, my mother among them, picked daffodils in the swamp across the Number 40 highway, and then stood on the shoulder, bare feet caked with black mud, and waved to the few British cars that passed by, selling the flowers to those who stopped.

My father's childhood home was small, with low ceilings and caramel walls seeped with the faint aroma of Yemeni soup. My grandmother, Savta Sarah, a petite, dark-skinned woman always in a headscarf and a shapeless dress that revealed her skinny ankles, would grab my hand and sneak a candy into it, folding my fingers over it and smiling as if we shared a secret. My grandfather regarded me with a vague nod, his head buried in holy books. I used to stare at his curly beard, stained yellow by turmeric, and the ringlets that coiled on the sides of his face.

My father was one of a few Yemeni students at Netsach Boys' School in downtown Petah Tikva, an area of town inhabited by European immigrants. It was there that he met Aaron Mahdoon, who lived a couple of blocks away in Sha'ariya. On the thirty-minute walk from school, they bonded over their love of soccer.

Aaron's family had emigrated from northern Yemen, while my father's parents came from the southern city of Taiz, home to the great seventeenth-century Jewish poet Rabbi Shalom Shabazi. Both families were poor but my father's family was worse off. Their house had no electricity, so my father studied for his exams under the streetlamp, sitting on the curb with his textbooks in the orange ring of light.

As his friendship with Aaron grew, my father became a frequent guest at the Mahdoons': a vivacious, friendly bunch blessed with sharp tongues and a flair for melodrama. The siblings laughed and gossiped, argued and teased each other. They huddled around the radio, a rare commodity in Sha'ariya (television, which was seen as a corrupting force, would not reach Israel until a decade later). My father stole glances at Aaron's younger sister, Yona, taken by her smile and fair skin, charmed by her witty retorts and fiery temper—a contrast to his dark complexion and wiry frame, his shy, gentle manners.

My mother can't remember when their friendship turned into romance. The local theater on Sha'ariya's main street showed three movies a week and my parents watched them all—Egyptian melodramas, Hollywood westerns, Indian movies starring Raj Kapoor. After the movies, they walked the streets and talked, the nights sweet with guava and citrus, the silence punctuated by the rhythmic chirping of crickets. In the distance, cars whispered from the highway.

IN 1959, MY father started writing poetry.

Israel was just recovering from years of austerity, the rationing of staple foods finally abolished. The Hollywood movie *Exodus*, starring Paul Newman, was being filmed in Israel, bringing international attention to the little country, no more than a dot on the world's map. In Haifa, the violent Wadi Salib riots erupted, their resonance reverberating throughout the nation. Israel was a young country, with two wars behind it already and a population that was growing rapidly, far surpassing its resources. The mass immigration of the fifties changed the ethnic ratio within Israel's Jewish population, which until then was predominantly Ashkenazi. The riots in Wadi Salib were the first civil protest against the mistreatment of Mizrahi in Israel. They were started by Moroccan immigrants who were housed in the formerly Arab neighborhood in slum-like conditions, while Polish immigrants who came at the same time were granted comfortable homes.

My father was twenty years old and fresh off his army service in the signal corps. During the day, he worked in menial jobs, and in the evenings took the bus to Tel Aviv, where he studied to be a lawyer. At night, he read books and wrote poetry. For my father, reading for pleasure was revolutionary: he wasn't raised to love books, wasn't recommended favorites by older siblings. His father read only religious texts and his mother was illiterate; like most Jewish Yemeni women of that generation, she communicated her joys and sorrows through oral storytelling and song.

My father wrote for an entire year, winter and summer. Whenever he saw my mother, who, despite her eighth-grade education, was a devoted bookworm and library dweller herself, he slipped handwritten notes into her palm. Then he mustered his courage and handed the poems to his literature teacher from high school. The teacher critiqued them mercilessly, littering the notebook with red ink. Crestfallen, my father concentrated on his studies and abandoned his literary aspirations.

* * *

Come to me
whole,
Come to me
unveiled,
Come to me
revealed . . .
. . . Come
and we shall go
—HAIM TSABARI, "Come to Me," 1959

. . .

ON THE FIRST day of 1961, my parents sat on an exposed water pipe near the local synagogue and made New Year's resolutions to an audience of stars. The night fell over the city, a silk handkerchief moist with perfume. My mother doesn't remember who said it first, just that right there and then, they decided to get married. They could live with her parents for a while before finding their own place, where my mother would hang curtains and my father would put up shelves for books. They set a date— a month away.

On their wedding day, my father wore a secondhand suit he'd bought at the flea market in Jaffa. My mother had received some money from her parents for a simple white dress. Her sisters had coiled her hair in rollers so it cascaded down her shoulders in loose ringlets. Family and friends were invited to an event hall in the city: long tables covered in maroon cloths and swan-shaped napkins tucked in wineglasses like a troupe of ballerinas. The guests dipped pita in hummus, nibbled on olives and pickles. Chicken legs in orange zest were served as a main course, and nondairy cakes were offered for dessert alongside muddy coffee spiced with cardamom. My parents did the twist, slow danced to Elvis Presley's "It's Now or Never," their foreheads gleaming, cigarette smoke floating above their heads like halos.

IN 1962 MY oldest brother was born. My father continued working during the day and studying in the evening. He no longer wrote poetry, just letters to Aaron, who was sailing to Greece and Turkey with the navy. The letters detailed soccer matches my father had watched, relayed neighborhood gossip, expressed his awe as he watched my brother's first steps, heard his first words.

Over the next decade, my parents had three more children

and moved four times, until they bought the apartment I was born in: a three-bedroom on the fifth floor of a six-story building overlooking the cluttered downtown, with a yellowish patch of lawn in the front. My father opened his own practice in a small office by the vegetable market, above a European deli. A few years later, he moved to a larger office with his brother in a more central location downtown.

My youngest brother was born in 1980. Soon after that, my parents started building our new home in Mahane Yehuda. Israel had just signed a peace agreement with Egypt, the first to be signed with an Arab country. A new decade loomed: people talked of the beginning of an era, of visiting the pyramids and drinking coffee in Cairo.

My father came home for lunch and siesta every day, before heading back to work. In those days, the city was shut down between two and four, when the sidewalks scorched your feet and the shadows folded into the houses. When we heard his key in the door, we sprinted from our rooms and jumped on him. He stood at the entrance with his briefcase at his feet, laughing. My mother waited her turn, smiling and wiping her hands on a kitchen towel.

I pause from writing, fingers hover over the keys.

I call my brother in Montreal. "Is this real? Were we really that happy?"

"I think we were," he says.

*   *   *

When I descend into oblivion
do not pull me back,
When I fall into the nether world
do not draw me out,

When I reach my grave
do not mourn me.
And on the day of my remembrance
do not visit me,
Remember me while I'm still on earth
—HAIM TSABARI, "Remember Me While I'm Still on Earth," 1967

THE DAY HE died, I dug out my sister's makeup from my closet, promising God that I wouldn't steal anymore. I called my best friend, Nurit. "My father is dead," I said, crying so hard that she couldn't make out my words. I remembered how he sang to me, "When you cry, you're not beautiful. Don't cry, little girl, don't cry."

"There's no such song," I protested, sniffling. "You're making it up!"

"I promise, it's a real song," he said, his hand to his heart. But he was laughing, and I didn't believe him.

HUNDREDS OF PEOPLE congregated outside our house on the day of his funeral, filled our home during the shiva, eager to tell us of the favors my father had done for them, the services he hadn't charged them for, the court fees he had paid on their behalf.

Hiding at the top of the stairs, a month shy of ten, I watched the men swaying back and forth in prayer, the living room rising and falling like waves at sea. I listened to the grown-ups talk about my father and it was like they were talking about somebody else. They said he was nearly deaf in one ear. I used to get frustrated with him for not answering when I called. They also said he was blind in one eye, the result of children's play that had gone terribly wrong; someone had thrown a sharp object that struck him in the eye. His mother, distrustful of Western medicine, hadn't taken him to a hospital until it was too late. That's why he'd always worn dark-tinted glasses. I reexamined my memories of him in the light of this new information, as if I were rereading a mystery book knowing all the clues. For days I walked around with a hand covering my eye, startled by the loss of depth and perspective.

My tenth birthday was a month after his death. Instead of a book of my writing, I got three Barbies from three different relatives, all desperately trying to cheer me up. My favorite was the black one. She had curly hair and brown skin, closer in shade to mine. She'd also lost her father. Together we hid in my father's closet, sitting between his hanging suits, hollow ghost dads that swayed and rubbed against my face, vaguely smelling of his cologne.

FOR THE NEXT few years, stories about my father's generosity and kindness followed us everywhere. Plumbers, electricians, and mechanics pushed my mother's hand away when she tried to pay. Packages arrived at our door, baskets full of chocolates and snacks. Being my father's daughter became a safety net, the inheritance he'd left behind. Taxi drivers did a double take as they dropped me off at home. "You're *his* daughter?" The big-muscled hot dog vendor outside my high school welled up in tears, and agreed to start a tab for me, a perk reserved for very few students, of which I took full advantage.

Years after his death, during my mandatory service in the IDF, I met an old Yemeni janitor, a civilian working for the army. We chatted. "I know only one man in Petah Tikva," he said. "Haim Tsabari, the lawyer."

I stared at him. "That's my father."

The man put his hand to his heart, his face crumpling. He used to work as a janitor at the courthouse in Tel Aviv. My father was the only lawyer who spoke to him, let alone befriended him. He would find the janitor in the hallways and ask him to take a break. The two of them would sit in the cafeteria and chat over coffee and a cigarette.

AFTER A FEW years the city decided to name the lane by our house after my father. A plaque was made, set into a rock; men in suits shook our hands, smiled at cameras. A photographer from the local paper snapped pictures of our family posing by the sign. My father became a public figure, a street name, a picture in history books.

As years passed his legend grew and my memories faded. I could no longer picture the way he walked, recall the sound of his voice. His facial expressions. His smell. I envied other people's stories, coveted them, and then I began borrowing them, second-hand stories I recited to others. My own memories seemed small, insignificant, often patched together from snapshots: my father and me in his Ford Cortina, driving on the beach highway to Haifa; the two of us sitting on a wooden bench outside a corner store, sipping Sprite from green glass bottles on a hot summer day.

* * *

ON THE PHONE from Israel, my mother answers my questions about my father until her voice starts to give. I write everything she tells me, collecting details the way I would for a fictional character. How did he drink his coffee? Did he really put salt on oranges? I see them walking the streets of Sha'ariya, my father in his black-rimmed glasses, my mother in her knee-length skirt and seamed stockings.

"Everybody loved him," she says. "He was the good one."

"What do you mean?"

"When people first met us, they thought, What a great guy. But his wife, she's such a snob."

"Why?"

"You know me, I don't always want to say hello to everybody. I have my own business to take care of. Your father—he had patience. He talked to everyone."

I realize that she has also lived in the shadow of his memory.

MY FATHER TOOK me to the beach in Tel Aviv once. He let me use his back as a float, my hands wrapped tightly around his neck and our feet kicking in unison. We swam far, past the wave breakers, to where the city buildings were as small as Lego. In the deep water, his eyeglasses slipped off. He watched them disappear into the murky green but couldn't dive for them with me holding on to his back.

My mother was furious when we got home late. "I was worried sick!" she yelled. "You drove back without your glasses?" From my hiding spot behind the couch, I watched my father work his charm. He spoke gently to her, stroked her hair, kissed her face. The wrinkle wedged in her forehead melted away and her lips formed a reluctant smile.

Sometimes, my father sang to my mother, "Yoanti, tamati, nishmati," which would make us giggle and her blush. He'd grab her hands, taking her away from the vegetables she was chopping or the soup she was stirring, and turn her around to face him, forcing her to join him in a dance. Her name, Yona, means "dove" in Hebrew and so this became their song. "My dove, my pure, my soul. My rose without thorns. You're mine and I'm yours."

"We all wanted a relationship like your mom and dad's," a cousin once told me.

Years later, Sean would sometimes grab my hands while I cooked, grumpy about something, and despite my protests would spin me around our kitchen in Vancouver while singing Otis Redding or Percy Sledge, until my frown turned into a smile, into joy and delight. And I'd think, All this time I was looking for my father in quiet, shy boys, but it was the boisterous, loud one who ended up giving me echoes of my parents' relationship, the kind of love I grew up watching and wishing for myself.

＊　＊　＊

With my pen I wander between thoughts
Pick through the riches of language
Join together forgotten words
into verse
Unravel the tangle
—HAIM TSABARI, "False Spring," 1959

WHEN I BEGAN writing about my father, I decided to revisit his poetry, perhaps take on the challenge of translating parts of it into English. I was nervous, afraid I might not like the book as much as I used to, now that I was older, more critical.

I also worried that I wouldn't be able to do his poetry justice. My father's language represented an era when Hebrew was fresh in people's mouths. A dead language for seventeen centuries, it was revived to serve a purpose: to unite Jews from disparate places who had no way of communicating but through the language of prayer. My father's generation reclaimed Hebrew as a language of poetry, finding ways to describe the ordinary, the secular, and the profane in words once considered sacred. In his poetry, my father fused modern Hebrew with words borrowed from the Bible, using antiquated phrasing and style, which lent the text a distinct, singular quality, making it near impossible to translate.

I studied my father's poetry, hoping that it would give me answers, that it would click and unlock, like a Japanese puzzle box. Maybe I'd see something that had been there all along, waiting to be revealed, the way my mother's memories were waiting for me to dust them off.

Eventually, something new did emerge. I could see my father as a young man: he smokes and drinks, falls in love but hesitates; he wants to write; he's full of doubt. In one poem, he hears whispers telling him to burn it all, a voice that says, "A poet's craft is an artist's realm / not for you, son of Yemen." That line broke my heart. I knew there were no published Yemeni poets in Israel at the time. Our celebrated poets were all Ashkenazi. Afikim, the publishing house that had released his book, was founded in 1964 by a collective of Yemeni authors and scholars, some of them friends of my father's, who wanted to provide a platform for Yemeni authors to showcase their work. It was their response to the hegemony, their way to carve their own space in Israel's literary landscape.

As I immersed myself in the poetic journal of my father's youth, it brought him down from the pedestal I'd placed him on. He became someone I could identify with, someone I could understand.

OVER THE YEARS, as the days of his absence grew longer than his time in my life—his memory a large, blinding, orbiting moon, and my longings for him new and reclaimed with every milestone he missed—I had reversed the promise my father made to me on his sickbed and vowed to publish a book in his honor. Along the way, I took some detours, moved across the world, stopped writing, and then started to write in another language. By the time the book I had dedicated to him was published, I was closer to the age he was when he died. I was proud of my accomplishment and imagined he would have been too, but a part of me was filled with trepidation and guilt: What would he think of my abandoning the language he loved so much? The language he breathed and dreamed in, the ink that flowed in his blood? Hebrew was the language of his poetry, the language of my childhood, with him. How would he feel about me writing in a foreign tongue whose words meant nothing to him? Would he be disappointed?

My father had built himself up from nothing, made a life for himself out of sheer determination and willpower, with no help from anyone. Shortly before his death, when he was in his early forties, he too decided to follow his passion, fulfill a fantasy that had been dormant for years, and signed up to study Hebrew literature at Tel Aviv University. He never made it. In hard times, as I put myself through writing school with student loans, working as a waitress and a housecleaner (although, unlike him, I had some support, from Sean), I thought of him, drew strength from his perseverance. I anxiously, senselessly wanted him to be proud of me. I wanted my dead father to recognize what it meant for me to write in English, to acknowledge that in choosing a second language, I had to commit to working harder than anyone else, to producing awful work, to coming last.

English was a place I fled to, an act of reinvention that echoed the anonymity and freedom I had felt when migrating to a new country, eliciting the same exhilarating thrill of stepping outside my comfort zone. I imagine my father must have felt something similar writing poetry in Hebrew, a language that was his native tongue, but not his mother's tongue. A language his parents spoke poorly and his mother couldn't read. A broken link between them, as English is—would have been—between us.

Losing him was the end and the beginning of everything, the cosmic explosion of my little universe. It was the reason I left my home, my family, and my language, and ran away from anything that threatened to tether me down, anything that could break me if it suddenly vanished, which, of course, was anything worth having. It was that loss that gave me permission to act as though I had nothing to lose and to make the mistakes he wasn't there to witness, but also the strength to eventually turn my life around and the inspiration, writing aside, to try (and sometimes fail) to be kind and give back, to strive for goodness, which may have been my father's true bequest, the thing that would truly make him proud.

*   *   *

IN MY FAVORITE picture of us, I'm wearing his hat. He's standing behind me in his dark glasses, hugging me, my hands crossed over his, pale against his dark skin. I don't remember when it was taken, or who took the picture. The feeling of his hands in mine.

HE WROTE TO me from his hospital bed a few days before he died. The folded lines are worn, the paper crumpled and thin. With his graceful stroke, his black pen, in his lyrical style, he writes, "My love, my precious, my smart, my beautiful. I miss you and I will see you soon."

THE ART OF STAYING

My DAUGHTER IS LEARNING about the passing of time, about the cyclical ways of the year. She's two and a half. Her memory doesn't span long. The future isn't vast and open yet. It's that glorious stage in life where there is only the moment, a mindset we spend much of our adult lives trying to re-access.

"When can I go trick-or-treating again?" she wants to know.

We are lying on the futon in her room, facing each other, limbs and breath entwined, a sweet moment, joyous, relaxed. "First we'll have Hanukkah and Christmas," I say. "Then it will be winter and it will snow, then Passover, then your birthday—you'll be three! Then summer, and we will go swimming, and then it's going to be fall again, and Rosh Hashanah and Sukkot, and *then* you will go trick-or-treating."

"And then we'll be done?" she asks, eyes round.

Done? Yeah, she's definitely not getting it yet.

"No," I say and repeat the whole thing again.

"And *then* we'll be done?"

"No." I laugh. "Then you'll be five and six and seven . . ." I count for a while, and then stop to inhale deeply. "Until you are a hundred!"

"And then what?"

I hesitate, not quite ready for that conversation. "Then you will be a savta!" I say.

But to her, Savta is my mother's name, not the Hebrew word for "grandmother." Her face crumbles and she begins to cry.

"Oh no! What's wrong?"

She sobs into me, inconsolable. "I don't want to be someone else. I want to be me."

I try to repair the damage, explain what I meant, soothe her until she trusts that she's not going to lose herself and become someone else. Two and a half years in this body and already her attachment to it is so strong, her fear of losing herself so great. I think of my reluctance for years to become a mother, for fear of having to give up the life I had made for myself, for fear of losing my individuality.

I didn't want to become someone else. I wanted to be me.

I AM A descendant of a bad mother. The worst kind. A mother who left. A mother—if you ask my grandmother, my mother, and my aunts—who was a selfish, horrible person. She had to be, because how else could you explain her actions? That mother was my great-grandmother Shama. Widowed twice by the time she was thirty, she deserted my grandmother and her twin sister in Yemen and moved to Israel with her third husband, never to see her twin daughters again.

I am also a descendant of good mothers. My grandmother Salha, or Esther, as she was called in Hebrew—abandoned at the tender age of two, married at twelve—carried her infant daughter, my aunt Rivka, as she walked the desert with my grandfather and his other wife for months, overcoming hunger, diseases, and adversities, all the way from their home in North Yemen to Aden. There, they boarded a boat to Port Said in Egypt, and then another one, filled with cattle, to Haifa. She raised six children in a new country while working as a maid and a laundress at the homes of the wealthy Ashkenazi to help support her family.

My mother also raised six children; the youngest was only two when my father passed away. My mother, with her eighth-grade education and no profession other than cleaning, cooking, baking, laundering, shopping, vacuuming, folding, washing, hugging, raised us on her own through grief, depression, and financial hardship.

The black-and-white family portrait I used to gaze at in my grandmother's house in Sha'ariya now hangs in my mother's new fifth-floor apartment. In it, my four-year-old mother is still sulking. It is a facial expression she carried into adulthood, childlike and endearing—an expression I remember from my grandmother's face, and one I sometimes see reflected in the mirror. Lately, my daughter has been mimicking it; her lips stick out in an exaggerated pout and her forehead wrinkles. It's an adorable gesture of discontent, honest in its rawness. "Look, Ima, I have your frown," she says.

These days, the similarities between me, my mother, and my grandmother, which I was loath to acknowledge as a surly adolescent, are a source of comfort. That likeness tells me I belong somewhere; I am a link on the lineage chain, a branch on the family tree. After years of feeling rootless and adrift, I take solace in knowing I can trace my history, my characteristics, back to them, to that little Yemeni neighborhood in Petah Tikva, to that mountainous village in North Yemen.

Like my mother and my grandmother, I am stubborn and argumentative, take too much space, and love to be right. My mother used to be a troublemaker in school, once running between the tables to avoid being spanked by a teacher, until she

reached the open window and leaped out. As a student, I was infamous for being a pest; a teacher once announced to the class
that if she ever suffered a heart attack, it would be my fault. I reflect on it sometimes when I watch my daughter's spectacular
tantrums, often carried out in airport terminals, supermarket
aisles, and subway platforms.

But the line ends—or begins—with a broken link. A chain that
hangs loose, a tree missing a branch. Nobody alive today knew my
great-grandmother, has even seen her picture. Rumor has it that
my grandmother is the spitting image of her mother, as fair and
as beautiful as she was, but we can't know for sure, and my grandmother, who never forgave her mother for leaving, did not care to
hear it. There must be other qualities we inherited, that survived
throughout the years, through famine, wars, and migration, a
gene pattern we can trace back to my great-grandmother. Maybe
it's our slight lisp, which I can detect only when I hear my voice
on tape, or those childbearing hips that my mother and grandmother put to good use. The witty retorts, the hot temper, that
pouting. How deeply we love our men. How deeply we love our
children.

What if some traits skip a generation or two? What if my great-
grandmother has something to do with my wanderlust, my itchy
feet, my commitment issues? My ambivalence about motherhood and raising children? Sometimes I wonder, dreadfully, what
if that great-grandmother I never knew is the woman I resemble
most?

＃　＃　＃

I FIRST IMAGINED leaving when my daughter was three days old.
The midwives said that this was normal. Baby blues. Not even

postpartum depression. Just ordinary, nothing-to-worry-about, hormone-induced turmoil. I was healing from a difficult birth, bleeding and sore, my breasts hurt and I was crying a lot and it felt like grief. And sometime during that third day (notorious, apparently, for its bouts of weepiness and anguish), I thought, What if I just take off? As if nothing happened? What if I could have my old life back? I glanced at Sean, who seemed to have a handle on this whole parenthood thing. He slipped into this role so easily. Early on in our relationship, during a carefree backpacking trip we now think of as our honeymoon, I had marveled as he held his hands up to a woman carrying a baby while she stepped off a boat in Malaysia. She beamed with gratitude and passed the infant to him. I watched him rocking our newborn baby. The two of them would be happy together, without me. They'd be better off.

This was three weeks before my fortieth birthday, a month after I published my first book. It took me years to find the right person, a few more to warm up to the idea of motherhood, and even then, it was with hesitation. The determining factor was that I couldn't envision *not* having a family, despite trying to give in to the idea of living child-free. Sean never pushed, but he never indulged my occasional childless fantasies either; it was clear to me that he wanted a family. Once we decided to try in earnest, it took a couple more years—due to Sean's impossible sailing schedule and my lazy thyroid—to conceive. We were thrilled and terrified.

In my first trimester and not yet showing, the fetus still a genderless secret in my belly, Sean and I were at a birthday party at a bar in Jaffa's flea market: a table set in a curving alley, painted warm amber by the soft beam of the streetlamp. I was having an intimate conversation with a man I had gone to high school with who happened to be there. Gal was handsome and charming and successful. He was living with a girlfriend in Jaffa, not far from there. "Any kids?" I asked, and he shook his head no.

"I always knew I didn't want kids," he said. And I blurted, without thinking, "Yeah, I never really wanted them either." It was mostly true, yet there was life inside my uterus, and my words felt like a betrayal. My baby might hear me, might feel unwanted. I was not yet a mother and already I had failed. Then Sean, who was chatting with our friend Omer, turned to me and said, "Omer's wife is pregnant too!" I froze, and took longer than necessary to turn back to Gal. From his face, I knew that he had heard, that he'd reached the obvious conclusion, that my words had puzzled him. I couldn't explain it, so I didn't.

Three weeks before my due date, I sat with my midwife in my Toronto kitchen. "You're not doing a reading in Guelph three days before you're supposed to give birth," she said.

"You don't understand," I said. "This is important. I just launched my first book."

"You'll never get the first days with your baby again," she said. "Nothing is more important than that."

But I hadn't given birth yet, hadn't met my baby. I almost resented hearing that my biggest achievement yet—an event I had dreamed of since childhood—could so easily be dismissed, outshined by this tiny creature in my belly.

I used to think love was the biggest entrapment of all, that nothing steals your freedom like a long-term, committed relationship. I was wrong. Motherhood was the one thing in my life I couldn't walk away from. I could not think of anything scarier.

\# \# \#

GROWING UP, THE story of my great-grandmother—the short version, that is—was one I heard often. My grandmother found no use or joy in storytelling, but the tale of her abandonment had shaped her life. It was the one story she never tired of relating, her hit song, her signature piece. My mother would mention it too, but mostly to boost her own image in our minds. "Can you believe it?" she would ask, incredulous. "Walking away from your two-year-old daughters? You're lucky you have such a good mother."

As far as I could tell, there was nothing more to the story, until a chance meeting at a restaurant in Varanasi, India, changed everything. I was twenty-two. A year earlier I had boarded a plane to India with a one-way ticket from Israel and still hadn't returned. One evening, while dining at a rooftop restaurant overlooking the murky Ganges River, I recognized Yifat from across the room: a beautiful, petite girl with the kind of typical Yemeni appearance I had often envied (once I gave up wanting to look more Ashkenazi)—her skin darker than mine, her hair in spirally, tight curls. She was my aunt's next-door neighbor in Sha'ariya. We had exchanged a few words in the past, played in a group of kids in the neighborhood. Politely, I crossed the room to greet her.

Over the next few weeks, Yifat and I kept running into each other, likely following the same route as other travelers. Then, in the airport in New Delhi, waiting for my flight home, I saw her again, frantically rummaging through her backpack. Her travel companion recognized me from across the terminal and beamed. He strode toward me and said, "Your cousin doesn't have enough rupees for the departure fee. Do you have some that she can borrow?"

I stared at him. "She's not my cousin."

"Right. Second cousin."

I said nothing. I gave him the money.

I said nothing because growing up in Israel in a large Yemeni family, I came to regard most Yemenis as relatives to some degree. I used to joke that all Yemenis were related unless proven otherwise.

On the flight, I found Yifat in the smoking section, slid into the seat next to her, and lit a cigarette. "So . . . we're cousins?"

She looked at me with surprise. "You didn't know?"

I shook my head.

"We have the same great-grandmother," she said. "Shama."

"The evil one? The one who left my grandmother in Yemen and moved to Israel with a new man?"

"Well, that's not exactly how it happened." Yifat shifted in her seat. "But yes. After she arrived in Israel with her third husband, she had another son. That son was my grandfather."

"So your grandfather and my grandmother are brother and sister?"

She nodded, squishing her cigarette in the metal ashtray between us. "You got it."

My knowledge of my family history was so scant that although I knew my grandmother had lost a brother in the 1948 war, it had never occurred to me to ask where that brother came from. Was he left in Yemen too? Was he a half-brother? I dismissed that detail as another complication in our family tree that I couldn't be bothered deciphering. Who could keep track? We were a big family, and there were plural marriages and marriages between cousins and, apparently, polygamy too. When I first discovered my grandfather had been married to two wives at the same time (rather than one after the other, as I had originally assumed), I asked my mother, "How come no one told me that?" and she said, "You never asked."

BACK IN ISRAEL, Yifat and I bonded over our reverse culture shock, spending our afternoons smoking pot and watching movies in her parents' house in Sha'ariya. We decided we needed a vacation to ease us back into the real world and hitchhiked to the Sinai desert in Egypt. Sinai offered a simpler existence, a world of primary colors: yellow dunes, blue water and skies, long black roads snaking through red mountains. We smoked desert weed full of sand and seeds that popped loudly, played backgammon with the Bedouins, swam in the warm sea—its floor slipping from under our feet into a wall of coral reef swarming with fish. We slept in a straw hut, the sand covered with striped rugs bleached by sunlight. We wondered if that was what Yemen looked like, if that was how our grandparents had lived.

One night, as we sat watching the string of gleaming lights across the Red Sea that underlined Saudi Arabia's shores—so close to the land of our ancestors—I said, "What did you mean on the plane? Why did Shama leave the twins behind?"

"She had no choice," Yifat said. "Her mother-in-law wouldn't let her take them. The twins were the only thing she had left from her dead son. She told Shama it was too dangerous; they were too little; they wouldn't survive the trip to Israel. She said, 'You can leave, but the twins must stay here.'"

OVER FRIDAY DINNER at my mother's, I told my family what Yifat had said. My mother was serving thin, yellow Yemeni soup with lahoh, a flat sticky pita that looked like a sponge speckled with holes.

"That's not true," my mother said. "That's not what happened."

"How do you know?"

My mother gave me a sharp look. "There's always a choice."

"Well, I just think it's interesting—"

"What's so interesting?" my mother interjected, waving a ladle. "She was a selfish bitch and a terrible mother, and that's all there is to it."

"And a bit of a harlot by the sound of it." My uncle laughed. "I mean, three husbands? That would be like six today!"

"There must be more to the story," I said. "Maybe I could write about it one day."

My uncle softened, wrapped his arm around my shoulder, and said, "I understand why you're curious, but there's no way to find out the truth, is there?"

It's hard to accept that some secrets really do end up in graves with the people who carried them, that the truth, like lahoh, is sticky and full of holes.

▪ ▪ ▪

WE DECIDED TO have a home birth, although we didn't tell our families that. During my hypno-birthing classes, I was coming around to the idea of birth as natural, something that has become unnecessarily medicalized, something my body knew how to do. I drew reassurance from my maternal ancestry: my mother's births were all natural and fairly easy; my grandmother gave birth to five of her six children at home. When my youngest uncle was born, my aunt Mazal ran to get the midwife in the middle of the night. She remembers my grandfather in the corner of their mud hut, making himself scarce, and the other kids sleeping through the whole thing.

I can do this, I thought. I am my mother's daughter. My grand-mother's granddaughter. I have their hips.

But after twenty-four hours of laboring at home, quietly, in-wardly, my midwife came to check on me. "Hmmm," she said with her hand inside my cervix.

"Hmmm? What are you feeling?"

She smiled and said something no woman wants to hear dur-ing labor: "I'm not sure. Something I haven't felt before."

An ambulance rushed me to the hospital through wet, sleepy Toronto streets. It turned out my baby was presenting her face first, looking out into the world, curious, impatient. It was a rarity, the doctor said. My midwife told me I was lucky; other doctors might have chosen to perform a cesarean at that point. Our daughter was born not in the intimacy of our home but in a room crowded with nurses and doctors who wanted to witness the un-usual delivery. She was not placed on my chest but whisked to the corner of the room to be examined. Sean went with her, held her little hand in his. It was he who was with her first. Not me.

I *was* lucky. If this were Yemen, we might not have made it.

When they finally placed her warm, wrinkled body on my breasts, she appeared to be smiling serenely, with a full head of jet-black hair that would later shed, be replaced by a lighter brown. Her head was bruised and swollen from the forceps. She was the newest thing I had ever seen, a whole world inside three and a half kilos, and I was terrified of her beauty and fragility.

In the middle of the night, I woke up startled by her absence. Sean and our baby were sleeping together on the folding bed be-side me, his body coiled around hers in a protective half circle. I remembered he took her for a walk while I slept, but it had been four hours and she needed to be fed. They looked so peaceful to-gether, father and daughter, her face a little, softer replication of his. But shouldn't she have slept with me on the first night of her life? Now she had gone too long without nursing. I felt, vaguely, that I was doing it all wrong, failing already.

And there was the question of love: I loved her, sometimes to tears, but it wasn't the instantaneous falling in love described by some of my friends, the elated ecstasy some mothers spoke about, like drugs, they said. This was nothing like drugs, and I knew drugs. I searched for it, desperately. Did I love her wrong, or just not enough? One day during that blurry first week, I called my friend Nancy, a mother of two, from the depths of my bed, crying. "What am I supposed to feel? Is this enough love?"

Those first days were dazed and stagnant, fragmented into strange, unnatural patterns of sleep and wakefulness, punctuated by diaper changes and brief forays into the kitchen to eat the food Sean had prepared. Much of my time was spent nursing in bed. Once I'd mastered breastfeeding (which had been a battle at first, yet more evidence of my incompetence), it became my answer for everything. My body kept my baby alive. It knew what to do even when I didn't.

Most of the time I felt like I was underwater, mute and un-gainly and out of breath, exiled into a new world where I was unversed in the native tongue and the local customs and the per-ception of time, stripped of my identity and my history. This sense of foreignness should have comforted me in its familiarity, but instead I felt profoundly alienated and invariably lonely— a stranger in my own skin, my own life.

I was also gripped by fear, disturbed by nightmares. I thought of my young mother raising all six of us on her own after my fa-ther died. She was only a year older than I was now. How did she manage? And then I worried about my own health, my heart, my genes, and felt guilty for waiting for as long as I had. Motherhood introduced a new degree of vulnerability I could have never conceived of, the kind of weakness I had spent my life trying to stave off. It made me lose my edge, peeled away my toughness. Underneath, I was completely exposed.

I was envious of Sean for being so adaptable, for being happy and unafraid, and for being the dad, a role that inherently allowed for more leeway, even though he had quit his job as a chief officer on a boat that sailed for six weeks at a time and taken paternity leave for ten months (thanks to Canada's generous parental leave policy). Even though he shared more than half the load, was more present than any father I had ever known. I may have done nights by myself (we figured at least one of us should be well rested and fully functioning), but he changed almost all diapers during the day, carried her more frequently than I did. At three months, he stayed with her two evenings a week while I taught continuing studies at the University of Toronto for extra cash. He was with her while I was promoting my newly released book, attending readings and interviews and launches. He knew what was in the diaper bag. I didn't.

In my mothers' group (all of them envious of me for this cushy introduction to parenting, which made me feel even more guilty for having the audacity to complain), one mother suggested they should invite Sean to the group, rather than me.

On the rare occasions that I took her out on my own, I was often flustered to the point of panic while trying to change her in public or calm her through her crying fits. Once, I burst into tears at the beach parking lot because Sean had sent me to get the car seat and I couldn't figure out how to unlatch it. It was a basic skill every mother had figured out by now, but I had never done it before.

I went to the park with a fellow writer who had given birth just a few months before me. Her face had the serene glow new mothers are known for, an expression of unruffled contentment. She spoke the whole way home about how happy she was, how she no longer cared about work or writing. "I just don't want to talk about anything other than my baby," she said. I nodded, but I couldn't relate. My old self was still there, dying to talk about books and literature. She was just trapped.

In the fall I went on a book tour with Sean and the baby in tow. They stayed in hotel rooms while I spoke onstage, mingled with authors in the hospitality suite, feeling like a fugitive on the loose, until my cellphone beeped, "She's up. Hurry," and I'd abandon everything mid-conversation and rush back to the hotel room, remove my fancy dress and my non-breastfeeding bra, and lie there, her hungry little mouth searching for my nipple.

While we visited the Vancouver Writers Festival, I also got to see Yifat. In yet another extraordinary string of events, she had fallen in love with my best friend from the photography program in Vancouver, whom I had brought to Israel for a visit in my late twenties. From that first chance meeting in Varanasi, our lives kept intersecting, interweaving. Then we were both pregnant at the same time, and gave birth a few weeks apart.

Motherhood suited Yifat; she appeared natural and relaxed. Like my grandmother, her great-aunt, she gave birth at home. "Aren't children fun?" she said as we watched our two babies babbling on the carpet.

We were descendants of the same great-grandmother. Was it all about perception? After all, Yifat wasn't told our great-grandmother was a bad mother. Or did it have nothing to do with her, and everything to do with me?

. . .

As soon as Sean's paternity leave ended and he went back to work, fortunately at a nearby port that allowed him to return home almost daily, I plummeted down a deep, dark hole. Was it possible to get postpartum depression ten months after birth? Google didn't offer a clear answer. Even with Sean around, I felt insulated and inept, bored and guilty for it; now I was feeling abandoned. Everyone left. Sean. My childless friends, which made for most of them. I had no family in the city. No support system. I wasn't good at asking for help; I was better at maintaining a semblance of competence and cheer. I missed my mother and my sister more than ever, wished I lived closer to them, wondered, as I often did during winter, why on earth I thought living in Canada was a good idea. My days with the baby were long and isolating, the two of us shipwrecked and alone. By the time Sean came home, he'd find me in the kitchen with eyes dimmed and lips downturned. I remembered that expression from my mother's face. But of course, she had six children and had lost the love of her life. What was my problem?

I posted a semi-comical cry for help on Facebook and an old friend said, "Many people can help you raise your child but only you can be the writer you are. Get childcare ASAP."

I nearly wept with gratitude. But another part of me thought, *Really?*

A few weeks after Sean went back to work, I landed a well-paying writer-in-residence gig at a school in Toronto. Our neighbor agreed to babysit and so I took the job. I cherished the short hours I spent there, particularly the times between consults, when I could write. In that little cluttered, tucked-away office I felt closest to my pre-maternal self, saw glimpses of her, longed to hold on to them.

On my first day there, I met with Aga, the writing teacher who had arranged for my gig. I had been thinking about her, remembering something she said when I was pregnant and going on about how I wanted more than one child. Coming from a large, close-knit family, I couldn't imagine having less than two. "Not me," she had said. "I'm selfish. I like to write. I like to travel. It's just so much easier with one." I had marveled at the nonchalant way in which she uttered those words.

When I arrived at the school, Aga was visibly pregnant. I was almost disappointed.

"You were so convincing!" I said. "What happened?"

"I love motherhood." She beamed. "I'm not like you. I don't *need* to write. I'd rather just hang out with my baby all day. I think writing is just more important to you than it is to me."

In her words I heard, "You're different." I heard, "Writing is more important to you than being a mother."

But I also heard a compliment. I was a *real* writer.

♯ ♯ ♯

IN MY MID-THIRTIES, after an almost decadelong writing block, I enrolled in a part-time writing program in Vancouver. Finally, I was writing and reading daily, living the life I had always wished for. I was the happiest I'd been in years.

Once I started writing, I knew I wanted to tell Yemeni stories, inspired by the tales I had coaxed out of my grandmother a few years ago. It was my chance to rectify my childhood experience of never seeing myself and my family in the books I admired, an opportunity to celebrate the rich traditions of my community. I began digging into our past, frequently calling my family with questions. Since my great-grandmother's character continued to fascinate me, her story became the focal point of my research.

Some families have diaries, old love letters wrapped in a string, yellow-edged photos of ancestors from the old country. Others have heirlooms that have been passed down for generations, a collection of porcelain knickknacks or a set of silverware that their grandmother would have them mark for inheritance. My family didn't even know how old my grandmother was. In Yemen, no birth certificates were issued, no recipes written, no photographs taken. My grandmother's village didn't appear on most maps, and an internet search for my maternal surname yielded zero results.

Browsing through history books, hoping to at least construct the background that would provide context to my family's past, has also proved futile. Little has been written about the lives of northern Yemeni Jews—a minority that lived, literally, on the margins of Yemeni society, in remote mountainous areas near the Saudi border, sometimes referred to as the "wild north."

Living in a place absent of my family history, a land that held none of our memories, I found myself drawn to Yemen. It was the only place—other than Israel—we could trace our past to. I remembered a trip Anand and I had taken to the Indian village from which his family descended, and how I envied him that experience, wishing it were possible for me to walk in the footsteps of my ancestors. But even though I was armed with my new Canadian passport, traveling to war-ravaged Yemen was extremely ill-advised. The improbability of such a visit lent the experience a magnified significance in my head. I didn't delude myself into believing it could feel like home, but I imagined a sense of relief, of closure, like a misalignment in my being would correct itself, a riddle solved.

ONCE I COMPLETED the writing program, I traveled to Israel for a lengthy research trip, determined to find some answers. It wasn't just the truth behind the story I was after; I needed to know more for the same reason I had wished to go to Yemen: to unlock the past as if it were a key to my present. A part of me believed that if I knew more about Shama, I'd understand a part of myself that I couldn't relate to my living ancestors. I drew parallels in our lives: I too had had many relationships; I'd left my loved ones and my country to follow a man. Maybe I could understand her choices.

My grandmother was in her late nineties by then and had moved into a home. When I came to visit, she sat slouched in a wheelchair, looking small and pale and clutching a handkerchief. She barely spoke, and when she did, she didn't always make sense. "When are we heading up to the second floor?" she said once. I was grateful for the time we had spent together a few years ago, the stories I captured her telling on video. Before I left, I kissed her wrinkly cheek and said, "Ma'asalama." *Go with peace.* I could swear her eyes lit up for a moment. She always loved it when I spoke Arabic.

It was the last time I saw her.

My extended family regarded my fascination with my great-grandmother with suspicion and annoyance. They also started openly probing me about my plans to spawn, rather than the thinly veiled hint "bekarov etsleh"—*soon at yours*—so often uttered at bris and birth celebrations. Israeli culture sanctified procreation, perhaps out of subconscious fear of being outnumbered by our enemies. Not having children was not an option. Even having one was considered an oddity. One day, a few aunts and female cousins ambushed me at my aunt Rivka's house, which had replaced Savta's home as the family gathering place. I was the oldest female cousin who hadn't bred yet.

"What are you waiting for?" they asked.

"I still have to write my book," I said, my voice whinier than I had intended.

"A book?" They exchanged glances. "The book can wait. A baby can't."

AFTER A FEW months of research, I managed to patch together an approximate time line of events, filled with overlapping dates and littered with question marks. I drew and redrew a family tree: it looked haunted, its branches entwined and tangled. Despite the many gaps and holes, and the lack of concrete evidence, a story began taking shape.

My great-grandmother Shama was born in Dawar il Yahood, the Jewish neighborhood in Sa'ada, a walled city in North Yemen, by the Saudi Arabian border. A stopover on the frankincense caravan route, the northwestern town was a cluster of mud houses that clung to each other in fear of the desert. Outside the city walls, a flat, arid land extended like a story with no ending.

Shama married her cousin Salim Harizi in her teens, as was the tradition in Yemen. After the wedding, she moved to his family home in Haidan a-Sham, a day's ride on a donkey's back. A couple of years after their wedding, Shama gave birth to a baby girl. But their joy was overshadowed by Salim's deteriorating health: a disease had taken over his guts and was eating at him rapidly.

A couple of years after Salim's untimely death, Shama married her second husband, Abraham Gurs, my great-grandfather. Abraham was already family—Shama's younger sister was married to his brother. Abraham's family was known in Haidan for their generosity and kindness. Word had it that travelers who knocked on the family door asking for a slice of bread were sent off with an entire loaf, which was how their last name, Gurs—a loaf of bread—came to be.

After the wedding, Shama and Abraham lived with Abraham's family, in the same house with her sister and her husband, who were unable to conceive. Shama, on the other hand, was blessed with healthy twin girls: one fair and one dark, my grandmother Salha and her sister, Saida.

Then Abraham fell ill too. It wasn't long before he passed away.

After the shiva, Abraham's mother sent Shama and her eldest daughter back to her mother in Sa'ada. "Times are hard," she said, "and with my son dead, we can no longer feed all of you. Your sister can take care of the twins in the meantime."

Shama was in her late twenties and already twice widowed. A woman in her position was considered bad luck. What man would risk becoming a third victim? Without a husband, she'd live in poverty, reduced to selling the rows of gold-plated silver coins that were sewn onto her wedding dress, altering clothes, and weaving baskets to get by. But then Salem-Zahir Madhala, a tall, handsome silversmith from Sa'ada who was taken by Shama's beauty, disregarded the curse and asked for her hand in marriage.

It was the beginning of a new century and more Jews were leaving Yemen for Jerusalem, the Holy Land they'd been praying for. The opening of the Suez Canal in 1869 had made traveling to Palestine easier, and Yemeni Jews could finally fulfill their centuries-long dream. For them, this was a time of redemption, the start of a messianic era. Groups of Jews walked through the desert for weeks, sometimes months, to Aden, where they boarded ships to Jaffa or Haifa.

In 1912, Salem-Zahir and Shama left their home with a few belongings and little money. They ignored the warnings of their Muslim friends and neighbors, who worried that the Arabs in Palestine might not be so welcoming. They took Shama's six-year-old daughter and Shama's mother with them and joined a group on their journey to Aden. On the way, they stopped at Haidan a-Sham, at the Gurs family house, to see Shama's twin girls.

For whatever reason, they left without the twins.

They would make it to Palestine a few months later. There, Shama would give birth to a boy, Yifat's grandfather. A couple of years after that, she would have a daughter who'd die at birth. A few weeks later, Shama would pass away too, succumbing to complications from the birth.

I think of Shama leaving my grandmother and her twin sister behind that day. Did she hug them? Cry? Bury her face in the nape of their necks and inhale their sweet smell? Did she beg her mother-in-law to let her take them? Did she try to fight for them? Did she believe she was doing the right thing, that by leaving them with her barren sister, she was offering her the best gift she could have given her? Or maybe she hoped that her sister could care for them until they grew up and were better suited for travel, that one day they would all be reunited in Israel?

I see her walking away, shoulders trembling, tears streaming. I imagine the mountains and the spirits who lived in them looking on as the family began their journey toward a new life. The mountains had witnessed the lives of the people for centuries. They watched patterns evolving through generations, old roles taken over by new faces, new husbands replacing the dead, girls becoming mothers and mothers becoming grandmothers. Nothing ever changed, but rather shifted ever so slightly, like an ancient folk song played in a new key.

* * *

ONE DAY, WHILE walking on Bloor Street in Toronto with my sleeping baby strapped to my chest, her cheek feathery soft against my skin, I saw a large cellphone ad in a bus shelter featuring a young backpacker against a tropical background, and I was over-whelmed by longing so severe it felt like a physical ache in my chest. I used to be that guy. The kind of person who takes off and leaves whenever she wants, a person with nothing to lose. I could never again be that person. And if I wasn't her, I wasn't sure who I was.

Of course, I didn't truly want to leave my family, yet I didn't know how to live without an imminent departure date, couldn't comprehend the nature of routine. It is human to dream of leav-ing, I told Sean. Men do it all the time. So many of my friends grew up with absent fathers. Men have their hero's journey, their *On the Road*. The image of the traveling man riding toward the sunset is a romantic one. But not women. Not mothers. Mothers stay.

When I was just over a year old, my mother went on vacation in Europe with my father and left me with her youngest sister. A small abandonment, hardly anything at all. By the time she came back, I was calling my aunt Ima. My mother still talks about it, eyes glistening, as if she was the one wronged in this story. How devastated she was when I refused to come to her, how she cried when I hid behind my aunt's leg as if my mother were a stranger.

When I was ten, a few months after my father's death, my mother traveled to New York for a few weeks with my baby brother. My uncle was working at the Israeli consulate in New York, and my mother needed to get away from the grief that was steeping in our house. I stayed with family, an uncle who had chil-dren around my age, only two blocks from our house. My two el-dest brothers were on their mandatory army service, returning only on weekends. My other brother was with relatives, and my sister stayed with friends. I missed my mother so much that some

THE ART OF LEAVING · 301

days I sneaked by myself into our vacant house and stayed for hours at a time. I slept there once—I had lied to my uncle, telling him my brother was there with me—a ten-year-old girl alone in her parents' bed, which still smelled of my mom's Nivea body lotion. I woke up sick with the flu, crawled to the window, and called for help. A neighbor I didn't know well walked by and heard me. She came in, made me tea, and scanned the surroundings. "Why are you here alone? Where is your mother?"

I was sick for two weeks. I wanted my mother, craved the softness and scent of her skin. In my feverish hallucinations, I felt her there, cradling me. I wished I could go to sleep and not wake up until she returned.

When I got better it was my eleventh birthday. My mother was still in New York. My uncle and aunt threw me a birthday party and I sat there among my many cousins, ate my cake, and wished I was in New York with my mother. I looked out the window and watched the blue sky, and there was grief and death written all over it, grief and death lurking in the trees and everywhere. Then, tired of self-pity, I replaced it with anger. I wanted to run away and never come back. I wanted to be the one doing the leaving.

*   *   *

THE WEEK BEFORE I returned to Canada from my research trip, Yifat's mom, Zehava, took me to the cemetery, the same one my father and grandparents are buried in, to visit Shama's grave. Zehava had been keen to help me with my research. Like me, she'd been haunted by the past. I knew better than to try offering her account to my family. Hers was the other family's narrative, the family Shama had chosen over us, the wrong story. My aunt had already taken to caustically calling Zehava my "new best friend."

The day was sweltering, the evanescent spring melting into an early summer. Zehava and I passed the ominous-looking funeral home at the cemetery's entrance and ignored the Orthodox men who loitered by it, hoping to make a buck by praying for your dead.

The lot was in the oldest part of the cemetery, on a little hill. Rows of shiny marble spread out in front of us like a gap-toothed grin. Plain stone-colored high-rises, the city's newest addition, bordered the cemetery on one end, like an extension of the gravestones they overlooked.

Zehava had been here before, over ten years ago. She had found a mound of old dirt with a handwritten wooden sign that read: *Shama Madhala*. "The Yemeni Jews believed the soul had gone elsewhere," Zehava said. "So why bother spending money on a stone?"

The cemetery had been renovated since Zehava's last visit, but she remembered the location of Shama's grave. I followed her as she counted steps until she paused, frowning. The mounds were gone. In their place, the cemetery had put up flat, body-sized castings of concrete with little square stones like pillows at the head. Some of them were engraved "Yemeni woman" or "Persian child." Others only had first names, like "Yaakov" or "Hava." One read: "Drowned in the Yarkon River." Another: "The Young Daughter of the Sharabi Family." But Shama's name was nowhere to be found.

A computerized system, recently set up to help visitors find their way in the maze of gravestones, was mounted into the wall of a booth in the parking lot, like an ATM. When we typed Shama's name, a message appeared: "There are no results for this deceased." We tried different spellings, previous surnames. Nothing. When we searched for Shama's sister, even her mother, the computer emitted a sheet with her name, date of death, lot and row number.

We went back and stood on the footpath, hands on our hips. "The sign must have fallen off before the renovation," I said. I pictured it being tipped over by a gust of wind, carried by a stream of rainwater down the hill, buried in mud and dirt. Lost forever.

Zehava walked back to the entrance and recalculated her steps. This time she found herself standing by a nameless headstone. A smaller grave, also unmarked, was right beside it: perhaps Shama's baby who died at birth?

"It's here," Zehava said. "I can feel it."

It was a blank slab of concrete, a nameless grave for a woman with no birth certificate, a woman who lived and died and left behind no picture or document. In my search, I found no evidence that my great-grandmother had ever existed. Everywhere I went, I hit a dead end. In the national archives' census records from those years, she wasn't listed. In one book, her son—Yifat's grandfather, who was killed in the war—was said to be the son of the wife who followed her.

"I'm sorry, Savta," Zehava said, voice shaking. "Please forgive us."

Forgive *us*? I squinted at Zehava. What was she talking about? I could hear my grandmother's voice in my head, and she was yelling, "We should be the ones forgiving *her* for what she's done. That's her punishment. For leaving us behind in Yemen, for choosing a man over her children."

"I wonder if she ever forgave herself." I knelt, touching the cool stone. "It's so sad. How could she have left so little behind?"

"What do you mean?" Zehava said. "She left us. She left a dynasty."

I found a large pebble and placed it on the grave. It's traditional, a way of saying, We were here. We visited you. We remember.

"WHAT KIND OF woman walks out on her children?" my mother had said to me over the years. During my fraught adolescence, she sometimes threatened to run away from home, phrasing it that way, which made her sound like a teenager herself. She grabbed her purse, made a big scene of her departure, then slipped in quietly later. I don't know what she did during those hours. We never took her seriously anyway. She couldn't leave us. She wouldn't. We knew that much.

But when I was a child, she was often absent, despite always being around. She disappeared into her sorrow and sadness, into her kitchen and housework. My mother and her sisters often described my grandmother in similar terms. Savta was distant, they said, angry sometimes, often cold.

Perhaps motherhood is a series of small abandonments, in the same way that life is a series of goodbyes. We are raising our children to survive without us in the world. We are raising them to leave us, raising them to endure our own departure.

I keep a tally of the times I've left my daughter. That first time I went to an industry party, for only two hours, when she was five weeks old and untrained to drink from the bottle of pumped breast milk. That time I didn't come when she cried because I wanted so badly to sleep, just that once. The first time I paid a caregiver to watch her so I could write. And every time after that. The first time I left her with my friend, just for a lunch meeting, and she clung to my leg and screamed her little heart out as I tried to get out the door. The first time I went away for an overnight speaking engagement in Houston, and I lay in my hotel room at night and, instead of enjoying my first uninterrupted sleep in over a year, felt lonely, missed her, and kept waking up from phantom cries, nipples leaking.

When she was two and a half, my grandmother's age when her mother left her, I went to a literary festival in Vancouver for five days. On the third day, I skyped her and she raised a sad look at me and concentrated on her drawing. "You don't want to speak to me?" I asked and she shook her head no.

When I came back, her behavior toward me changed. Already, before that, she had displayed a clear preference for her father, which I had done my best to deal with maturely, but now, when I tried to console her after a fall, she pushed me away, squeezed out of my arms. "I want Aba," she said. "I like Aba better."

One day, when I picked her up at daycare, she shoved me and said, "Go away. I don't want you." I broke down and cried in the daycare's hallways. Her rejection made me feel like an unloved child, the way I sometimes felt when my mother retreated to her grief.

"You're an exception," a friend from my mothers' group said. "Usually it's the fathers who get rejected that way."

Sometimes when I watched the two of them together, both Canadian-born, both native English speakers, I felt like the odd one out. Despite my efforts, she was growing up with his cultural references, not mine—I was the only mother at swimming lessons who didn't know the lyrics to "Itsy Bitsy Spider." They had the same eyes, the same hair color (brown with tones of auburn and threads of summer blond), the same skin tone. ("You're her mother?" a young girl in the park asked in disbelief. "But she's *normal* and you're . . ." and she stopped, blushing.)

Sometimes, against my better judgment, I felt abandoned, displaced within my own little family unit. Like many immigrants, I am bound to watch my child grow farther away from me, away from my traditions, my language, and my memories of an Israeli childhood she will never know. I imagine my grandmother must have felt the same way with my mother.

Scientists have been saying that it may be possible for some emotional inheritance to be passed on biologically through our DNA, that our ancestors' experience may be hereditary—their traumas and phobias, their love of spicy food, their fear of spiders, and their aversion to patchouli. What they suggest is that we carry with us not just our ancestors' personality traits, but their memories and emotions. Memories of being abandoned, memories of walking away. I am both the mother who left and the child who was left behind. We all are.

* * *

LATELY, MY DAUGHTER, who's always been a daddy's girl, has turned her affections toward me. There's no real reason for that change of heart—toddlers are fickle like that—and this may just be a temporary phase, but sometimes Sean catches me suppressing a smile, not so secretly pleased. She tells him that she wants me, only me, that she loves me most. She crawls over me, kisses me, snuggles into me in bed, can't seem to have enough of my touch. She caresses my cheek while gazing into my eyes and whispers, "Ahuva sheli." *My love.* It is the purest form of love I have ever known, and I am filled to the brim with it. This bond, this love, is precious and blissful, and there is nothing even remotely like it. These days, motherhood feels like joy. These days, I have no qualms telling people I love being a mother. Perhaps it's time, or perhaps it's her age: getting to watch her personality develop and evolve, her interests and her quirks, listening to her speak and form complex thoughts.

One day, I catch her pretend-writing on our kitchen table,

wearing fake plastic glasses. She glances at me unsmiling. "I am writing my book, Ima," she says. Another day, she's lit up by the sound of Yemeni music, jumping onto her feet and dancing like this beat has been latent in her all along, and we hold hands and twirl. In moments like that, I am reminded in awe that we are a part of something bigger than the two of us, bigger than the present moment. In my daughter's body, I see a connection to something both ancient and unwritten. A link on a lineage chain, a branch on a family tree.

I look at her and I think, This is what it means to belong.

The other day, before I took off to give a talk out of town—one of those trips I embark on often that both satisfy my travel bug and make me intensely miss my family—she snuggled up to me in bed and whispered, "I wish you stayed forever." I squeezed her tight. "I'm not leaving for long," I told her. "I always come back." I wanted to tell her that nothing had ever made me want to stay put the way she did, that nothing had ever made me happier, truly nothing. I wanted to tell her, If I leave, we leave together.

ACKNOWLEDGMENTS

"Writing a book should take longer than a day," my father said to me when I presented him with my very first book, a school notebook filled with my handwriting. He was right. In fact, from the moment I started writing stories from my own life—the first writing I had done in English—it took twelve years until they shaped themselves into a memoir. Twelve years is a long time. During that period, I published another book, my first, moved across Canada, enrolled in two writing programs, had a child. Writing a book over the span of that many years also makes for an exceptionally long list of acknowledgments: I have been fortunate to have had many people help me along the way. All deserve my gratitude.

I am deeply indebted to my brilliant editors, Jennifer Lambert at HarperCollins Canada and Andrea Walker at Random House in the United States, for their enthusiasm and insight. Thank you for pushing me to make this book the best it could be. I am grateful to the team at HarperCollins Canada: Iris Tupholme for championing my work from the start, Noelle Zitzer for overseeing the production stages, and Catherine Dorton for her meticulous copyediting. At Random House, I'm grateful to Susan Kamil for taking a chance on me and Emma Caruso for her help with the production process. To my wonderful agents, David Forrer and Kimberly Witherspoon, thank you for your guidance, smarts, and faith in me. Eternal gratitude to the Sami Rohr family for their enormous generosity. The Sami Rohr Prize for Jewish Literature changed my life and allowed me to concentrate on writing this book. Thank you to everyone at the Jewish Book Council, especially Carolyn Hessel, for their ongoing support.

I have been blessed with several inspiring mentors over the years. Wayde Compton was the best first champion an emerging writer could have hoped for. He believed in me before I dared to believe in myself, and I am forever indebted to him. Thanks also to Betsy Warland, Catherine Bush, Camilla Gibb, Janice Kulyk Keefer, and Nancy Lee for sharing their wisdom and making me a better writer; to my cohort at the Writer's Studio at Simon Fraser University and my classmates at the University of Guelph MFA in Creative Writing, who read parts of this book when it was first written; to the supportive communities of writers I've been lucky to be a part of in Toronto, Vancouver, and Israel; and to my writing students for continuing to inspire and challenge me.

I am immensely thankful to the many excellent readers and friends who've read the book or parts of it at different stages and provided invaluable feedback: Kathy Friedman, Becky Blake, Janet Hong, Anna Chatterton, Nancy Jo Cullen, Nazanine Hozar, Alison Pick, Amanda Leduc, Rachel Knudsen, Alev Ersan, Jan Redford, Leslie Hill, Sue Anne Linde, Jen Caldwell, Fiona Scott, and Clarissa Green. Special thanks to the incomparable Eufemia Fantetti, who's read numerous drafts of this book and commented on them tirelessly, brainstormed story arcs and themes with me, and discussed everything from the title to covers to epigraphs. I am humbled by your friendship.

This book was written mostly in the homes I inhabited in Vancouver, Toronto, and Israel, but also at Toronto Writers' Center, at Sage Hill Writing Residency in Saskatchewan, and at Crescent School in Toronto during my term as writer in residence. Most of the copy-edits were completed during my residency at the Toronto Reference Library. Heartfelt thanks to all who have made it possible for me to write comfortably, especially Aga Maksimowska and Trish Cislak for arranging the Crescent School gig; Sage Hill Writing for their financial support and Ted Barris for his encouragement; Nissim Mizrahi, my mother's loving partner, for creating an awesome room with a view for me at their new home; and my brother, who allotted me an office at his place of work. Immense gratitude also to Sonia Finseth and Karin Randoja for babysitting, and to Becky, Eufemia, and Gabrielle Zilkha for helping out. Special thanks to Taunya Gaum, the delightful Doda T., who volunteered to watch my kid once a week so I could write and allowed me to escape to her downstairs apartment at other times to use her desk while my baby was with her sitter upstairs. It may be the kindest thing you can do for a writer who's also a mother, and I'm lucky to have you as a friend.

For their generous support of this project and my career, I'm indebted to the Canada Council for the Arts, the Ontario Arts Council, and the Toronto Arts Council.

For more than a decade, I have been conducting extensive research into Jewish Yemeni history. During those years of research, I was aided by numerous people—first and foremost, my extended family, especially my beloved aunts and uncles. Gratitude also to Tuvya Sulami, Gila Beshari, Shlomi Hatuka, Menashe Anzi, Amnon Ma'abi, Yossi Zabari, Zion Ozeri (whose amazing photographs of Haidan a-Sham are still the only ones I've ever seen), and many others from the Yemeni community who opened their homes and hearts to me. I am thankful to the many librarians, scholars, and researchers who assisted me at the city archives in Petah Tikva and Rehovot, the Yad Ben Zvi Institute and the Central Zionist Archives in Jerusalem, the Museum of Yemeni Jewry in Rosh HaAyin, and the Museum of the Jewish People at Beit Hatfutsot in Tel Aviv. Thanks to Kamal Al-Solaylee for his help with Yemeni words and spellings. For their generous support of my research, I am grateful to Yosef Wosk, the Access Copyright Foundation, and the Chalmers Family Fund and the Ontario Arts Council for awarding me a Chalmers Art Fellowship.

I am deeply grateful to everyone who appears in the book, by either their real name or pseudonym, and to my many wonderful friends—too many to name, many of whom didn't make it into the memoir—for their unwavering love and support. I am limiting my individual thanks to those who helped me in specific ways while I was writing the book. Orit Mosseri (Kreskas), Yael Levinger, Carlin Sandor, Sacha Levin, Danielle Nakouz, Marie Belzil, Nadia Hedar, Sarah Hedar, Riyadh Hashim, Stefania Gilardi, Jane Warren, Doron Sagie, Einat Katz Kaplan, Tsvika Kaplan, Limor Iron, Gurjinder Basran, Homeyra Javadi Panah, Cecilia Mutti, Jill Moffett, Elanor Waslander, Hayim Raclaw, Mona Krayem and her family. I love you all.

Special thanks to the Brereton-Creer clan for their love and encouragement. To Michal Shavit, my most enduring heart-sister. To Tal Savoray, my earliest reader and writing partner and a steady source of solace in my life. To Yifat Jovani for her boundless support and companionship since our chance meeting in India. To Elsin Davidi, my partner in crime and grief, for her friendship and inspiration. To Maya Tevet Dayan, for her poetry and camaraderie. To Yonit Naaman, granddaughter to Saida, my grandmother's twin, for her brilliance and friendship, and for her amazing essay

"Everyone Knows Yemenites Are Great in Bed" (available online!), which was the inspiration for my essay "A Simple Girl." And to Aya Ortal and her mother, Shuli Haza—who look like family because they are—I dedicate that essay.

Parts of this memoir have appeared in different forms in the following magazines: *Event, Room, PRISM International, Paper Brigade, The New Quarterly,* and *Grain.* I'm grateful for the editors who've helped shape these essays. I've also included in this book bits and pieces from essays I've published in the *National Post, Lit Hub,* and *Jewish Book Week.*

Infinite gratitude and love to my immediate family: To my beloved brothers, for trusting me to write this book and for having my back, always and forever. I apologize for anything you may have remembered differently. To my sister—my best friend— who transcribed my first stories into a notebook when I was five and she was twelve, and bought me my very first diary at the age of six and said, "Write." To my nephews and nieces, whom I love more than they know. Most of all, I am immensely grateful to my mother, who understood my need to write this memoir; while she couldn't read this book in the language I wrote it in, she approved a translated summary of the parts in which she's mentioned. Thank you for nurturing, feeding, and loving me. I love you. You're an amazing mother. Don't be mad about the drugs.

To my father, who instilled in me his love of writing and books and people: this book, like everything I write, is in your memory.

To my grandmother, who loved me with few words: I'm grateful for the time we spent together and the stories you (reluctantly) shared. Ma'asalama.

And finally, profound gratitude to my daughter, the best human who has ever happened to me, for giving me perspective, inspiration, and so much love and joy. I'm in awe of you every single day. And to Sean Brereton, my love, for pushing me to write and making it possible, for helping me with funny English expressions, and for being, hands down, the best partner a writer could ask for. Now everyone knows how awesome you are.

AUTHOR'S NOTE

Writing a memoir is a work of memory, not a work of history. And though I often like to brag about my freakishly good memory (my partner, Sean, calls me his external hard drive), I am also well aware that memory is a shifty, unreliable character who shouldn't be trusted. While I researched facts and interviewed other people whenever I could, this book relies mostly on my recollections, journals, and letters, and therefore is a subjective telling of my own story. I have changed some names and a few details to protect people's privacy. I have also taken some creative liberties: I re-created dialogue based on my recollections and, in some cases, compressed time for the sake of a tighter narrative.

In "A Simple Girl," I mentioned Mizrahi activists who have been calling the media out on their under-representation of Mizrahi characters. You can follow the Web series *HaMishmar HaMizrahi* by Shlomi Hatuka for examples (in Hebrew only) on Kan Israeli Public Broadcasting Corporation (https://www.kan.org .il/program/?catid=16).

Also in "A Simple Girl" I remarked on young Mizrahi poets who have sidestepped the gatekeepers by launching their own poetry readings. I was referring specifically to Ars Poetica, which was founded by poet Adi Keissar in 2013. The name of the series is a wordplay reclaiming the word "Ars"—Arabic for "pimp," and a derogatory name for Mizrahi men in Israel. Google "Ars Poetica Israel" to find more information.

In "Not for the Faint-Hearted," I mentioned the Yemenite Children Affair as a trauma that shaped Jewish Yemeni history. However, expanding on this devastating topic was beyond the scope of this book. If you'd like to know more, the only book written in English on the topic is *Israeli Media and the Framing of Internal Conflict: The Yemenite Babies Affair* by S. Madmoni-Gerber (Palgrave Macmillan, 2009). In Israel, the Amram Association has been doing amazing work collecting survivors' testimonies and fighting for justice and recognition. You can find and support them online. You can also watch the powerful Web series *Neviim Docu-Shorts* on YouTube for interviews with survivors and activists. (English subtitles are available.)

In "If I Forget You," I tell the story of dealing with the hordes of books in my childhood home. A couple of years after I gave away my brother's books, I found a pile of the Young Technician series at a used bookstore by the port in Haifa and bought them for him. I think he's forgiven me.

Transliteration and Language

Transliterating Hebrew or Arabic words is a tricky business. Most people simply follow their ear and attempt to write the word as phonetically as possible. As a result, some common words may have competing spellings. The letter *Tsadik*, for example, which is the first letter of my last name (or *Tsade*, as it appears in Wikipedia), may also be spelled *Tzaddik*, *Tzadi*, or *Sadhe*. When I was little and couldn't pronounce the letter *Tsadik*, I was told to put *T* and *S* together, which is how the spelling of my last name came to be.

Yet others with my last name may choose to spell it with *Tz,* *S,* or *Z.*

I decided to use *H* to represent the letter *Het* (also spelled *Chet* or *Heth*) in Hebrew and the letter *Ha* in Arabic. These guttural letters have no English equivalent. I chose the *H* over *Ch,* which is another common way—misleading, in my opinion—of transliterating *Het* (so you'll see *Hanukkah* sometimes spelled as *Chanukah*). To further complicate things, there's one exception in this book: the name of the Yemeni dish jichnoon. For this word, I chose to use *Ch* to denote the *H.* Yemeni Jews from different regions pronounce the name of the dish slightly differently, so if you look for the recipe online, you may find it under *jachnun,* which is the most common pronunciation and spelling. But those who call it jichnoon, like my family, tend to feel strongly about the name, as this staple dish also represents home, history, and identity. To the copy editor who suggested changing it, I explained that my family might disown me. On a similar note, if you're looking for a bisbas recipe, you might find it under *schug* or *zhug.* If I called it schug in my mother's home, I'd be asked to leave.

The Arabic words in this book are words my grandmother used in her conversations with me, which I've transcribed from video and confirmed with my mother. As this is a Judeo-Arabic Yemeni dialect rarely used nowadays and also colored by geography, I couldn't always find a way to verify them.

SOURCES

In "A Simple Girl," the quote by Dr. Vicki Shiran (p. 36) appeared in an op-ed she published in *Tel Aviv Magazine* in the eighties.

In "Not for the Faint-Hearted," the quote by David Ben-Gurion (p. 184) from his letter to Chief of Staff Yigael Yadin on November 27, 1950, appeared in *1949: The First Israelis* by Tom Segev (The Domino Press, 1984), p. 181. The quote from the *HaTzvi* newspaper (p. 184) appeared in an article titled "On the Yemenites," set on its front page, on January 27, 1909. The scanned original paper is available online at the Historical Jewish Press website (http://jpress.org.il/), which was initiated by Tel Aviv University and the National Library of Israel. The final quote, taken from a memo written by Jacob Thon (p. 184) in October 1908, titled "Memorandum for Workers' Regulation in Palestine," appears in *History of Zionist Settlement* by Alex Bien (Masada, 1942), p. 98, as well as in the article "HaTeimanim" ("The Yemenite") by Haim Hanegbi, *Matzpen,* April 10, 1971.

In "Yemeni Soup and Other Recipes," I mention a fundraising film from the fifties (p. 235) meant to highlight the work of Moetzet HaPoalot (Working Women's Council). The film is titled *Bederech Halev (The Way of the Heart).* The specific excerpt that I refer to is available online (https://www.facebook.com/uri.rosenwaks/).

In "Unravel the Tangle," my father's poems "False Spring" and "Come to Me" (pp. 275 and 268) are taken from the book *Sihey Tsabar Svuhim (Tangled Prickly Pear Shrubs)*, published by Afikim in 1984 and edited by Tuvya Sulami. The poem "Remember Me While I'm Still on Earth" (pp. 270–71) is from *Afikim* magazine, issue 18, March 24, 1967.

The opening epigraph (p. ix) is from James Baldwin's *Giovanni's Room* (Vintage Books, 1956). The epigraph for Part I (p. 1) is from Maya Tevet Dayan's poem "Home," translated from her Hebrew book of poetry, *Floating Home* (Kvar Series, Mosad Bialik, 2017). The epigraph for Part II (p. 77) is from an interview with Cynthia Ozick by Eleanor Wachtel on CBC Radio, which appeared in the book *Writers & Company* (Alfred A. Knopf Canada, 1993). The epigraph for Part III (p. 191) is from Esi Edugyan's book *Dreaming of Elsewhere: Observations on Home* (University of Alberta Press, 2014).

All Hebrew quotes, poems, and song excerpts are my own translations.

Publication History

Excerpts from this memoir were previously published in different, usually shorter, forms:

"A Simple Girl" appeared in *Paper Brigade* (2018).

"You and What Army" appeared in *Event: Poetry and Prose* 36, no. 3 (2007), and *Slice Me Some Truth: An Anthology of Canadian Creative Nonfiction* (Wolsak & Wynn, 2011).

"Missing in Action" appeared in *PRISM International* 49, no. 3 (2011).

"The Marrying Kind" appeared in *Room* 33, no. 2 (2010); *Making Room: Forty Years of Room Magazine* (West Coast Feminist Literary Magazine Society and Caitlin Press, 2017); and *Love Me True: Writers Reflect on the Ins, Outs, Ups and Downs of Marriage* (Caitlin Press, 2018).

"Soldiers" appeared in *The New Quarterly* 131 (2014) and *Wherever I Find Myself: Stories by Canadian Immigrant Women* (Caitlin Press, 2017).

An excerpt from "Tough Chick" was first published under the title "Victim" in *Event: Poetry and Prose* 38, no. 3 (2009).

An excerpt from "Hornets" appeared in *PRISM International* 53, no. 2 (2015).

"Yemeni Soup and Other Recipes" appeared in *Grain* 39, no. 4 (2012), and an excerpt from it also appeared in *Sustenance: Writers from BC and Beyond on the Subject of Food* (Anvil Press, 2017).

"Unravel the Tangle" appeared in *Room* 36, no. 2 (2013).

ABOUT THE AUTHOR

AYELET TSABARI was born in Israel to a large family of Yemeni descent. After serving in the Israeli army, she traveled extensively throughout Southeast Asia and North America, and now lives in Tel Aviv. She teaches creative writing at the University of King's College's MFA Program in Creative Nonfiction and at Tel Aviv University. Tsabari's first book, *The Best Place on Earth,* won the Sami Rohr Prize for Jewish Literature and the Edward Lewis Wallant Award for Jewish Fiction, and was nominated for the Frank O'Connor International Short Story Award. It was also a *New York Times* Editors' Choice pick and included in *Kirkus Reviews'* Best Debut Fiction of 2016. Essays from this book have also won several awards, including a National Magazine Award. In addition to writing, Tsabari has worked as a photographer and a journalist.

ayelettsabari.com
Facebook.com/ayeletsabari
Twitter: @AyeletTsabari